BEN HECHT'S THEATRE OF JEWISH PROTEST

# BEN HECHT'S THEATRE OF JEWISH PROTEST

GARRETT EISLER

RUTGERS UNIVERSITY PRESS
NEW BRUNSWICK, CAMDEN, AND NEWARK, NEW JERSEY
LONDON AND OXFORD

Rutgers University Press is a department of Rutgers, The State University of New Jersey, one of the leading public research universities in the nation. By publishing worldwide, it furthers the University's mission of dedication to excellence in teaching, scholarship, research, and clinical care.

Library of Congress Cataloging-in-Publication Data

Names: Eisler, Garrett, author. | Hecht, Ben, 1894–1964. We will never die. | Hecht, Ben, 1894–1964. Jewish fairy tale. | Hecht, Ben, 1894–1964. Flag is born. | Hecht, Ben, 1894–1964. Terrorist.
Title: Ben Hecht's theatre of Jewish protest / Garrett Eisler.
Description: New Brunswick : Rutgers University Press, 2025. | Includes bibliographical references and index.
Identifiers: LCCN 2024019635 | ISBN 9781978835948 (paperback) | ISBN 9781978835955 (hardcover) | ISBN 9781978835962 (epub) | ISBN 9781978835979 (pdf)
Subjects: LCSH: Hecht, Ben, 1894–1964—Criticism and interpretation. | Jews in literature. | Holocaust, Jewish (1939–1945), in literature. | LCGFT: Literary criticism. | Drama.
Classification: LCC PS3515.E18 Z64 2025 | DDC 812/.52—dc23/eng/20240701
LC record available at https://lccn.loc.gov/2024019635

A British Cataloging-in-Publication record for this book is available from the British Library.

Copyright © 2025 by Garrett Eisler
All rights reserved

No part of this book may be reproduced or utilized in any form or by any means, electronic or mechanical, or by any information storage and retrieval system, without written permission from the publisher. Please contact Rutgers University Press, 106 Somerset Street, New Brunswick, NJ 08901. The only exception to this prohibition is "fair use" as defined by U.S. copyright law.

References to internet websites (URLs) were accurate at the time of writing. Neither the author nor Rutgers University Press is responsible for URLs that may have expired or changed since the manuscript was prepared.

∞ The paper used in this publication meets the requirements of the American National Standard for Information Sciences—Permanence of Paper for Printed Library Materials, ANSI Z39.48-1992.

rutgersuniversitypress.org

For three great mentors: David Savran, Marvin Carlson, and Morris Dickstein.

And for a great actor and friend Vincent Beck (1924–1984), whom I knew as a child and rediscovered when I saw his name in the cast lists of some of these plays. If only he or I knew of the possibility of this book back then.

# Contents

Introduction . . . 1

**Part I    From "Vanishing" to Visible: Barriers to Jewish Representation, 1933–1943**

1  Protesting Antisemitism via Antifascism . . . 15
2  Breaking the Silence: *We Will Never Die* . . . 28

**Part II   Tevye and the Terrorists: Plays for Palestine, 1944–1947**

3  The Assassination of "Lord Moisha": *A Jewish Fairy Tale* and the Pivot to Palestine . . . 63
4  The Death of Tevye and the Birth of Israel: *A Flag Is Born* on Broadway . . . 78
5  Passion Play for a Jewish "Terrorist" . . . 105

Conclusion . . . 117

APPENDIX 1: *WE WILL NEVER DIE* (1943) . . . 125
APPENDIX 2: *A JEWISH FAIRY TALE* (1944) . . . 153
APPENDIX 3: *A FLAG IS BORN* (1946) . . . 165
APPENDIX 4: *THE TERRORIST* (1947) . . . 203
ACKNOWLEDGMENTS . . . 223
NOTES . . . 225
BIBLIOGRAPHY . . . 249
INDEX . . . 255

BEN HECHT'S THEATRE OF JEWISH PROTEST

# Introduction

WHEN I FIRST learned about Ben Hecht's *We Will Never Die*, I was stunned. Here was a large-scale theatrical performance in one of New York City's largest venues (Madison Square Garden) exposing the horrors of the Holocaust to a wartime American audience in March 1943, more than two years before the war's end. Moreover, the artists involved in creating and performing it were marquee-name Broadway and Hollywood celebrities, many of them Jewish themselves. Hecht, a renowned playwright and screenwriter, was its instigator, Moss Hart directed, Kurt Weill provided the musical score, and among the actors appearing either that night or during a subsequent national tour were Paul Muni, Edward G. Robinson, John Garfield, Luther Adler, and Sylvia Sidney. The performance was thus groundbreaking in two ways. First, at a time when stories about Jewish massacres in Europe were only beginning to appear in the American press, *We Will Never Die* exposed the horrors of the "Final Solution" long before they became more widely known after the war. It also broke another silence in the context of the era's popular culture: addressing Jewish concerns on the American stage from a Jewish point of view.[1]

The prominent contributions of Jewish performers, writers, and producers to the American entertainment industry of the early twentieth century are legendary. But success as workers within the field did not always translate into representation of Jewish life in their given medium. Those who were actors were still usually pressured to adopt new stage names if their given names were deemed "too Jewish" to appear on a movie poster. After some flourishing of ethnically specific storylines and characters in the early decades of the century, American mass culture came under increased pressure to deracinate during the mid-1930s, partially as a result of anti-immigrant sentiment enshrined by Congress in the restrictive quotas of the 1924 "National Origins Act," which severely restricted further U.S. immigration of Jews and other ethnic minorities. As a result, writes Harley Erdman in his historical study *Staging the Jew*, "after 1920 . . . performing Jewishness in mass culture increasingly required varieties of masking."[2] Writing in 1952, the drama critic Henry Popkin reflected on this phenomenon in an essay titled "The Vanishing Jew." Popkin attributed the paucity of Jewish visibility in popular culture over the preceding two decades to a preemptive self-censoring by the entertainment industry, an overcautious reaction to Nazism: "The American answer to the banishment of Jews from public life in Germany was the banishment of Jewish figures from the popular arts—in the United States."[3] In Hollywood—especially after 1934, when a new Production Code sought to homogenize all content for an implied Christian audience—Jewish signifiers in stories and characters (and even the word "Jew") were carefully screened for and excised from screenplays.[4] While no such formal constraints applied on Broadway, a chill toward Jewish subject matter was evident nonetheless. When the young Arthur Miller was submitting his first play to producers in the late 1930s, it was rejected, he would recall, "for the stated reason that it was not a time to come forward with a play about Jews."[5] Between nativism, fear of antisemitic backlash, and presumptions of a mostly parochial American audience, all appeared to have contributed to what Edna Nahshon characterizes as "the reluctance of Jewish dramatists to tackle Jewish themes . . . well into the mid-twentieth century."[6]

And yet, despite all the era's barriers to representation, here was Hecht in 1943 breaking what in effect had become a code of silence by assembling an all-star cast of Jewish actors to demand (to quote a later Miller play) that "attention must be paid" to Jewish subjects on the American stage. *We Will Never Die* was only the first of many Jewish-centered theatre works Hecht wrote and produced over the next four years, as the horrors of the Holocaust were revealed, the war came to an end, and the fight for a Jewish homeland in Palestine intensified. His play *A Flag Is Born* (1946) brought the postwar Jewish refugee crisis to Broadway, running for four months followed by a national tour. Less publicized were two one-act plays, *A Jewish Fairy Tale* (1944) and *The Terrorist* (1947), occasional pieces written for one-night Zionist fundraising benefits, but nevertheless performed at the prominent venue of New York's Carnegie Hall. Working outside the commercial theatre industry, Hecht authored and essentially self-

INTRODUCTION

produced four dramatic works that gave unprecedented voice and visibility to contemporary Jewish issues on the American stage.

Regardless of how little this oeuvre is known today, its existence challenges the notion of a "vanishing" of openly Jewish American dramatic expression during the era of the Holocaust. There is historical basis for that perception—but Hecht deserves credit for acting on that absence and doing his best to remedy it. In the field of Jewish American theatre studies, this book aims to fill a gap between Erdman's *Staging the Jew* about the rise and fall of Jewish visibility between 1860 and 1920 and Henry Bial's *Acting Jewish* which resumes that topic "in the aftermath of World War II" when "the importance of cultural difference began to reassert itself" and the performing arts again became a site for "negotiating [Jewish] ethnicity on the American stage and screen."[7] "Acting Jewish," even militantly Jewish, was still possible during the war years, but, as Hecht demonstrated, one had to go around the usual show business cultural apparatus to do so.

Hecht's Jewish theatre works are not new discoveries, but most of the scholarly attention they have received to date has been in historical contexts other than Jewish American drama. *We Will Never Die* is routinely cited in histories of the Holocaust and American responses to it. Ever since David Wyman highlighted the performance in his landmark 1984 study *The Abandonment of the Jews*, Hecht's theatrical activism has been part of the discourse over the failure of the U.S. government under President Franklin D. Roosevelt to rescue European Jewry. In the four decades since that book, Wyman and his colleague Rafael Medoff have chronicled the movement led by the wartime Zionist activist Peter Bergson, who commissioned and produced *We Will Never Die* and the three subsequent plays. Their research into Bergson's tireless lobbying for U.S. intervention both in Nazi-controlled Europe and British-ruled Palestine has, by extension, documented his collaboration with Hecht.[8] This connection has forever enmeshed these texts in the ideology of Bergson's cause of "Revisionist Zionism," a nationalist and militaristic movement considered to be on the right wing of the political spectrum. (The "Revisionists" were the direct antecedents to the Likud party of later Israeli politics.) The influence of Revisionist Zionist thinking on Hecht's Jewish writing may be evident in his "ends justify the means" embrace of political violence and its anti-Diasporic renunciation of assimilation as an answer to antisemitism. But to classify these works as merely propaganda for right-wing Zionism is reductionist and overlooks Hecht's equally committed involvement with left-leaning "Popular Front" causes of the era, which, as I will demonstrate, significantly informed his Jewish theatre pieces as well. The politics of these works is most accurately seen in the domestic American terms of its time, not the foreign policy divisions of the future. Hecht was always first and foremost an American writer, not a foreign agent.[9]

Another limitation of the Bergson-centered accounts of Hecht's Jewish theatrical work is that they become subsumed under the much broader public relations campaign Hecht engaged in as the in-house propagandist for Bergson's political action committees. Hecht's output over six years of editorials, paid newspaper advertisements, and pamphlets—as well as his 1944 book on antisemitism, *A Guide for the Bedevilled*—is a remarkable body of work, and Wyman and Medoff have compellingly described it, as have recent Hecht biographies by Adina Hoffman and Julien Gorbach. This study, however, is strictly a work of theatre history, situating *We Will Never Die*, *A Flag Is Born*, and its companion pieces in a context not previously considered—the culture and practices of mid-twentieth-century American theatre and show business.

Another context Hecht's Jewish theatre has been presented in (by Stephen J. Whitfield, Erika Fischer-Lichte, and others) is in comparison to other contemporaneous examples of Jewish "pageantry" in America, particularly the three biblical epics presented by the Zionist impresario Meyer Weisgal during the 1930s.[10] Hecht's works did share some common elements and personnel with Weisgal's, but the differences are instructive. Weisgal's *Israel Reborn* (1932) and *The Romance of a People* (1933) were performed only in Chicago, as promotional events for the Zionist Organization of America, of which Weisgal was a leading official. *Romance* was a feature attraction of the 1933 Chicago World's Fair, the theme of which was "A Century of Progress." Conceived of and performed only on the cusp of Hitler's rise to power in January 1933, these were optimistic celebrations of Judaism's past and promising Zionist future.[11]

*The Eternal Road* (1937), an operatic treatment of the Hebrew Bible that Weisgal commissioned from the author Franz Werfel and the composer Kurt Weill, bears a stronger connection to Hecht's work due to Weill's involvement with both. (They not only shared the same composer but much of the same music, since Weill repurposed extracts from *The Eternal Road* for *We Will Never Die* and *A Flag Is Born*.) Adding the German director Max Reinhardt to the artistic team, Weisgal promoted the opera as a timely work by a trio of European Jewish refugee artists and presented its world premiere at New York's Manhattan Opera House. But *The Eternal Road*'s status as an antifascist or proto-Holocaust work owes more to the life circumstances of its creators than the content of the libretto itself—whose only nod to the present is a framing device in which modern-day European Jews, hiding from a local pogrom, introduce the scriptural episodes that comprise the main action. While presented as part of the New York theatrical season, it is better understood as an imported Jewish European work than an original product of American Jewish culture. Although Weill had left Germany in 1933 and was already writing Broadway musicals by 1937, Werfel remained in Vienna until the 1938 Anschluss and composed the *Eternal Road* libretto in German since he could not write in English.[12]

Because of their frequent comparisons to Weisgal's productions, the label "pageant" has stuck to Hecht's formally and substantively very different Jewish theatre pieces—not just *We Will Never Die* (which Hecht did call a pageant) but also his three ensuing Zionist plays, which all vary in form. Filing them all under "pageantry" has had the effect of displacing this body of work from the mainstream of American theatre history. While "pageantry" has often connoted amateur and community-based performance, Hecht—a commercially successful playwright and screenwriter—leaned heavily on his Broadway and Hollywood colleagues to participate in and headline his projects. *A Flag Is Born*, for instance, was literally a Broadway play, opening at the Alvin Theatre with a professional Equity cast led by a major star, Paul Muni.

Recent theatre and performance scholars have recuperated pageantry as a distinct and important theatrical form, but in Hecht's time the term could be quite pejorative in dramatic criticism.[13] (In his *New York Times* review of Hecht's *A Flag Is Born*, Brooks Atkinson's harshest words characterize the play as "after the fashion of pageants, which at best are untalented theatre.")[14] As I will demonstrate by close readings of the original texts, pageantry is just one of many theatrical idioms Hecht drew upon in his unusually eclectic brand of dramaturgy—one that constantly alternated between pageantry, religious ritual, documentary realism, heroic tragedy, symbolist drama, and even carnivalesque satire.

Another major distinction I make between Hecht's project and pageantry is the immediacy with which these works addressed the present, even as they paid tribute to the past. In *We Will Never Die*, the opening section—a "Roll Call of the Great Jews"—channels pageantry with its procession of supernumeraries representing centuries of famous historic individuals. But its remaining three scenes intensely engage with the specific moment of 1943: the participation of Jewish soldiers in the Allied forces; the massacres of Eastern European Jews by the German Army; and even the Warsaw Ghetto uprising, which occurred while *We Will Never Die* was on tour, leading Hecht to make a last-minute addition to the final performance. Such "straight from the headlines" urgency made *We Will Never Die* more akin to the 1930s "Living Newspaper" plays of the Federal Theatre Project than the ornate historical reenactments of Weisgal's pageants.

Similarly, *A Flag Is Born* does feature biblical reenactments akin to *The Eternal Road*'s, but Hecht's present-day protagonist (an elderly Holocaust survivor) directly engages in time-traveling dialogue with the Hebrew patriarchs and kings. *A Jewish Fairy Tale*, written hastily in response to the 1944 assassination of the British official Lord Moyne by Jewish Palestinian militants, staged a debate over the controversy between a dead Jew and Winston Churchill. In *The Terrorist*, he memorialized the April 1947 execution of another Zionist soldier, Dov Gruner, in a script that he brought to the stage that September.

Because these texts were never widely published, they are more known about than known. *We Will Never Die* and *A Flag Is Born* were issued in limited editions long out of print, *The Terrorist* appeared in a long defunct newsletter, and *A Jewish Fairy Tale* was never published at all. To study them in detail requires tracking down the relatively few extant copies in far-flung libraries or consulting Hecht's original typescripts scattered across different archival collections. Many of the available commentaries have mainly relied on the primary-source research of a small number of dedicated Hecht historians and biographers. This is why I am including all four scripts in the appendices of this book, so that they can finally be accessible firsthand in their entirety and so they may finally be considered as a cohesive body of dramatic work produced by a significant Jewish American dramatist during the tumultuous and tragic years of 1943 to 1947.

My explorations of these texts are organized chronologically into two parts. In part 1, I trace Hecht's efforts during the prewar and wartime eras to sound an alarm about Nazi antisemitism and the oncoming Jewish genocide and to galvanize his fellow American Jews. Part 2 follows Hecht's postwar pivot—in the wake of the Holocaust and the failure of the United States and its allies to stop it—to the Palestine conflict, a cause for which he wrote (and Bergson produced) three plays of increasing outrage and militancy, collectively dramatizing the replacement of the dying Jewish culture of the Diaspora with the vigorous Zionist ideal of the Jewish soldier.

In chapter 1, I review how the American theatre of the 1930s and '40s had been responding to the rise of Nazism before Hecht entered the fray. Many plays addressed the issue in some way, but few did so from an expressly Jewish perspective. (In fact, some settings were so abstract or allegorical that Germany itself was not identified.) The Hollywood studios (Hecht's main employer) even more adamantly avoided content about antisemitism, only doing so through veiled references. Hecht's initial Jewish activism, therefore, consisted of joining various antifascist campaigns, bringing him into the fold of "Popular Front" politics, the 1930s coalition of liberal and radical forces advocating many progressive causes, including religious tolerance. During the period between 1939 and 1941—after the war had begun in Europe but while the United States was still neutral—

INTRODUCTION

Hecht became a prominent spokesman of the "interventionist" cause, writing a daily newspaper column for *PM* and, in October 1941, staging his first political "pageant," the anti-isolationist *It's Fun to Be Free*.

Chapter 2 examines the gestation, performance, and reception of *We Will Never Die*, Hecht's first theatrical response to the Holocaust, coming, as it did, just a few months after U.S. newspapers began confirming reports of mass killings of European Jews by German troops. It also marked the beginning of his theatrical partnership with the Zionist activist Bergson, who served as the de facto producer of all Hecht's stage productions in support of their joint efforts on behalf of European and Palestinian Jews. Billed as a "Mass Memorial Dedicated to the Two Million Jewish Dead of Europe," *We Will Never Die* combined several dramatic forms and performance practices in a unique evening of both mourning and protest. Part pageant, part religious service, it also channeled "documentary theatre" techniques, symbolist drama, and even Hollywood war movies—all in the service of an ultimately heroic portrayal of Jewish identity, from the patriarchs and scholars of the past to the soldiers and resistance fighters of the present. Even the concluding episode of recent massacre victims testifying before an imagined war crimes tribunal ("Remember Us") shifts attention away from mere sympathy to demands for justice. The performance's aspirations to achieve tangible results in saving European Jews and stopping the Holocaust may not have materialized, but after seven performances around the country in large arenas, in addition to accompanying news coverage and three radio broadcasts, Hecht's "memorial pageant" had broken two silences: the dearth of news media coverage of the massacres of Jews abroad and the entertainment industry's continued "masking" of Jewish identity at home.

Chapter 3 documents the shift in Hecht's focus to the struggle of Jews in Palestine against British rule. His first play to address this was *A Jewish Fairy Tale* (1944), a one-act comedy prompted by the shocking assassination of a British imperial officer by Jewish militants. Despite America's important wartime alliance with Great Britain, Hecht makes Winston Churchill the villain of the play in response to the prime minister's crackdown on Jews in Palestine in retribution for the killing. To make the case for the Jews—even Jewish "terrorists"—Hecht enlists a familiar figure from modern Yiddish literature, Sholem-Aleichem's Tevye (transliterated as "Tevya"), a character he would continue to utilize in his subsequent plays as an avatar for the vanishing "Old Country" of Eastern European shtetl culture. While the original Tevye is an inherently comic character, Hecht conjures him as a ghost (after his murder in a gas chamber) who finds himself answering for his life not to God but to Churchill. Despite the dark premise, the scene takes the form of a satirical revue sketch, given its topicality and broad spoofing of Churchill's famous mannerisms. Performed just twice at Bergson-organized fundraising events, A Jewish Fairy Tale was seen by much smaller audiences than We Will Never Die and received far less press attention, but remains notable as an escalation in Hecht's theatrical rhetoric in support of Jewish liberation at any cost.

Chapter 4 recounts the peak achievement of Hecht's Jewish theatrical activism: his Broadway play A Flag Is Born, which opened in September 1946 and enjoyed a four-month run before a national tour early the following year, achieving significant exposure of the Palestine conflict to American theatre audiences. In Flag, Hecht's Tevya returns, along with his wife, this time as a survivor of the camps. In a setting owing much to symbolist drama, the couple wanders through the wasteland of postwar Europe, represented onstage as a graveyard, where they search for an imagined "bridge" to Palestine. As they await divine guidance, Tevya has visions of the past glories of "Eretz Israel" (the play's one element of "pageantry") and receives guidance from the kings Saul and Solomon. In the end, Tevya and his wife die before they can ever reach their destination, but their young traveling companion (another camp survivor) finally sees the foretold "bridge" and is led across it by a band of Zionist soldiers while holding aloft Tevya's old *talis* on which he has emblazoned the Star of David—a vision of the flag of Israel over a year before that nation came to be.

The staging of A Flag Is Born reflected the influence of multiple theatrical genres, including political satire (when Tevya addresses the stodgy diplomats of the United Nations) and, poignantly, the then fading art form of the Yiddish Theatre. Its director, Luther Adler, and stars, Paul Muni and Celia Adler, all came from that tradition—as did the figure of Sholem-Aleichem's Tevye. Hecht subtly used comforting and familiar Yiddish Theatre tropes and stylings of the past as a dramaturgical analog to the dying world of European Jewry, while switching to more jarring satiric and agitprop modes to engage the audience with the political crisis of the time. And as embodied by the unknown young (non-Jewish) actor playing the role of David—Marlon Brando—the play even benefited from the emotional rawness of modern "method acting" that was itself an outgrowth of Jewish American culture.

Hecht's last Jewish play, The Terrorist (discussed in chapter 5), received far less public attention than Flag due to its staging as part of a longer benefit performance for Bergson's committee. But historically it may be the most remarkable of these texts in demonstrating the escalation of Hecht's engagement with what was then known as "Palestinian [i.e., Jewish] Terrorism." Through

INTRODUCTION

Bergson, Hecht found himself allied with the most controversial of those militant groups, the *Irgun Zvai Leumi*, and it was the *Irgun* commander Menachem Begin himself who personally commissioned *The Terrorist* as a tribute to a soldier recently executed by the British. The resulting play dramatizes the overcoming of past Jewish suffering—again embodied onstage in a ghostly Tevya figure—by the embrace of new ideals of "muscular Judaism" and an uncompromising pursuit of victory over persecution by any means necessary. Another dramaturgical hybrid, *The Terrorist* contains at its center a realist prison drama about the last days of the hero awaiting execution, as witnessed by a ghostly chorus reciting centuries of past anti-Jewish violence. When the martyr of this Jewish Passion Play is finally hanged, Hecht again dramatizes rebirth through death and sacrifice.

I conclude by showing how Jewish representation and visibility in popular culture began to change after the war with films like *Gentleman's Agreement* (1947) and the stage adaptation of *The Diary of Anne Frank* (1955) finally confronting the evils of antisemitism on the commercial American stage and screen. Hecht's small but strident oeuvre on the same subject paved the way for these and other famous titles and even anticipated some of their most notable elements. It also presaged the emergence of a new assertive Jewish American identity in popular performance.

Finally, a historian's disclaimer. Dealing as they do with the events leading to the creation of the State of Israel, Hecht's militantly Zionist plays discussed in part 2 have only grown more politically volatile with time. They invited controversy from the very beginning, but initially from rival Zionist factions decrying Hecht's alleged celebration of violence and the recklessness of his *Irgun* sponsors in diverting attention and funding away from more peaceful and "productive" Palestine campaigns. But the role of Palestinian Arabs as another player in the struggle over that land appears nowhere in the contemporary critical discourse on these plays. In the American press leading up to 1948, the Palestine "story" was largely one about Jews versus the British—a two-way conflict, not three. Accordingly, the question of an Arab role in Palestine's future is raised just once in *A Flag Is Born*, late in the play, where Tevya downplays any tension by insisting Jews and Arabs are "brothers" united against their British "masters."[15] The play may never explicitly assert Jewish precedence in Palestine, but the absence of a credible Arab perspective suggests a blind spot (deliberate or not) toward an issue that risked complicating the play's otherwise freedom-fighting message of human rights.

It may be difficult for readers today to separate these texts from the ultranationalistic ideology of their Revisionist Zionist sponsors, one that has informed the policies of right-wing Israeli politics from 1948 through the twenty-first century. Hecht knew of his *Irgun* colleagues' fervent anti-Arab antipathy. Upon their first meeting Bergson boasted, "The Irgun policy is we kill two Arabs for every Jew who is murdered."[16] The "Eretz Israel" Tevya longs for in *A Flag Is Born* clearly reflects the Revisionists' "territorial maximalist" demand for the "Greater Israel" of ancient times, spanning both sides of the Jordan River—entailing an extreme displacement of Arabs no other Zionist group was advocating. The biases inherent in the Revisionists' influence on Hecht certainly infuse many passages in these works.

For most of Hecht's American audience circa 1945, though, Zionism was still an abstraction untethered to the policies of an Israeli state that did not yet exist. Even among American Jews, Zionism had been slow to take hold in the decades before World War II. (Combined membership in U.S. Zionist organizations grew from an estimated combined membership of 65,000 in 1933 to approximately one million by 1948.)[17] The Revisionists in particular "existed only on the fringes of the American Zionist community," overshadowed by much larger and more politically liberal groups like Hadassah, Zionist Organization of America, and American Jewish Congress.[18] When Zionism's following in the United States grew, it was due to the broader goals of saving Jewish refugees in the present and creating a still hypothetical Jewish homeland in the future. "The political machinations of American Zionist leaders and the multiple factions splintering the movement," writes Hasia Diner, "did not resonate with American Jews, who concerned themselves more with making a comfortable place for themselves in America than with arguing points of Zionist ideology."[19]

By considering Hecht's Jewish theatre works from the historical perspective of his time (not retrospectively from the fraught Israeli-Palestinian future), they emerge more clearly in an American Popular Front context of fights for freedom among oppressed groups. The revolution Hecht was creating onstage may have aspired to effect change abroad, but it also did the necessary cultural work of asserting Jewish identity at home. This is why no less a progressive than Victor Navasky—later the longtime editor of *The Nation* and a historian of McCarthyism—invoked Hecht in remembering the great cultural shift afoot in social equality at large in that postwar moment: "My political awakening had begun with two events: watching (and cheering) when Branch Rickey hired Jackie Robinson to play for the Brooklyn Dodgers, the first African-American in major league baseball, and my being hired as a 'volunteer' (at $2.50 an hour)—my first real job—to pass out a contribution basket at Ben Hecht's play *A Flag Is Born*, which opened in 1946, the year after my bar mitzvah."[20] Navasky's link-

INTRODUCTION

age in his memory between Hecht and Robinson reveals how these plays could be experienced in the greater context of postwar "civil rights" in the broadest sense. Hecht's personal focus may have been on influencing overseas outcomes, but his writing also served to prompt American Jews to look at themselves and their identity as part of a larger movement toward social equality and liberation from prejudice.

# Part I

# From "Vanishing" to Visible

## Barriers to Jewish Representation, 1933–1943

# 1
# Protesting Antisemitism via Antifascism

THE VISIBILITY BEN HECHT gave to the plight of European Jews when he wrote *We Will Never Die* in 1943 was the most significant exposure the issue had received on the American stage in the ten years since Hitler's rise to power. Broadway had broached the subject of the Nazi regime only occasionally and often obliquely. The issue was sometimes the butt of satirical ridicule, a marginal subplot, or removed from its German context in dramatic abstraction. And even within those examples, the foregrounding of Jewish characters in the narrative was even rarer. Much has been written by film historians about the frustrated efforts of screenwriters and producers to make anti-Nazi films in the face of cautious studio executives determined not to buck popular isolationist sentiment or to endanger German and European markets for their product.[1] But even without a Hollywood-style "production code" mandating neutrality in foreign affairs, Broadway fared not much better in sounding an alarm of the impending crisis.

The lack of prominent attention to antisemitism in the American drama of the era goes hand in hand with a declining visibility of Jewishness onstage in general. Jewish identity remained prominent offstage as American Jews continued to work and thrive in the Broadway industry, but it was a decreasingly popular topic for playwrights to write about—which, in turn, meant fewer Jewish-identified characters for actors to play. Harley Erdman notes a "blossoming of Jewish-American stage representation in the second half of the nineteenth century," which remained "widespread in the years right after the turn of the century," but one which gave way by the 1920s to a "transition toward decreased Jewish visibility" where "performing Jewishness in mass culture increasingly required varieties of masking."[2] The cultural pluralism of the melting pot ethos of the earlier era extended into the roaring twenties, producing a range of representations from broadly stereotypical comedies by non-Jewish writers like Anne Nichols's long-running hit *Abie's Irish Rose* (1922) to more sincerely empathetic Jewish-authored dramas like Samson Raphaelson's *The Jazz Singer* (1925). But alongside continuing cultural tolerance ran an increasing strain of anti-immigrant sentiment that gradually had a chilling effect on the embrace of ethnic and religious diversity in popular culture. In 1920, the country's leading automobile manufacturer, Henry Ford, published the first in a widely disseminated series of antisemitic screeds under the title *The International Jew*, which targeted the "Jewish Influence in American Life" and the country's "Jew-controlled" film industry in particular.[3] "The widespread perception among anti-Semites that Jews controlled the American entertainment industry," writes Henry Bial, "caused many Jewish actors, directors, and playwrights to feel deeply ambivalent about publicly acknowledging their Jewishness."[4] As a result, "Jewish dramatic activity during the 1920s and particularly in the 1930s," argues Edna Nahshon, "must be seen within the context of the period's nativism."[5]

The differences between the presentation of Jewish identity in *The Jazz Singer* and another canonical Jewish American drama written a decade later, Clifford Odets's *Awake and Sing!* (1935), are instructive. Not only are Raphaelson's characters clearly identified as Jewish but the hero is a cantor's son who ends up singing Kol Nidre in his place at the conclusion. Despite such ethnically specific cultural markers, *The Jazz Singer* was a major cinematic success when Warner Brothers chose to film it as their first sound picture in 1927. *Awake and Sing!* is about a multigenerational family named Berger who live in the Bronx and speak in Yiddish-inflected cadences, but its central conflict is between utopian aspiration and capitalist materialism, and the characters' Jewishness has no distinctly measurable impact on their lives. Despite being considered a canonical playwright of Jewish American drama, *Awake and Sing!* was Odets's only play primarily about modern Jewish characters. He followed it up with a more commercially successful drama about the immigrant experience, *Golden Boy* (1937), in which he made the central family Italian American. *Golden Boy* was adapted by Hollywood into a hit movie; *Awake and Sing!* was not.[6]

These examples, of course, are all from the English-speaking American drama. Any overview of Jewish performance in America during the early twentieth century must also take into account the contributions of the Yiddish Theatre, which was still presenting a vibrant repertoire of expressly Jewish-centered drama in New York well into the 1930s and 1940s until the city's Jewish population became increasingly American-born. While it lasted, the Yiddish Theatre provided a variety of empowering narratives and character types far beyond the narrow stereotypes of mainstream popular culture. The drop in Jewish representation on the Broadway stage during these years was somewhat offset by the continued availability of a more ethnic-friendly alternative on the "Yiddish Broadway" of downtown Second Avenue. But Yiddish Theatre could never compete with Broadway for attention in the larger public discourse. The language barrier rendered it an art form forever "facing in" on its own implied audience, not "facing out" to the general public—as the younger generation of American-born Jewish playwrights sought to do.[7]

In the face of anti-immigrant social pressures, the early attempts of American dramatists to contend with the Nazi regime are notable, even when they did not focus on its racial policies. Some of the first productions came from the ranks of the New York Workers Theatre movement, which, through its connections to the Communist Party, were among the first artists to rally behind the cause of antifascism due to an investment in the communist-fascist conflicts arising in Europe. Odets's *Till the Day I Die* (1935)—written as a curtain-raiser for his more celebrated labor play *Waiting for Lefty*—was typical of that strain, focusing on the oppression of German communist cells after Hitler's rise to power. (Antisemitism factors only in a subplot about a conflicted part-Jewish SS officer.) A year earlier, two of Odets's Communist Party (but non-Jewish) colleagues, Elia Kazan and Art Smith, presented *Dimitroff*, an agitprop piece memorializing the German communist framed and executed by the Nazis for the Reichstag fire. The Broadway hit *Pins and Needles* (1937), a satirical revue performed by members of the International Ladies' Garment Workers' Union, frequently ridiculed Hitler and other fascist leaders in its constantly updated topical material over a three-year run.[8]

Non-labor-affiliated playwrights treated the topic as well, but mostly with little commercial or critical success. The very first Broadway play about Hitler appears to have been *Kultur*, which opened in September 1933. Written by Adolf Philipp, a sixty-nine-year-old German Jewish immigrant from an earlier era (and the onetime musical star of New York's bygone "Little Germany" circuit), the play was a farcical story of a Jewish doctor called upon to operate on an unnamed antisemitic "Chancellor." It ran one week. Another short-lived play in the fall of 1933 was *Birthright*, a more sober drama by Richard Maibaum (a young American-born Jewish playwright who later became a celebrated screenwriter) about a bourgeois family in Berlin facing sudden antisemitic discrimination despite years of military service and even religious conversion. Elmer Rice, a more seasoned Jewish American playwright, wrote three antifascist plays throughout the decade. He offered his own version of the Reichstag fire case in *Judgment Day* (1934), but one which fictionalized and abstracted the setting to an unnamed "capital of Southeastern Europe." His *American Landscape* (1938) turned the focus to homegrown Nazi sympathizers as a historic Connecticut estate is passed down through the generations until landing in the hands of a Bundist group. His most direct treatment of the conflict came in 1940—after war began in Europe but before Pearl Harbor—with the suspense thriller *Flight to the West*, in which fleeing refugees (including Jews) find themselves on the same transatlantic airliner as some Nazi officials, bound for the still neutral United States.[9]

The presence of Jewish characters in the prewar antifascist plays became even less central as the decade wore on. Like Rice's *American Landscape*, George S. Kaufman and Moss Hart's drama *The American Way* (1939) also brings onstage a German American Bund–type group, but their victims are a Gentile German immigrant family. Lillian Hellman's *Watch on the Rhine*, which opened in April 1941, is perhaps the most famous of the anti-Nazi titles of the era, but, as Julius Novick quips, she "managed to write a play about refugees from Nazi Europe . . . in which there are no Jewish characters."[10] (The play, set in the Gentile home of a Washington, D.C., socialite, features an exiled resistance fighter of unspecified racial origin.) The most Jewish antifascist Broadway play of the era was arguably written by a non-Jew: Clare Boothe Luce's comedy *Margin for Error* (1939), which starred Sam Levene as "Officer Finkelstein," a New York cop assigned to guard the city's German consulate.

## BEN HECHT'S JEWISH POLITICAL JOURNEY

No one was more aware of the decline in Jewish visibility than Ben Hecht. Writing in 1944, he lashed out against the "exorcising of the Jew from literature and the stage" and laid the blame squarely at the feet of Jewish show business producers:[11]

> The greatest single Jewish phenomenon in our country in the last twenty years has been the almost complete disappearance of the Jew from American fiction, stage, radio, and movies. Were the Jews a totally extinct race surviving only as a few Passover cups and saucers in the Metropolitan Museum, they could have hardly less representation in the cultural and entertainment media of our land. . . . When I was young, the stage was full of Jewish dialect comedians, of Jewish family plays, . . . of tales of Jewish struggle and comedy. . . . Whereupon the two great media of mass entertainment appear, the movie and the radio, both dominated by Jews—and

the Jew vanishes. He vanishes not only from the screen and the air waves, but he is also out of print and gone from the footlights. No greater kidnapping has ever been witnessed.[12]

Given these circumstances (as Hecht perceived them, at least), it is no wonder that the only way he found to make Jews visible on the stage again was to go outside of the Broadway establishment, team up with such nonconventional producers as Bergson and his Revisionist Zionist political action committees, and create works that defied expectations of conventional drama.

Ironically, Hecht himself had rarely treated Jewish subjects in his own work prior to the rise of Nazism, despite professing a long-standing connection to his ancestral roots. He was born in 1893 in New York City to Russian Jewish immigrants and spent his early childhood on the city's Lower East Side "speaking Yiddish almost as fluently as English."[13] His father, a tailor, moved his family to Chicago when Hecht was six and then to Racine, Wisconsin, four years later. Racine took Hecht far from the diversity of turn-of-the-century urban life (he recalled only two other Jewish children in his public school), but his largely unacculturated parents and the extended family that moved with them created a home environment that Hecht described as "a sort of Yiddish Canterbury Tales" of old-world memories and customs.[14]

Hecht quickly assimilated into cosmopolitan American society when he left home for Chicago at age seventeen and embarked on a writing career that would take him from journalism to literary fiction to theatre and, most lucratively, to the movies. As a playwright, he made his Broadway debut in 1922 (with a short-lived comedy, *The Egoist*), but it was not until 1928, when he began collaborating with his fellow newspaperman Charles MacArthur, that he finally scored a major theatrical success with *The Front Page*, a satire of tabloid journalism based on the two men's experiences in Chicago. This catapulted him into screenwriting, where he soon found success across genres, from gangster stories like *Underworld* (1927) and *Scarface* (1932) to screwball comedies like *Design for Living* (1933) and *Nothing Sacred* (1937). His ongoing collaboration with MacArthur led to successful screen adaptations of their plays *The Front Page* (1931)—remade as *His Girl Friday* in 1939—and *Twentieth Century* (1934), and the two teamed up on such Hollywood blockbusters as *Gunga Din* (1939) and *Wuthering Heights* (1939). (The critic George Jean Nathan dubbed the duo "the two most publicized scenario writers in Hollywood.")[15] During the peak of his demand, Hecht claimed to have been earning up to $5,000 a week for his services (sometimes even $10,000) at a time when the median professional salary in America ranged between only $1,000 and $3,000 per year.[16] The uncredited "script doctor" contributions he made to such major Hollywood classics as *Stagecoach* (1939) and *Gone with the Wind* (1939) further indicate his elite status as an in-demand screenwriter who helped define what critics now laud as "Classical Hollywood Cinema."[17]

While Jewishness was absent from his plays and screenplays of the 1930s, it did keep recurring in his literary work, even if sometimes in an ambivalent or outright negative light. In Chicago, some of his first dramatic efforts for the local "Little Theatre" movement (co-written with Kenneth Sawyer Goodman) were "poignant studies of life in Chicago's Jewish tenements."[18] He revealed an affinity for Yiddishkeit, but only in attempts at stereotypical ethnic humor, including mock doggerel he wrote in the persona of an "Alfred Pupick" with titles like "Oi Yenta, Oi My Yenta!"[19] The most prominent Jewish-themed work of his early career was also his most notorious—the darkly comic novel *A Jew in Love* (1931), whose predatory and facially grotesque protagonist repelled readers, especially Jewish ones.[20] (A Manhattan rabbi condemned the book as "an atrocious malignment of Jews" by a "reckless" author.)[21] But by 1936, when he adapted the novel for his film *The Scoundrel*, the lead character's Jewish origins were erased and the role was played by Noël Coward—perhaps a sign of Hecht's increased view of his Jewish identity as no longer a laughing matter.

Hecht first found his Jewish voice as a polemicist. While he would later claim that he "turned into a Jew in 1939," he first spoke out publicly in an editorial for the *New York Daily Mirror* in July 1935.[22] As a guest contributor to Walter Winchell's "On Broadway" column—a feature usually devoted to promotional items about show business celebrities—Hecht delivered an 800-word essay on the significance of Hitlerism to Jews in America. Even at this relatively early stage of anti-Jewish persecution in Germany (the Nuremburg Race Laws would not be proclaimed for another two months), Hecht had clearly taken notice already of the centrality of racial purity to the Nazi regime.[23] But his column that day focused less on events abroad than on the reaction of his fellow American Jews to the resurfacing of an old prejudice many had been content to forget about. Already in 1935, Hecht zeroed in on what would become a primary theme of his later propaganda writings—the complacency and denialism of Jews who felt safe from antisemitism: "There are quite a number of Jews in New York who have . . . shed their Jewish stamp and for several generations emerged as individualists. . . . The Hitler howl is like a lash driving them back in to the Ghetto. They who have preened themselves as Americans, as world citizens, as individualists long emancipated from the little cul-de-sac civilization of Israel, find themselves abruptly returned to a race they have outgrown. . . . Painful though it is, I have a feeling that this Jew consciousness is rather good for the seemingly assimilated Jew."[24]

The necessity of one's own personal embrace of Jewish identity as a precondition to effective protest remained central to Hecht's activism. "Jew consciousness" at home was to him essential for saving Jews abroad.

While Hecht failed to immediately follow up the stridency of this column with direct Jewish political content in his creative work, he embarked on a series of scripts that found more oblique ways of condemning fascism. His play *To Quito and Back* (1937), produced on Broadway by the Theatre Guild, was about a popular uprising in Ecuador and the cynical reporter-screenwriter who finds himself swept up in it. The revolution is opposed by imperialistic capitalists who, to safeguard their profits from the country's natural resources, create what Hecht refers to as a fighting force of counterrevolutionary "fascists."[25] Hecht planned to go even further in linking antagonists to current events in Europe, but he claimed that some Theatre Guild board members requested that "some of the anti-fascism be cut down because it could outrage Hitler and kill a lot of Jews."[26] This first foray of his into explicitly political theatre was largely received with critical scorn—some from reviewers disappointed that he strayed from his more successful satirical comedy vein, some from more overtly radical critics skeptical of this commercially successful writer's supposed political conversion. (Mary McCarthy, in *Partisan Review*, accused Hecht of only "giving lip-service to radicalism.")[27] But another reviewer appreciated the play's focus on "one of the most vital and provocative of present-day problems: the plight of an unstable intellectual liberal in a world of violently shifting social forces."[28]

Opportunities to dramatize the antifascist struggle were significantly more curtailed in Hollywood, where not even as lucrative and trusted a screenwriter as Hecht could get past the stifling limits of the governing "Production Code" that movie studios adopted in 1934 as self-censorship to avoid any controversy in cinematic content. All screenwriters were hired hands, their product the property of the studios to revise or censor as they wished, and Hecht was no exception. As long as the United States remained officially neutral toward Germany, the Production Code called for the "respectful treatment" of the "history, institutions, prominent people and citizenry of other nations."[29] One factor behind this provision was the studios' fear of alienating the still profitable German-speaking market, where some continued to export their films as late as 1940, even after Hitler was at war with much of Europe. (The fact that two of these studios were Hecht's most regular employers at the time—MGM and Paramount—even further limited his freedom of political expression in his work as a screenwriter for hire.) To address antisemitism, screenwriters working under such constraints had to resort to such subterfuges as only having the word "Jew" appear in writing, not spoken (as in *The Life of Emile Zola*), or referring to persecuted characters as "non-Aryan" (*The Mortal Storm*) or "people of his faith" (*Dr. Ehrlich's Magic Bullet*).[30]

In this context one can appreciate Hecht's efforts to infuse antifascism into the unlikely project of a musical Western he was hired to write for popular singer Nelson Eddy, *Let Freedom Ring* (1939). Hecht's plot concerns a Wall Street tycoon who descends on a frontier town to buy up its land and people while Eddy plays an intrepid journalist who publishes a subversive newspaper to oppose the robber baron. Filming began in November 1938, just days after the Nazis' *Kristallnacht* pogroms against Jews in Germany and German-occupied lands—a fact that adds special meaning to the film's opening moments showing ranchers' houses being set aflame by the villain's henchmen, as Hecht's introductory title cards pay tribute to "the eternal struggle against oppression."[31] Hecht's commitment to *Let Freedom Ring* as an antifascist parable is evident in the telegram he sent his wife after the first screening the completed film on January 16, 1939: "Just saw *Let Freedom Ring* in the projection room. It made everybody cry and looked and sounded like the best picture I've ever done for effectiveness. It is more patriotic than a Madison Square Garden meeting and all the rhetoric about freedom and humanity goes over like a cannonball. . . . I wouldn't be surprised if it reelected Roosevelt and overthrew Hitler."[32] As hyperbolic as Hecht's ambitions for the film might have been, the antifascist implications of *Let Freedom Ring* were not entirely lost on 1939 audiences, especially those already motivated to seek them out. The *Daily Worker*, for example, praised it as "a resounding statement of the American people's will to democracy" and said it "does at least a little to purify the New York air so recently polluted by the vaporings of Fritz Kuhn," referring to the leader of the pro-Nazi German American Bund organization, which had just held its own "Madison Square Garden meeting" the week before the film opened.[33]

After the outbreak of hostilities in Europe in late 1939, Hecht began pursuing more explicitly antifascist and war-related projects, but none came to fruition—at least not with his name on them. William MacAdams reports that he discussed collaborating on an "anti-Nazi screenplay" with actor-director Erich von Stroheim in the spring of 1940.[34] In January 1941, British Hungarian producer Alexander Korda announced his purchase of the rights to a scenario by Hecht for a film set in German-occupied Paris to be titled "Forbidden City," which was never made.[35] Most promising was an adaptation of Eric Ambler's antifascist espionage novel *Journey into Fear* he had been hired to write for RKO, but when Orson Welles took over the project in July 1941, he declined to use Hecht's script.[36]

One completed film he did contribute to, albeit uncredited, was Alfred Hitchcock's *Foreign Correspondent* (1940), a thriller about an American reporter's perilous adventures in Europe on the eve of war.[37] Throughout filming, which began in early 1940, the original script was forced to keep the nationality of the obviously German antagonists vague. But by the time shooting had completed in early summer, the war had drastically escalated after the surrender of France and the first air attacks of the Battle of Britain. Hitchcock and producer Walter Wanger decided to insert a last-minute epilogue depicting the German bombing of England and hired Hecht to write it. In this new ending, the journalist hero is in a London radio studio, broadcasting live amid the sounds of Luftwaffe bombers. The speech functions as a direct-to-camera plea for America to end its isolationism and join the fight against fascism:

> All that noise you hear isn't static. It's death, coming to London. Yes, they're coming here now. You can hear the bombs falling on the streets and in the homes. Don't tune me out. Hang on a while, this is a big story and you're part of it. . . . It's as if the lights were all out everywhere. Except in America. Keep those lights burning, cover them with steel, ring them with guns, build a canopy of battleships and bombing planes around them. Hello, America! Hang on to your lights. They're the only lights left in the world.[38]

At the time of the film's release in August 1940, Hecht's call for "battleships" would have struck many as premature, since military support for Britain was still controversial in Washington. (It would be another six months before President Roosevelt convinced Congress to pass the first Lend-Lease Act.) But Hecht's speech—delivered onscreen by the movie's star, Joel McCrea, to the accompaniment of "The Star-Spangled Banner"—put an American face on the "big story" of the fight against fascism. As McCrea says to both his (fictional) radio and (real) cinema audiences, "You're part of it."

## THE INTERVENTION CAMPAIGN

By the time of his work on *Foreign Correspondent*, Hecht had already become involved with several of the antifascist groups and campaigns that proliferated under the auspices of the Popular Front—the political coalition between labor-allied leftists and bourgeois liberals that emerged in the mid-thirties to present a "united front" again fascism worldwide. Sparked by a Communist International declaration in the summer of 1935 encouraging its members to seek such alliances, the movement took on a life of its own in the United States, building on the New Deal coalition already forged by President Roosevelt as well as the advancement of organized labor into the mainstream of American life.

It also manifested itself extensively in the performing arts, through what became known as the "cultural front," defined by Michael Denning as "the terrain where the Popular Front social movement met the cultural apparatus."[39] Two chief examples of that "apparatus" were the New York stage and Hollywood film industries. From the "social issue" movies of the Warner Brothers studio to labor-centered Broadway hits like *Waiting for Lefty*, *The Cradle Will Rock*, and *Pins and Needles*, theatre and film artists made a major contribution to the dissemination and promotion of Popular Front ideals—including antifascism.

To organize and demonstrate against fascism in the United States during the 1930s inevitably entailed joining forces with the Left in American politics. Hecht had previously stayed out of politics in both his life and work during his early career, and he was never at home with the more radical circles of Broadway and Hollywood writers. ("I could understand almost anybody espousing Communism except a writing man," he once wrote. "In a Communist state I would be either jailed or shot for speaking my mind.")[40] But the Popular Front provided Hecht a venue for his specific concerns without requiring fealty to any specific partisan ideology. Moreover, it fostered bonds with other like-minded Jewish American artists—like Edward G. Robinson, Paul Muni, and Kurt Weill—with whom he would continue to collaborate in the coming years on his more explicitly Jewish-themed projects.

While never joining the Communist Party, Hecht did interact with several Popular Front organizations, including some—the Hollywood Anti-Nazi League, the League of American Writers, and the Motion Picture Artists Committee—that were later infamously labeled "Communist Front Organizations" during later investigations by the House of Representatives Committee on Un-American Activities.[41] His most significant engagement with the movement came in early 1941, when he was recruited by left-wing publisher Ralph Ingersoll as a columnist for his new newspaper *PM*, which soon became "perhaps the most successful organ of the New York Popular Front."[42] *PM* gave Hecht a prominent platform in the still isolationist climate of 1941 to write prolifically about European fascism and the threat it posed to Jews abroad and at home. One of his first columns took on Hollywood's reluctance to make anti-Nazi films by reporting on the efforts of Joseph P. Kennedy to steer studio executives away from such subject matter. Kennedy, then Ambassador to Great Britain but also an outspoken isolationist, had worked in the movie business and was now, according to Hecht, "giving advice to his Semitic Hollywood pals . . . to lie low, not to attract attention to themselves, and not to use their powerful medium of expression as a propaganda weapon against the Nazis."[43]

Hecht's activism continued to intensify in the months leading up to Pearl Harbor, especially on the question of American intervention in the European war to prevent a German victory—something that seemed quite possible after the fall of France and the bombing of Britain. In April 1941, he joined Fight for Freedom, a pro-intervention advocacy group launched in opposition to the isolationist America First Committee.[44] Hecht took a leading role in the organization's "Stage, Screen, Radio, and Arts Division," and by the summer of 1941 began planning a mass rally for the fall. The resulting "mammoth revue" (as advertisements promised) was billed as "Fun to Be Free" and featured celebrity appearances by, among others, Jack Benny, Eddie Cantor, Helen Hayes, Tallulah Bankhead, Melvin Douglas, and Burgess Meredith—all frequent participants in Popular Front campaigns.[45] It was co-produced by Labor Stage, the theatrical arm of the International Ladies Garment Workers Union (ILGWU), which produced the Broadway "workers' musical" *Pins and Needles*. Performed at Madison Square Garden on October 5, 1941, the event began with a variety show featuring such timely acts as Bill "Bojangles" Robinson dancing on a coffin representing Hitler's grave to the accompaniment of Irving Berlin's "When That Man Is Dead and Gone." In a sketch called "The Verboten Overture," the orchestra played a medley of songs by Jewish composers that was constantly interrupted by "a burly gent in a Nazi storm trooper's uniform" who "stepped forward and apoplectically bellowed, 'Verboten!'"[46]

The centerpiece of the rally was *It's Fun to Be Free*, a "historical pageant" by Hecht and MacArthur.[47] Like earlier Progressive Era civic pageants, this work featured enactments of iconic scenes from American history reframed as conflicts between militant liberalism and corrupt "appeasement." Its nine historical episodes retell familiar tales of patriotic lore in distinctly contemporary political terms. Patrick Henry is harassed by a mob that the stage directions label "a gallery of appeasers."[48] Next, Thomas Jefferson is shown triumphing over those in the Continental Congress who "yammered for appeasement" of King George (241). Even Abraham Lincoln is pitted against isolationist stand-ins like a northern pro-Confederate "Copperhead" who advocates "acquiescence in the doctrine of secession" (249). That the Copperheads, like 1941 "appeasers," were also countenancing racial persecution (in the form of slavery) made the implicit parallels between the Civil War and World War II even stronger.

Hecht makes the pageant's historical relevance more personal by including a Jewish hero of the American Revolution—Haym Salomon, a financial backer of Washington's Continental Army. As the narrator announces: "There were Jews in the American Revolution—thousands of them. They went without food, stood by shoeless, and with guns in their hands—and fought for the new idea for freedom and liberty for all. . . . Here is one of them—the Jewish warmonger of 1776, Colonial Soldier, the Paul Revere of the Jews" (244). In the scene, Salomon interrupts the holiest of all synagogue services, Yom Kippur, to collect funds from his community for General Washington. (The stage directions set the scene: "Synagogue—Jewish music playing. All Jews are in their praying shawls, and present is Rabbi leading them in their chanting.") The ensuing dialogue between Salomon and his rabbi encapsulates a common Jewish American dilemma—how to practice modern civic duty without interfering with ancient pious observance. "Forgive me, Rabbi," Salomon entreats, "but on this Sabbath we can do more than pray to God—we can fight for Him. . . . Jews, the world knows how you love God. Do you also love liberty?" (244–245).

The most arresting and confrontational part of the pageant was its conclusion: a simulated "air raid" announcing German planes over Manhattan. After the historical scenes concluded, the pageant's narrator warned the audience of "a present of tomorrow—the tomorrow that rides on the Panzer tanks and on the dive bombers of the Luftwaffe" (250–251). Sounds of flying bomber planes began to fill the hall, air raid sirens blared, and miniature parachutes were released from the rafters, carrying small cardboard cutouts of German infantrymen. This theatrical "New York Blitz" established a visceral audience identification with the victims of the London bombings at a time when aid to Britain was the most contentious issue of the day in the isolationist-interventionist debate. Putting the Madison Square Garden audience at an imagined ground zero compelled these Americans to identify, for at least a few minutes, with besieged Londoners—and, by extension, all the other populations across the Atlantic currently under very real attack by German forces. Press accounts testified to at least a momentary credulity within the hall of seventeen thousand. "Searchlights flashed, gunfire sounded, women screamed," reported *Life* magazine.[49]

Fight for Freedom considered the "Fun to Be Free" rally so successful that it announced a tour of several cities, starting in Washington, D.C., on November 4. Even on December 10, three days after Pearl Harbor, a planned performance in St. Louis went ahead as scheduled, with Humphrey Bogart joining the cast of narrators. But further performances were canceled when U.S. entry into the war fulfilled the goals of the organization, which soon dissolved. Hecht continued his own "fight for freedom" by aiding the war effort however he could. He wrote for the National War Fund and the Office of War Information and joined committees to promote the cause of Russian War Relief. But by the end of 1942, with the first confirmed reports of mass killings of Jews in Europe, Hecht devoted himself full time to the cause of Jewish rescue. By that point, in the seven years since his first anti-Nazi editorial, he had become a national spokesman for the antifascist cause and, with "Fun to Be Free," an expert propagandist of the stage. With his newfound prominence and theatrical resourcefulness, he was poised to become a uniquely effective advocate for European Jewry as well as an unprecedentedly outspoken Jewish voice in the American theatre.

# 2

# Breaking the Silence

## *We Will Never Die*

ON NOVEMBER 25, 1942, an Associated Press report appeared in both the *New York Times* and the *Washington Post* claiming that "approximately half the estimated four million Jews in Nazi-occupied Europe had been slain in an 'extermination campaign'" and that "Hitler has ordered the extermination of all Jews in Nazi-ruled Europe in 1942."[1] This news—announced by Rabbi Stephen Wise (leader of the American Jewish Congress), based on European sources and confirmed by the U.S. State Department—became the first published report in major American newspapers confirming the basic facts of what only later would be called the Holocaust. For the time being, however, it remained only one of many ongoing stories about the multiple fronts of World War II. (The *Post* ran the AP story on page six, and the *Times* on page ten.) No immediate government action was taken, and, with no Allied forces yet deployed in Europe, it had no impact on the military conduct of the war.

The Japanese attack on Pearl Harbor on December 7, 1941, may have finally stirred the United States out of isolationism and committed the American public to entering the war, but the battle most Americans rallied to fight that day had nothing to do with the Jews of Europe. With American forces not directly engaging with German forces until the North African campaign of late 1942, public attention was more focused on the immediate fate of U.S. servicemen in the Pacific than events across the Atlantic. As Paul Fussell recalls of the nation's mood at that time, "The slogan was conspicuously 'Remember Pearl Harbor.' No one ever shouted or sang 'Remember Poland.'"[2]

Given the low priority accorded to the unfolding catastrophe of Hitler's Final Solution, it was all the more remarkable in March 1943—less than four months after those ominous headlines first appeared—when the actor Jacob Ben-Ami, dressed in the ceremonial white *kittel* and *kippah* of a rabbi, stepped onto the stage of New York's Madison Square Garden and addressed a sold-out audience of 20,000 spectators in prayer: "Almighty God, Father of the poor and the weak, Strength of the Righteous and Hope of all who dream of goodness and justice; Almighty God who favored the children of Israel with his light—we are here to affirm that this light still shines in us. We are here to say our prayers for the two million who have been killed in Europe, because they bear the name of your first children—the Jews."[3] This was the opening prologue of Hecht's *We Will Never Die: A Memorial Dedicated to the 2,000,000 Jewish Dead of Europe*, the first representation of the Holocaust on the American stage.

A product of Hecht's new partnership with the militant Zionist leader Bergson, *We Will Never Die* was an unusual collaboration between a band of renegade Jewish nationalists from Palestine and a group of American show business celebrities politically active in the Popular Front. They joined forces not only to save the Jews of Europe but also to change American perceptions of Jews as defenseless victims—a stereotype they believed only encouraged neglect of and indifference toward their cause. As expressed in a stagecraft that mixed elements of pageantry, religious ritual, symbolist drama, and 1930s agitprop theatre, Hecht's theatre of Jewish empowerment, agency, and self-determination marked a turning point in the representation of Jews on the American stage.

## MUSCULAR JUDAISM

Before U.S. entry into the war, Hecht's political rhetoric regarding Nazism was generally more antifascist than pro-Jewish. His 1941 interventionist pageant *It's Fun to Be Free*, for example, argued for war against Germany in broad terms of America's historical values of liberty, equality, and opposition to tyranny (see chapter 1). But as Germany proceeded to advance through Europe, he began to advocate more openly for the cause of Jews directly. His first major platform for doing so was *PM*, a progressive daily paper launched by the editor and publisher Ralph Ingersoll in 1940. Seeking a broad coalition to promote the paper's interventionist stance, Ingersoll hired Hecht to write (beginning in January 1941) a column called "A Thousand and One Afternoons in New York," a space Hecht frequently used (despite the localized title) as a forum for his antifascist advocacy and denouncing of antisemitism. As he later said of his time at *PM*, "I was as much Jew as reporter."[4]

Hecht's most powerful personal statement to date of his own Jewish identity was his *PM* column "My Tribe Is Called Israel" from April 15, 1941, in which he stated, "I write of Jews today, I who never knew himself as one before, because that part of me which is Jewish is under a violent and ape-like attack."[5] The column is less about overseas "apes," though, than his fellow American Jews, particularly "those Jews who think they can remove themselves as targets by turning their foolish backs to the battle." His previous columns about antisemitism, he says, have led to a "barrage of strangely nervous and sadly sensitive letters" from Jewish readers who were "sick to death of such efforts as mine to Judaize them and ghettoize them again and increase generally the Jew-consciousness of the world."[6] But it is too late to worry about any self-exposure, Hecht argues, because "we are Jews in the eyes of our enemies." "My way of defending myself," he challenges his implied Jewish readers, "is to answer as a Jew."[7]

One Jewish reader of that column he did not expect was a visitor from Palestine, Peter Bergson, who had arrived a year earlier to lobby the still neutral U.S. government for aid to Jewish refugees. Surprised and frustrated by the indifference he encountered in the halls of power, Bergson was relieved to find in Hecht's *PM* columns a voice of unusually forceful and explicit Jewish advocacy in the mainstream American press. He reached out to Hecht shortly after reading "My Tribe Is Called Israel," and the two met in late April 1941, launching the partnership that became the primary driver of Hecht's Jewish activism throughout the war and after. Together they produced a highly visible propaganda campaign to raise American awareness of the Holocaust as it happened, a campaign whose two main weapons were print newspaper ads and live theatrical performance.

"Peter Bergson" was the American alias of Hillel Kook, born in Lithuania in 1915 before his family resettled in British-ruled Mandatory Palestine. As a young man he became an acolyte of Vladimir (Ze'ev) Jabotinsky and his Revisionist Zionist movement, which had splintered off from the dominant Labor Zionist party over Jabotinsky's insistence on maximal territorial demands for Jewish settlement in Palestine and his call for violent resistance to British governance. Central to Jabotinsky's appeal to his followers was his promotion of "Muscular Judaism," a philosophy that challenged the antisemitic stereotype of Jews (especially Jewish men) as physically weak by projecting a more dynamic and militant image on the world stage. He put this idea into practice during World War I, when he successfully lobbied the British military in 1917 to create a division of Palestinian Jews (a "Jewish Legion") to fight Ottoman forces under the British flag. As a result, Jabotinsky cemented a reputation as "the first military hero of the Zionist revival" and a "theoretician of Jewish militarism."[8]

Bergson first came to the United States in 1940 accompanying Jabotinsky on a speaking tour, but when his mentor died on the trip, Bergson remained as the movement's chief American representative. In the summer of 1941, inspired by the Jewish Legion, Bergson founded his own Committee for a Jewish Army, an organization he immediately recruited Hecht to join as its chief propagandist in the American media. "Hecht and Bergson were a perfect match from the start," according to the Bergson chronicler Rafael Medoff. "Both men were fired by a determination to shatter the image of the Jew as weakling, and replace it with the image of Jew as soldier."[9] Outside of their common dedication to Jewish empowerment, though, the Bergson-Hecht partnership was an unusual one. The Revisionist Zionist movement was on an ultranationalist trajectory that ultimately took form in the right-wing *Herut* and *Likud* parties of modern Israeli politics. Hecht shunned political labels of right and left, but he had been very active since the thirties in liberal and progressive politics under the antifascist platform of the Popular Front. Other, more established Zionist organizations in the United States were, at the time, more closely allied with American liberalism (Zionist Organization of America, American Jewish Congress), but Hecht had grown impatient with their cautious approach to political lobbying and their reluctance to aggressively pressure public officials. The Revisionists were virtually unknown in the United States and had no following, but Bergson's penchant for bold political rhetoric better suited Hecht's own approach to public relations and his sense of showmanship. Ironically, therefore, Bergson "won a surprising level of support from American progressives" and "succeeded in creating an almost impossible synthesis between . . . left-wing Jews and [his] right-wing Zionist organization."[10]

As an executive board co-chairman of Bergson's Committee for a Jewish Army, Hecht spent the fall of 1941 and much of 1942 writing press releases and newspaper advertisements promoting it, as well as hosting fundraising meetings amongst his Broadway and Hollywood colleagues. But when the "extermination" reports started appearing in the American press later that autumn, the committee's mission changed. Outraged that American newspapers were only running brief items about the rapid escalation of Nazi atrocities (and not even on their front pages), Bergson and his colleagues vowed to raise public awareness and shock the American public as much as the news had shocked them.

The committee had already benefited from Hecht's copywriting assistance and connections to Hollywood donors, but now, recalls Bergson's colleague Yitshaq Ben-Ami, they needed "Hecht's dramatic talents" to "break through the apathy and wariness of the Jews of America."[11] Hecht agreed that "a theatrical representation of the extermination might shake up the Jewish community and exert some pressure on the [Roosevelt] administration," and, perhaps recalling the success of *It's Fun to Be Free*, "had an inspiration for a possible dramatic presentation at Madison Square Garden which would also be shown in Washington and elsewhere."[12]

## A DIVIDED FRONT

Hecht initially envisioned this "theatrical representation" as a collaborative effort of the entire Broadway Jewish community. But unlike in the prewar antifascist campaign of the thirties, he now found his otherwise politically active colleagues more reluctant when the cause focused specifically on Jews. In his 1954 memoir *A Child of the Century*, Hecht tells the story of a meeting he convened in January 1943 at the home of George S. Kaufman, one of Broadway's leading playwrights, where he invited a few dozen theatre artists, people he describes as "the box-office flower of American culture" who "could command the press of the world," and who, "in addition to wit, success, and influence, they had in common the fact that they were all Jews."[13] According to Hecht, he made an impassioned plea that they, as prominent American Jews, use their status to make a significant intervention in the fate of the war: "What would happen if these brilliant Jews cried out with passion against the German butchers? If these socially and artistically celebrated Jews spoke up in rage at the murder of their people! How they could dramatize the German crime! How loudly they could present the nightmare to America and the world! . . . I recited all the facts I knew about the Jewish killings. I said I felt certain that if we banded together and let loose our talents and our moral passion against the Germans, we might halt the massacre."[14] According to Hecht, this speech was met with a surprising silence, some walkouts, and even hostility. He recalls the playwright and novelist Edna Ferber as particularly affronted, asking him, "Who is paying you to do this wretched propaganda, Mister Hitler? Or is it Mister Goebbels?"[15] Hecht attributed this instant negative reaction to his audience's fears of being identified as Jews to the greater American public after having enjoyed the social acceptance of show business success. He quotes his hostess, Kaufman's wife Beatrice, offering a private apology: "You asked them to throw away the most valuable thing they own—the fact that they are Americans." To which Hecht replied, "Did they think they would be mistaken for 'real' Americans if they proved they had no hearts?"[16]

The anxiety Hecht encountered that evening reflected that of many Jewish Americans at the time who feared that if they called for precious war resources to be directed to saving other Jews, they would be seen as selfishly pursuing a

"Jewish war"—just as "America First" isolationists of the 1930s had warned against. (Charles Lindbergh in 1941 accused American Jews of "agitating for war," for "reasons which are not American.")[17] They worried that protesting antisemitic violence abroad would only fan the potential flames of it at home, and they had reason to believe so. According to Leonard Dinnerstein, antisemitism on the home front actually increased during the war years: "By 1943 hostility toward Jews in the United States had grown enormously," making the wartime period actually one of "anti-Semitism at high tide" in America.[18] In the thirties, Hecht's Jewish American antifascist colleagues labored to reassure the rest of the country that a war against Germany was in the interest of the entire nation, a typically American "fight for freedom." Now Hecht was telling them to focus on the uniquely Jewish plight after all.

Fortunately for Hecht, his appeal to what he called "the thirty Jewish geniuses of New York" was not completely in vain, since Moss Hart and Kurt Weill were in attendance and pledged their support to do "anything definite in the way of Jewish propaganda."[19] Both men were veterans of the prewar Popular Front and had continued engaging in war-related benefit performances since Pearl Harbor. Weill had already worked with Hecht providing music for *It's Fun to Be Free*; Hart's political involvement dated back to his 1933 topical revue *As Thousands Cheer*, and he was currently developing a pageant-like Broadway spectacle of his own featuring active Air Force servicemen (*Winged Victory*). As *We Will Never Die* progressed, Hart agreed to direct, taking on the challenge of realizing Hecht's vision of a "mass memorial pageant" onstage. Weill was able to quickly supply a score infused with Jewish liturgical music by borrowing from his 1937 opera *The Eternal Road*, an earlier theatrical defense of Jewish heritage under the threat of antisemitism.

Another instrumental show business icon Hecht succeeded in enlisting was Billy Rose, a producer who specialized in "spectaculars" at large venues such as the circus-musical *Jumbo* at the New York Hippodrome (co-written by Hecht) and his "Aquacade" show at the 1939 World's Fair. (He even produced a musical spectacle based on Sinclair Lewis's antifascist novel *It Can't Happen Here*.)[20] In contrast to his usual fare, Rose was careful to publicize *We Will Never Die* not as an entertainment but as a civic and religious event. He successfully lobbied Governor Thomas Dewey of New York to declare the day of the Madison Square Garden premiere (March 9) an official "Day of Mourning"—"a day to be set aside by the citizens of our State to offer prayer to Almighty God for the Jews who have been brutally massacred."[21]

Even more notable were some of the performers Hecht ultimately convinced to appear on stage. Almost as bold a statement as the written pleas and polemics in Hecht's script was the sheer presence of successful Jewish American actors who, after years of acceding to Hollywood deracinating norms, were now embracing their Jewish identity more publicly than ever before. Not all of the leading actors in the event's six different casts in New York and on tour were Jewish; but for those who were, their appearance provided them a powerful opportunity to embrace a dual Jewish American identity in the course of advocating for both European Jews and the American war effort. This was especially true for Paul Muni, Edward G. Robinson, and John Garfield, all major stars of the Warner Brothers studio. All three had been highly active in Hollywood Popular Front circles, especially in antifascist organizations like the Hollywood Anti-Nazi League. *We Will Never Die* provided these icons of stage and screen a unique opportunity not only to publicly acknowledge their own Jewishness (which in many cases had been obscured by studio-mandated name changes) but to model a new Jewish identity in America along the lines of Hecht and Bergson's "Muscular Judaism."

## A "MASS MEMORIAL"

In envisioning *We Will Never Die* as, in his words, a "pageant," Hecht was drawing on a theatrical form prominent both in American popular culture and in recent Zionist activism. American civic pageantry of the early twentieth-century Progressive Era was a familiar vehicle for communities to document and enact their histories, as well as for more outwardly political demonstrations, such as the 1913 Paterson Strike Pageant presented by the International Workers of the World (IWW). In the early 1930s, the American Zionist leader Meyer Weisgal produced two large-scale pageants in Chicago celebrating Jewish heritage, *Israel Reborn* (1932) and *The Romance of a People* (1933), as well as Kurt Weill and Franz Werfel's opera, *The Eternal Road* (1937), which retained many elements of pageantry in its series of biblical reenactments. But what distinguished *We Will Never Die* formally from all these predecessors was its explicit framing as a religious service, specifically a "Mass Memorial Dedicated to the Two Million Jewish Dead of Europe." Hecht announced to the press his intention "to bring a Madison Square Garden audience to the large grave of Jewry and let them stand for two hours looking into its remarkable contents."[22] And yet, the event would have failed its producers' intentions if it left audiences merely despondent. Instead, it strove to embody the Bergson group's motto, "Action, not Pity." *We Will Never Die* balanced acts of mourning and remembrance with episodes of valor and vengeance. It opened with a rabbinical prayer, followed by a tribute to the heroes of Jewish history (the "Roll Call"). The present-day heroics of

Jewish soldiers and resistance fighters were then dramatized ("Jews in the War" and the subsequently added "Battle of the Warsaw Ghetto"). The evening concluded with a return to mourning but also an act of bearing witness, with ghosts of Jewish victims testifying at a future war crimes trial against the Axis nations ("Remember Us").

In its staging, the performance enacted the rituals of a memorial service in several ways—starting with the transformation of Madison Square Garden, a venue that usually hosted sporting events and political conventions, into a sacred space. (Ironically, the hall had been the site of controversial rallies of the German American Bund in 1939 and the America First Committee in 1941.) Two accomplished Broadway stage designers, Sointu Syrjala and Lemuel Ayers, collaborated on the elaborate setting, which draped the auditorium in black curtains and erected on the stage platform two forty-foot "tablets" bearing the Ten Commandments.[23] In a signal embracing both Jewish and American identities, a Star of David hung atop the tablets alongside an American flag.

Hecht sets the scene in his opening stage directions: "The lights of the meeting hall are dim. Two towering Tablets containing the Ten Commandments loom at the back of the stage. A flight of stairs leads down from them to the stage level. There is a space of four feet between the two Tablets. When the Tablets are lighted the music begins. It is the Yom Kippur music. A cantor appears in the orchestra and sings Kol Nidre" (11). The "Yom Kippur music" refers to Weill's seven-minute overture to the pageant, which powerfully set the tone for the evening's "mass memorial" framing. As with nearly all of Weill's music for *We Will Never Die*, the overture drew from his score for *The Eternal Road*, for which he had conducted extensive research into Jewish liturgical music.[24] (Weill also knew this tradition intimately as the son of a cantor.) It opens with brass notes imitating the call of the shofar, the traditional ram's horn associated with the celebration of the Jewish new year at Rosh Hashanah, but (as the printed program reminded audiences) has also historically represented "the Hebrews' clarion call for battle."[25] Weill then introduces the Kol Nidre melody of the Yom Kippur service, but as part of a haunting medley in which it alternates with the Zionist anthem "Hatikvah"—creating a tension between the mourning of the Jewish "Day of Atonement" and the utopian aspirations of Zionism.[26]

Weill's arrangement of the Kol Nidre, however, is not set to the traditional Aramaic text. He transforms the prayer (in English) from an appeal for forgiveness into a plea for rescue by substituting lines from Psalm 22, beginning with its famous opening entreaty, "My God, my God, why hast thou forsaken me?"[27] Popularly known in Western culture as the dying words of Christ (Jesus quotes the psalm from the cross in the gospels of Mark and Matthew), the original prayer is a lament over God's silence in the face of suffering. Jewish tradition also associates the text explicitly with political upheaval, as "a lament by David over the future exile" and "the threat against the Jews by Haman in the book of Esther."[28] The rest of Weill's new lyrics (presumably composed in collaboration or consultation with Hecht) emphasize the psalm's evocation of persecution and abandonment.

> I cry unto thee and thou hearest me not.
> Deliver my soul from the sword of the dog.
> Remember thou me for thy goodness' sake.
> I cry for thee.[29]

Unlike the psalms, *We Will Never Die* was not addressed to God but to humanity. In the hall of Madison Square Garden, the "thee" and "thou" addressed by the figure of the cantor referenced the audience and the American public at large—it was their silence Hecht was indicting and their help he was entreating. In performance, this message was amplified bodily in the singing of the Kol Nidre by Kurt Baum, a Metropolitan Opera tenor and a recent Jewish refugee from Czechoslovakia.[30]

## "THE VICTORY OF THEIR DYING"

Continuing in the ritualistic stages of a synagogue service, Hecht follows the song of a cantor with the prayer of a rabbi. "From between the Tablets appears the figure of a Rabbi in a satin robe and a white satin hat," he writes. "The Rabbi walks down the steps and takes his place at the central altar near the front of the stage" (11). The "Rabbi" here was actually an actor: Jacob Ben-Ami, longtime star of the New York Yiddish Theatre.[31] The poetic two-page monologue Hecht wrote for the evening's prologue required a performer of Ben-Ami's commanding presence and oratorical gifts, and he continued to perform the role of "Rabbi" on tour across the country.

In the spirit of "Action, not Pity," the rabbi presents the Jewish dead as martyrs, not helpless victims, even to the extent of finding a "victory" in their suffering—a victory defined in the biblical prophecy that Hecht adopted as his title: "We are not here to weep for them although our eyes are stricken with this picture and our hearts burdened with their fate. We are here to honor them and to proclaim the victory of their dying. For in our Testament are written the words of Habakkuk, prophet of Israel, 'They shall never die'" (11). Hecht again alternates between alarming the audience about the reality of the calamity facing European Jewry and emboldening them not to surrender to despair or

Figure 1. *We Will Never Die* at New York's Madison Square Garden. The Shema Yisrael prayer is "led by our rabbis who have come from the dead ghettos of Europe." Source: Ben Hecht, *We Will Never Die: A Memorial Dedicated to the 2,000,000 Jewish Dead of Europe* (published script), New York: Committee for a Jewish Army of Stateless and Palestinian Jews, 1943. Newberry Library, Ben Hecht Papers.

accept the success of Hitler's Final Solution as inevitable. It may be too late for those already dead to emerge victorious; but their loss can still inspire victory in their name. And it is America—and American Jews—who must take up their fight: "We are here to strengthen our hearts, to take into our veins the pride and courage of the millions of innocent people who have fallen and are still to fall before the German massacre. They were unarmed. But not we! We live in a land whose arm is stronger than the arm of the German Goliath. This land is our David" (12). The rhetorical shift from Habakkuk's "they" to the "we" of Hecht's title mirrors this implied act of the audience taking on the identity of the dead and acting in their place.

Hecht concludes the rabbi's sermon with another formal prayer, the *Shema Yisrael*, and in a striking theatrical moment, calls for "twenty rabbis, dressed in the various costumes of their sects and countries," to take the stage (12).[32] Unlike the actor Ben-Ami, Hecht meant these to be real refugees drawn from the local community wherever the performance was taking place: "The prayer, Shema Israel will be led by our rabbis who have come from the dead ghettos of Europe. They are among the few who have survived. They were witnesses of the killing of our folk in Germany, Poland, Holland, France, Czecho-Slovakia,

Roumania, Russia and all the places overrun by the Germans" (13). The singing of the prayer—in Hebrew—then followed, with the rabbis backed by a full chorus.[33] In a performance so concerned with marking the absence of the victims, it was important to assert presence as well, to demonstrate that the Jews as a people "will never die."

## "THE ROLL OF THE GREAT JEWS"

Another way *We Will Never Die* works to combat fatalism in the present is by reclaiming the glories of the Jewish past. The pageant's second episode, the "Roll Call," celebrated over one hundred figures from Jewish history, from biblical patriarchs to contemporary popular culture icons. As onstage narrators called out their names, a procession of candle bearers gradually filled the auditorium with light in a gesture akin to a memorial service, yet also triumphant. The purpose, as Hecht's narration says, was "to give strength to hearts that have forgotten in their sorrow the shield, the sword, the valor and the indestructibility of their people."[34]

As historical pageantry, the "Roll Call" section of *We Will Never Die* elevated Jews from marginalized victims to integral players in Western Civilization. "The halls of fame of a hundred nations hold the names of Jews who have given value to life," the narrators' say and, indeed, Hecht's selection stretches across centuries and continents (21).[35] His biblical personae run from Moses up through Jesus; next come two millennia of Jewish scholars, from rabbis and commentators (Hillel, Akiva, Rashi) to giants of medieval and Renaissance science and philosophy (Halevi, Spinoza, Maimonides) and on to nineteenth-century revolutionary thinkers (Marx, Freud). Figures from the arts dominate the modern period: writers (Heinrich Heine, Sholem-Aleichem), composers (Giacomo Meyerbeer, Jacques Offenbach), painters (Camille Pissarro, Amedeo Modigliani), and actors (Sarah Bernhardt and Rachel Félix). Hecht ends with twenty-one winners of the Nobel Prize ("our world champions," he calls them), including the, at the time, living scientists Albert Einstein and Niels Bohr, both refugees who had fled Hitler's Europe for America.[36]

The presence on the list of people who were still alive may seem out of place amid the trappings of a memorial service, but the continuity Hecht stresses of Jewish culture over the centuries only strengthens the promise behind the pageant's title. Hecht even includes some contemporaries from the literary and performing arts: the classical musicians Vladimir Horowitz and Jascha Heifetz, the Broadway composers George Gershwin and Jerome Kern, and the playwright Ferenc Molnár. There are even names of historical figures whose Jewish identity is either tenuous or completely unfounded (e.g., Michel de Montaigne, Nostradamus, Georges Bizet, Camille Saint-Saëns, and even Pablo Picasso).[37]

In writing *We Will Never Die*, "Hecht immersed himself in research," Yitshaq Ben-Ami recalls, "delving into Jewish history and lore with a vengeance."[38] One specific source Hecht appears to have consulted was the Oxford professor Cecil Roth's *The Jewish Contribution to Civilization*, published in America in 1940. (Seventy-five percent of the names from Hecht's roll call are cited in Roth's book, and some lines from the script clearly paraphrase or copy from it verbatim.)[39] Roth's book would have been especially valuable to Hecht due to its stated mission of supplanting a common "lachrymose" narrative of Jewish history with one that publicized the various successes of Jews within Western Christian society and their lasting positive impact upon it.[40] The "Roll Call" also continued the work of *It's Fun to Be Free* in reminding audiences of Jews' integral role in American history. Haym Salomon—a hero of the earlier pageant—receives mention here, as does the Revolutionary War soldier Isaac Franks, "one of the hundreds of Jewish heroes of '76" (17). The inclusion of two writers of nineteenth-century Americana—the California Gold Rush chronicler Brett Harte and John Howard Payne, the composer of "Home, Sweet Home"—goes further in arguing how intertwined Jews have been in even the most seemingly "white" aspects of American heritage (even when claims of their Jewish lineage were questionable).[41] Even reminders of Americans already widely known to be Jewish reinforced their links to American folklore and patriotism. Not only is Emma Lazarus mentioned, for instance, but the final lines of her verses for the Statue of Liberty are recited. The mention of Irving Berlin, the composer of the wartime anthem "God Bless America" (and the previous Broadway season's hit revue *This Is the Army*), reminded audiences of American Jews' contributions to the nation's war effort.

In performance, the theatricality of the "Roll Call" went beyond a recited list; it was an embodied demonstration that filled the arena with Jewish history. Hecht originally imagined that "as the Narrators call the roll of the great Jews, each of them appears" and that "the costumes and faces of all the centuries light up one by one," but this pageant-like presentation was abandoned in performance in favor of a more symbolic approach.[42] The director Moss Hart staged a procession of over one hundred "black robed figures" carrying lit candles through the auditorium, "offer[ing] themselves to the audience as symbols of the light the Jews have brought into the world" (15). The *Washington Post* described the torchbearers as "a black-veiled choir ... with a candle for each of the dead Jewish luminaries."[43] The effect on stage of the first few candles might have been indiscernible, but gradually the light spread throughout the arena as the

FROM "VANISHING" TO VISIBLE

Figure 2. "Symbols of the light the Jews have brought into the world." Moss Hart's visually striking staging of the "Roll Call" scene in *We Will Never Die*. Source: Ben Hecht, *We Will Never Die: A Memorial Dedicated to the 2,000,000 Jewish Dead of Europe* (published script), New York: Committee for a Jewish Army of Stateless and Palestinian Jews, 1943. Newberry Library, Ben Hecht Papers.

hundred-plus names were called.[44] "The scroll overruns," say the narrators of the final stage picture. "The prophet Hosiah spoke of Israel that it was destined to bloom and bud and fill the world with its fruit. Here is that fruit. Here is that Jew who shall never die" (21). The powerful image of hundreds of candles emerging from the darkness of the auditorium to illuminate the stage realized the idea of Jewish visibility in a uniquely theatrical way.[45]

Jewish visibility was also embodied in the "Roll Call" by the actors narrating it at the New York premiere: Muni and Robinson, two of Hollywood's biggest stars and most prominent antifascist activists. But not until this appearance had their activism addressed Jewish issues explicitly, making their appearance in *We Will Never Die* a significant act of self-identification, a gesture they had been denied so often in their movie careers. Born Meshilem Meier Weisenfreund in the Galicia region of Austria-Hungary (now Western Ukraine) in 1895, Muni began his acting career in New York's Yiddish Theatre and became a Broadway star in 1931 as the Jewish protagonist in Elmer Rice's *Counselor-At-Law*, a play about the spiritual cost of assimilation.[46] (So identified was Muni with this role that he reprised it in a 1942 revival that was still playing on Broadway during

*We Will Never Die.*) He catapulted to movie celebrity in 1932 as the Al Capone–inspired gangster in *Scarface*, with a screenplay by Hecht. It would be the first of many "ethnic" roles for an actor who made a specialty of them in a succession of Warner Brothers films playing almost every race but his own.[47] (He did not play an expressly Jewish character on-screen until 1959 in his final film, *The Last Angry Man*.) With *The Life of Emile Zola* (1937), a project he actively pursued, he brought to the screen that landmark case of antisemitism, the Dreyfus affair, even though he himself played the "righteous gentile" role of Zola instead of the wrongly accused Jewish officer.

Though not always as critically lauded as Muni, Robinson was just as in demand in Hollywood, and the two men shared many personal parallels. Born in Romania in 1893 as Emmanuel Goldenberg (the family name lived on in his invented middle initial), Robinson likewise began in Yiddish Theatre and even co-authored *The Kibitzer*, a 1929 Broadway comedy. Like Muni, Robinson made his film debut as an Italian gangster, in 1930's *Little Caesar*, and continued to play various ruffians of indeterminate ethnicity for Warner Brothers throughout the decade before graduating to more dignified roles.[48] *Dr. Ehrlich's Magic Bullet* (1940) was another historical biography of social conscience, but with Robinson as the historical Jewish figure (the biologist Paul Ehrlich) in the central, not supporting, role. In *Confessions of a Nazi Spy* (1939), the first major studio release to seriously treat the German threat to America, Robinson starred as an FBI investigator chasing a network of German "fifth columnists"—a role matching the actor's own off-screen antifascist activism as a leader of the Hollywood Anti-Nazi League.

As narrators of the "Roll Call," Muni and Robinson were called on to deliver a kind of stage pageant equivalent of the progressive Warner Brothers historical biopics they were both often associated with. (Paul Ehrlich's name is even in the "Roll Call," spoken by Robinson himself at some performances.) But *We Will Never Die* allowed them to provide a primary and explicit Jewish focus that had not been permitted them in Hollywood. Moreover, as modern-day successful Jewish American artists themselves, they effectively took their own place in the "roll of the great Jews" in the eyes of their audience.

## FROM BAR KOCHBA TO BARNEY ROSS

In referring to the Jewish Nobel laureates in the "Roll Call" as "our world champions," Hecht inadvertently reinforced a stereotype of Jews being athletes of the brain and not the body. Jews had long gained respect for intellectual and artistic achievements, but not physical. For centuries, writes Paul Breines, "virtually the only operative images of Jewish force, strength, or power involved the Jewish brain, which would typically be housed in frail (the Jewish scholar) or fat (the Jewish merchant) male bodies, but never in rugged, muscular or lithe ones."[49] At a time of crisis like the Holocaust, this old mythology contributed to a popular perception of essential weakness and victimhood in Jews, as if their persecution were inevitable since they could not defend themselves. It was necessary in the next scene, then, for Hecht to refute the enduring "anti-Semitic critique of the Jewish body as inherently unfit for military service" with a theatrical demonstration of Jewish physical vitality and martial heroism.[50] The choice was a theatrical as well as a social intervention, since American audiences had rarely seen onstage Jewish characters in uniform. As a 1951 critical survey of Jewish American dramatic representation observed, "Considering the part Jewish soldiers have played in the wars of the United States, it is noteworthy that they have slight mention in drama."[51]

*We Will Never Die*'s second scene, "Jews in the War," begins in a more dramatic fashion than the processional pageantry of the "Roll Call," with an enactment of the recent heroics of one Jewish American GI, Corporal Irving Strobing. In May 1942, Strobing was the Army Signal Corps operator during the Battle of Corregidor, where American forces lost their last stronghold against Japanese invaders for control of the Philippines. At the time, it was a devastating setback for the Pacific campaign in the early months of the U.S. war effort. But Strobing's efforts to continue sending out telegraph dispatches from the front under heavy fire soon became famous when released by the War Department in an effort to salvage an uplifting tale of American morale from the defeat.[52] One aspect of Strobing's messages that stood out from the usual war reporting was his bursts of irreverent humor during lulls in the action, many of which revealed his Brooklyn roots. ("We are waiting for God only knows what. How about a chocolate soda?")[53] His last message, tapped out amid the panic of the battle's final moments before surrender, resonated especially with Jewish Americans with its invocation of home: "Get this to my mother, Mrs. Minnie Strobing, 605 Barbey Street, Brooklyn, NY. They are to get along OK."

In Strobing's account of the battle, Hecht saw a unique opportunity to dramatize the experience of a Jewish soldier in his own words, employing a "documentary theatre" approach akin to the stagecraft of the "Living Newspaper" plays of the Federal Theatre Project in the 1930s. At the start of "Jews in the War," "three soldiers, in torn and soiled uniforms, appear quickly and throw themselves down upon the upper stage," Hecht writes. "They carry a field telegraph set . . . [and] we hear the clicking of a telegraph key" (21). Then, "two narrators, dressed in soldier uniforms" read from the dispatches and tell Strobing's story:

SECOND SOLDIER: A twenty-two year old Jewish boy from Brooklyn, by name Irving Strobing sits at his post and pounds away at his wireless key. He's sending a last message to the world. Corregidor is saying goodbye to the folks back home.

FIRST SOLDIER: Listen to it. This is how an American soldier sounds in defeat. Here's how a Jewish Boy from Brooklyn sends in his last words. We'll translate the Morse code for you. Irving is telling the world. (22)

According to the *New York World*, Hecht mined the exciting battle reportage in Strobing's messages for full dramatic effect: "With a telegraph key clicking in the darkness of the Garden . . . the assemblage listened in emotional silence as a narrator gave the last words."[54] The real Strobing was captured as a prisoner of war by the Japanese, not killed in action, but Hecht takes the dramatic license of treating him as a martyr. After his final words to his family are read, the telegraphic "clicking" sound that had been underscoring the scene suddenly stops, leaving the audience in a moment of silence, followed by the playing of "Taps" (22). "That was the army's hail and farewell from Corregidor," the narrators say, "the salute from the dying delivered by Irving Strobing" (23).

After Strobing's story, Hecht expands the focus to the Jewish soldiers currently fighting across all the Allied forces internationally. "Hundreds of Jewish soldiers, sailors, fliers and marines have been decorated and cited for valor," say the narrators. "They are under the fighting flags now. They have been under them since the first guns sounded in Poland" (23). A procession of actors dressed in the uniforms and, literally, bearing the flags of each nation are then introduced. "They were under the brave flags of the Greeks," begins the litany, followed by men representing the French, Dutch, Soviet, British, and, finally, American armies. (Each soldier's entrance is accompanied by his nation's anthem or signature march song, as arranged by Weill: "The Marseillaise" signals the French soldier, "Tipperary" the British, "Song of the Plains" the Russian, and George M. Cohan's "Over There" announces the American GI.) There is even a figure representing a Palestinian "Jewish Army," as promoted by Bergson. (Weill uses the "Hatikvah" to stand for the Palestinian soldier.) The Palestinian Jews, say the narrators, "have a flag of their own—the Star of David raised above the reclaimed deserts of Palestine. . . . There are another hundred thousand sturdy pioneers of Palestine and they cry for the right to fight. . . . 'We Jews of Europe are being killed as Jews. Give us the right to strike back as Jews. Let the Star of David be one of the flags that enters Berlin'" (24–25).

The procession ends with a call from the narrators for a moment of silence in the audience—"in honor of our soldiers. All our soldiers, Jewish and Gentile, who have died in this war."[55] The linking of the Jewish soldier's sacrifice to the greater national cause is a sentiment reinforced by the singing of the "Battle Hymn of the Republic" that immediately follows. Ending the "Jews in the War" segment with this iconic abolitionist anthem, a symbol of America's own Civil War sacrifices on behalf of racial equality, returns the focus of *We Will Never Die* to the broader American "Fight for Freedom" that Hecht had championed in *It's Fun to Be Free*.

One reason Hecht considered "Jews in the War" essential to *We Will Never Die* was to dispel antisemitic accusations that Jewish Americans were avoiding military service due to cowardice, physical weakness, or even a selfish desire to let others fight for "their" cause. In reality, according to Deborah Dash Moore, "approximately 550,000 Jewish men and women served in the United States armed forces during World War II, the equivalent of thirty-seven divisions."[56] But such facts did not put the accusations to rest. Public opinion polls taken throughout the war years signaled a continuing distrust of Jews' willingness to serve: "About a third of the population thought Jews wanted to avoid military service and Jews were far more frequently accused of such desires than any other ethnic group."[57] Even within the ranks of the military itself, many officers initially argued against the integration of Jewish and Christian troops, and antisemitic literature unofficially circulated on bases.[58]

The "Jews in the War" procession of nations, therefore, climaxes with a reminder of the Jewish *American* sacrifice in particular, presenting it in recognizably traditional patriotic ways:

SECOND SOLDIER: And under the flag of the U.S.A., three hundred thousand Jews are marching and sailing and flying forth to battle. And their spirit is the spirit of Washington, Lincoln and Roosevelt—of Yankee Doodle and the Battle Hymn of the Republic—of Bar Kochba and Irving Strobing—
FIRST SOLDIER (*in a ringing voice*): and Meyer Levin.
(*The soldiers dip their flags and all stand silent for a minute.*) (25–26)

The name of Meyer Levin receives special emphasis (and prompts the "moment of silence" concluding the scene) because Levin, unlike Strobing, was a true casualty of the war and a particularly famous one. In December 1941, he had won renown as the bombardier of the first American air raid on Japanese forces, three days after Pearl Harbor. (He survived that mission, but perished in another battle in January 1943.) The tribute to Levin was especially poignant at the Madison Square Garden premiere when Levin's parents were known to be in attendance.[59]

Hecht's reference to Bar Kochba in his salute to Jewish American soldiers is even more striking. The figure of this ancient Judean warrior (who briefly overthrew Roman rule in 132 C.E.) was central to the Muscular Judaism movement and was invoked frequently by Nordau, Jabotinsky, and other early Zionist leaders. Hecht first mentions Bar Kochba in the "Roll Call": "If you would know whence the Jewish soldiers in the fox holes, tanks and bombers of today derive their fierceness, look on Bar Kochba. Bar Kochba, the mighty warrior who marched forth against the Roman legions and scattered and terrified them for three years. And who for a year stood with his small army against the entire might of the Roman world and died with all his soldiers on the ramparts of the ancient city of Bethar" (15). Through the ages, Bar Kochba has actually been a controversial figure who has long divided Jewish scholars over whether his failed revolt should inspire Jews to permanently take up arms or instead caution them against reckless violence.[60] But in *We Will Never Die*, Hecht's narrators proudly proclaim, "Bar Kochba's boys are scattered in a hundred armies," transforming that complicated story into a defiant triumph (23).

In addition to Strobing and Levin, another of those "boys" mentioned is Private Barney Ross of the Marines—better known to the audience as one of the most famous American prizefighters of the 1930s. "In Ross's boxing prime, he'd been seen by Jews around the world as a living embodiment of what Max Nordau had spoken of," writes Ross's biographer Douglas Century.[61] Shortly after Pearl Harbor, Ross enlisted at the age of thirty-two and was decorated for bravery after fighting in the battle of Guadalcanal in November 1942. Four months later, Hecht capitalized on his fame in "Jews in the War": "The Jew, said the Nazis, cannot fight. Wait till Barney Ross gets to Berlin" (23). As a modern exemplar of the "Fighting Jew" ideal of Muscular Judaism, the figure of Ross fused ancient Judean iconography with the contemporary Jewish American experience.[62]

The invocation of Ross in "Jews in the War" took on added dimensions in the Los Angeles performance, when it was uttered by the movie star John Garfield—who was actually in negotiations at that time to play Ross on-screen.[63] Garfield's participation in *We Will Never Die* cemented his already well-established public image as a "Fighting Jew" of American popular culture.[64] Born in 1913 in New York City as Jacob Julius Garfinkle and discovered by the Group Theatre in the early thirties, Garfield's elevation to movie stardom at Warner Brothers in 1938 reflected how naturally he fit the studio's mold of ethnic masculinity as established by Muni and Robinson.[65] Initially typecast as an urban criminal, he rose in studio casting during the war from hoodlum to hero, especially in a series of successful combat pictures beginning with *Air Force*, which opened February 3,

1943, and was still playing in cinemas throughout the tour of *We Will Never Die*.⁶⁶ As an on-screen embodiment of the GI Joe, Garfield was a perfect Hollywood analog to real-life Jewish servicemen like Strobing and Ross. (A weak heart rendered him ineligible to serve overseas himself.)

*We Will Never Die* was a rare opportunity for Garfield not only to campaign for a Jewish cause but—in his enactment of the Strobing dispatches—to play a Jewish character.⁶⁷ While his Ross movie never materialized, Garfield did finally play a Jewish soldier in the postwar drama *Gentleman's Agreement* (1947), one of Hollywood's first films directly addressing American antisemitism. (The screenplay was by *We Will Never Die*'s director, Moss Hart.) Not only does his character, Dave Goldman, not hide his ethnicity, in one scene he expresses it with physical force by lunging at a patron in a restaurant over an antisemitic slur. As a decorated officer seen throughout the film in uniform, Dave Goldman marked the culmination of Garfield's wartime Fighting Jew persona.

## "REMEMBER US": A SYMBOLIST REVENGE TRAGEDY

*We Will Never Die*'s final scene completes its journey from the Jewish past to the present and into the future. But it is a bleak future, despite its prediction of a German defeat at war's end. In imagining a future "peace conference," Hecht presents a prophetic warning of what will happen to the Jews of Europe if no one stops the current massacre, even with an Allied victory. The scene's opening image of a long conference table creates a stage picture eerily anticipating (in retrospect) the Nuremburg war crime trials of 1945–1946. "We come to tomorrow," the narrators announce. "There will be a great meeting hall with tall windows. In this hall will stand a long table. It will be the table of judgment." The stage directions call for "three Germans, two in frock coats and one in uniform, with the swastika on their sleeves," to "go to the empty table and sit down with their backs to the audience."⁶⁸ Hecht had been developing the concept of a fictional trial against Germany for a while. In December 1942, he received a delivery of dispatches from Hayim Greenberg, an émigré activist and editor of the New York–based journal *Jewish Frontier*. These were eyewitness accounts from European sources documenting massacres not yet reported in the American press.⁶⁹ Hecht decided to publish these in the form of an article written in the voice of the victims to maximize the emotional impact of the gruesome reports. Entitled "Remember Us," it consisted of imagined first-person accounts of fifteen real massacres from across Eastern Europe. First appearing in *American Mercury*'s February 1943 issue (one month before *We Will Never Die*), thousands more readers saw it when *Reader's Digest* published an abridged version later that month.[70] It was one of the most detailed accounts of the Holocaust to have appeared in the American press by that time.[71]

The article's presentation of ghosts bearing witness at the trial of their murderers was already inherently dramatic, and Hecht instantly saw the potential for adapting it to the stage. ("Reading it in the magazine, I thought of a larger idea and set out to test its practicality.")[72] Again adopting the form of documentary theatre—where reportage is foregrounded as reportage and not filtered through the conventions of realist drama—the staging of "Remember Us" in *We Will Never Die* maintained the distant voices of the dead rather than stage the atrocities referenced in the dispatches through direct visual representation. "Out of the Tablets come seven Jews, two men, a rabbi, two women and a child," Hecht's stage directions read. "Their faces are grey. They move slowly, and stiffly the fingers of their hands are curled inward. They advance down two steps and remain motionless facing the peace table. They are the dead and their heads are bowed. One of the dead raises his head. He speaks in emotionless tones." This ghostly figure then says, "Remember us. In the town of Freiberg in the Black Forest two hundred of us were hanged and left dangling out of our kitchen windows. We watched our synagogue burn and our rabbi flogged to death" (33). Eight more stories follow, told by more ghosts as "a stream of dead figures comes, one by one, out of the tablets . . . form[ing] a rough circle around the brightly lighted peace table." They tell of a massacre at a Yom Kippur service ("all of us were killed before our Atonement day was done"); of old men forced to "clean out German latrines" with their prayer shawls; of 500 women and children gunned down in the marketplace of a Polish town; of Jewish prisoners dying from starvation while being transported across Europe in locked freight cars; and of a hundred teenage girls in Warsaw who poisoned themselves rather than serve as prostitutes for German occupiers. This steady accumulation of graphic details over the scene's three pages of dialogue provided audiences more information about the Holocaust than most Americans at the time could have found in their daily newspaper. Presenting their stories as more than just "routine" German atrocities, Hecht again "destroyed the anonymity of the victim" by foregrounding the uniquely antisemitic nature of the attacks, leaving no doubt that what marked these people for death was their Jewishness.

By this point in the scene, the "peace conference" has become a courtroom prosecution, and it is not just Germany on trial. Positioning the defeated Axis Power representatives facing upstage, "sit[ting] down with their backs to the audience," Hecht placed the audience in the dock as well (34). The actors playing the victims, facing downstage, looked out over the heads of their persecutors into the auditorium. In performance, their repeated refrain of "remember us" clearly addressed the spectators of 1943, not a fictional jury of the postwar future. A correspondent for the *Philadelphia Record* perceived the intimation of collective guilt: "The bare and crippled feet of the dead faltered across the stage of Convention Hall last night, and their haunting wail, 'Remember Us,' rose to the rafters that have echoed so many promises never kept . . . always whipping into its 15,000 listeners the message that we, too, have failed those who will never die."[73] The gradual filling of the stage with the Jewish dead, completely surrounding the peace table by the end, echoed the staging of the "Roll Call" in once again overwhelming the scene with Jewish bodies, suggesting the ultimate prevailing of Jewish victims over their enemies. But theatrically, the haunting effect of these ghosts countered any easy optimism. The scene's conception and staging were not just symbolic but specifically "symbolist" in style—a theatrical mode popularized by modernist poet-playwrights like Maurice Maeterlinck and W. B. Yeats that featured "representations of imagined psychic states between life and death" through silence and "static" action "to evoke a reverie in the spectator necessary for the contemplation of the higher realms of existence."[74] Hecht, an aspiring modernist as a young writer, knew the form well. In his original draft, he conceived of the speeches as voice-overs, disembodied from the onstage actors, as if to fulfill the symbolist depiction of characters as ethereal abstractions.[75] As radio and newsreel footage of *We Will Never Die* reveals, no offstage voices were ultimately used here, but the actors delivered these speeches in a deliberately slow and almost monotonous cadence.[76] While the text of the scene may suggest the spirits of the dead seek peace, the eerie stillness of the scene in performance would have evoked a disquieting uncanniness, leaving the audience more disturbed than merely sad or mournful.

The repetition of the words "remember us" in the scene channels another dramaturgical context as well: the revenge tragedy. The phrase recalls many such utterances in plays of that genre—none more so than *Hamlet*, where the ghost of the prince's father, after recounting his own death in graphic detail, commands his son to "remember me" (1.5.91) and "revenge his foul and most unnatural murder" (1.5.25). While the "perturbed spirits" of the revenge tragedies address an onstage hero, in *We Will Never Die* it is the audience that the spectral figures rouse to action. This parallel to classical dramatic tradition is further strengthened by the feelings of disempowerment encoded in the revenge tragedy genre, where "revengers are typically frustrated victims who want retribution for a crime that goes unpunished."[77] Just as the revenge tragedy protagonist "tak[es] matters into his own hands because the institutions by which criminals are made to pay for their offences are either systematically defective or unable to cope," Hecht and his collaborators appoint themselves avengers in light of the failure of the United

States and its Allies (and their governmental "institutions") to halt the progress of Hitler's Final Solution.[78] The narrators of "Remember Us" remind the audience that Jews will not even have a seat at the table at any "peace conference," since they have no nation to represent them: "Absent from the table of judgment will be the Jew. . . . For no homeland is ever theirs. . . . The dead of many lands will speak for justice through their spokesmen around the table of judgement. The Jew alone will have no one to speak for him. His voice will remain outside the hall of judgment, to be heard only when the window is opened and the sad faint phrase drifts in, 'Remember Us'" (32–33). Here the Zionist roots of the pageant and its sponsor (the Committee for a Jewish Army of Stateless and Palestinian Jews) come to the fore. The fundamental argument behind Bergson's mission was that in the realities of geopolitics, a people without a nation have no voice in international relations.

After "Remember Us," *We Will Never Die* ended as it began, with a formal prayer. Returning to the frame of a memorial service, Hecht calls for the singing of the Kaddish. The rabbi from the prologue reenters and says, "The Jews have a prayer for their dead. It is the prayer called the Kaddish, the prayer that begins Yis-ga-dall v-yis-ka-dash. . . . Let us sing this prayer for the voiceless and the Jewish dead of Europe" (37).[79] Unlike the Kol Nidre that opened the evening, the Kaddish was sung untranslated in its original Aramaic text, a striking instance of unassimilated Jewish liturgical ritual on the American stage at the time.

## "RALLY, JEWS!": THE BATTLE OF THE WARSAW GHETTO

The first performance of *We Will Never Die* was in New York on March 9, 1943, at Madison Square Garden, which was then located in the heart of the Times Square theatre district.[80] In addition to Muni, Robinson, and Ben-Ami, the cast included such Broadway stars as Luther Adler and Sylvia Sidney (who were married at the time). Weill's score was played by the NBC Symphony Orchestra, conducted by Isaac Van Grove. The demand for tickets was so high that a second showing was added at 11:00 P.M. to follow the 8:30 premiere. With both performances playing to full capacity, a total of nearly 40,000 people saw *We Will Never Die* on its first night. (Hundreds more reportedly stood on the street outside the hall to listen to the performance over loudspeakers when they could not buy tickets.)[81]

Given the immediate interest from audiences, plans were already underway by opening night to send *We Will Never Die* on tour to other major cities. On April 12, the New York cast repeated their performance at Constitution Hall in Washington, D.C. This was followed by showings at Convention Hall in Philadelphia (April 22), Chicago Stadium (May 19), Boston Garden (June 6), and the Hollywood Bowl in Los Angeles (July 21). New cast members joined the production on tour and some of the most notable actors were non-Jewish Hollywood stars whose allegiance to Hecht and Bergson's cause stemmed from their longtime Popular Front activism: Burgess Meredith, Claude Rains, Ralph Bellamy, Edward Arnold, and Joan Leslie. Their celebrity helped attract local media attention on tour, and such publicity was as crucial to Hecht's mission as ticket sales, since every newspaper article about *We Will Never Die* added to the limited press coverage of the Holocaust itself.

The tour also enabled Hecht to update the script with new information from the continually developing story of the persecution of the Jews of Europe. In Chicago, he added the names of two more Jewish servicemen to "Jews in the War," both casualties of recent battles in New Guinea and both well known to the local audience: Maurice Levy, a Chicago-born sharpshooter decorated posthumously with a Distinguished Service Cross; and Hymie Epstein, a medic who sacrificed himself in the process of treating wounded GIs.[82]

By the time *We Will Never Die* reached Los Angeles in July, Hecht added an entirely new scene. During the tour, word spread about the Warsaw Ghetto Uprising that began in April. By mid-May, the rebellion had been crushed by German forces, but Hecht saw an opportunity to include something that had been missing in *We Will Never Die*—an example of contemporary Jews taking up arms and fighting back against their oppressors. His new scene, placed after the "Roll Call" and "Jews in the War," set the Jewish resistance fighters of the Warsaw streets alongside the ancient Israelite warriors already mentioned and the uniformed Jewish soldiers of the Allied armies in a battle scene of cinematic proportions—part Hollywood war movie, part Epic Theatre.

The three original episodes of *We Will Never Die* relied to various degrees on presentational processions (the candle bearers, the parading soldiers, and the dead massacre victims), but Hecht conceived of "The Battle of the Warsaw Ghetto" as an action-driven war narrative that would visually bring the battle to life onstage. It begins with the appearance of a new set piece, a ten-foot-high "wall" that "extends across the stage center" (26). Onstage narrators are again utilized in the scene to tell the story of the uprising; but as they set the scene, an ensemble of silent supernumeraries begins to appear, playing out the events. Hecht's opening stage directions for the scene—its atmospheric detail probably not visible to most of the Hollywood Bowl audience—seem more fitting for a fade-in from one of his film scenarios than a stage play: "We see a street inside the ghetto wall. It is night. The street is empty. . . . Groups of men, women and children have been appearing in the street. Old men with prayer books in their hands have appeared and stand facing the wall and praying. Women, holding fast to their children have appeared and stand in huddles.... The street continues to fill. Ragged gaunt figures appear. In the corner a woman falls dead. Her children sit crouched around her until she is picked up and carried away. Women sit weeping against the wall" (26–27). Amid the squalor and suffering, the rebellion quietly begins: "Four men pass through the crowd in the street, bearing a coffin on their shoulders. They lower the coffin and open it. They remove old rifles and ammunition from it and distribute these to the men and women" (27). Recorded sound effects then signal the approach of German tanks, and the stage action escalates; "groups of twenty and thirty men and women, carrying various arms, run through the street, shouting and waving their guns" as "the street inside the ghetto wall becomes a hospital [where] wounded are brought and laid out" and "fires light up the city beyond the wall" (29). For a scene written specifically for performance at the Hollywood Bowl, located at the heart of the "film colony," Hecht deployed an appropriately cinematic mise-en-scène.

"Warsaw Ghetto" evokes not just war movies in general but the very topical "European resistance" genre that had become a staple of wartime studio releases—most famously *Casablanca*, which opened nationwide in January 1943 and was still playing in some cinemas when *We Will Never Die* began its tour.[83] (Hecht even cast Paul Henreid, the actor who played *Casablanca*'s French resistance fighter, Victor Laszlo, as one of the scene's narrators.)[84] Because studios still remained reluctant throughout the war to explicitly address antisemitism, Hecht's "Battle of the Warsaw Ghetto" rewrites the genre of the European resistance narrative, recasting it with Jewish heroes.

Another 1943 resistance film that may have been on Hecht's mind at the time was Fritz Lang's *Hangmen Also Die*, released April 15, 1943. (The film is especially notable for bearing Bertolt Brecht's only screen credit during his Hollywood exile.) It depicted the May 1942 assassination in Prague of Reinhard Heydrich, one of the highest-ranking officers in the SS and Hitler's handpicked "Protector of the Reich" over conquered Eastern European lands. The Nazis' retaliatory mass execution of suspected Czech insurgents in the nearby village of Lidice had quickly become a cause of international outrage—one often cited by Hecht and Bergson as a sign of the Allies' hypocrisy regarding their relative silence about the ongoing massacres of Jews in the same region. "When they burned Lidice," read a Bergson committee ad (possibly written by Hecht), "a cry of horror went up from the civilized world. The Jew ... has witnessed and experienced the horrors of a thousand Lidices."[85]

Further linking the Warsaw Ghetto scene to contemporary cinema was its elaborate musical underscoring by the famed Hollywood composer Franz

Waxman, who also conducted the Los Angeles performance.[86] (Kurt Weill was busy rehearsing his next Broadway musical, *One Touch of Venus*.) Waxman even wrote the Warsaw fighters a "battle song" with lyrics by Frank Loesser, the Jewish American songwriter later famous for his postwar Broadway hit *Guys and Dolls*.[87] Their "Battle Hymn of the Ghetto"—its title echoing the "Battle Hymn of the Republic"—resounds with defiance:

> We the scum of the human chattel
> We of everlasting flight
> We will rise in fearless battle
> We who cannot live the night.
> Tears no longer—
> Tears no longer
> Let them taste the death they deal.
> And though we die, we die in battle
> Not beneath the tyrant heel.[88]

Such ballads—often written by Jewish songwriters—were a common feature of Hollywood resistance movies. *Hangmen Also Die* featured a very similar *kampflied* by Brecht and the exiled German-Jewish composer Hanns Eisler called "No Surrender."[89] They also showed up in some of the era's pro-Soviet war films; Aaron Copland and Ira Gershwin wrote "Song of the Guerillas" for *The North Star* (1943) and E. Y. Harburg and Jerome Kern wrote "And Russia Is Her Name" for *Song of Russia* (1944). The "Battle Song" may have been de rigueur when dramatizing antifascist resistance in Hollywood, but the Waxman-Loesser "Battle Hymn of the Ghetto" was the only one sung by Jewish battlers.

Aside from its cinematic influences and aspirations, the scene was equally informed by the legacy of the American political theatre of the 1930s—evident in the links of many of its participants to three prominent organs of that movement: the Group Theatre, Labor Stage, and the Federal Theatre Project. With Hart otherwise occupied in New York, the responsibility for staging the Hollywood Bowl performance fell to his assistant Herman Rotsten, who had previously directed the national tour for Labor Stage's *Pins and Needles*.[90] Rotsten was one of three *Pins and Needles* alumni to play a key role in *We Will Never Die*; Syrjala conceived of the original stage design and Louis Schaeffer, the head of Labor Stage, served on the New York producing committee.

Another participating group with links back to the thirties was the Actors' Laboratory Theatre, a Los Angeles company founded in 1941 by former Group Theatre members who had moved west to work in the film industry. (Three of those actors—J. Edward Bromberg, Roman Bohnen, and Art Smith—performed in the "Remember Us" scene in Los Angeles.) Actors' Laboratory Theatre also ran a school, which supplied the large number of supernumeraries required for the Warsaw Ghetto crowd scenes.[91] Founded as it was by politically engaged actors (many of whom were later blacklisted), Actors' Laboratory expressly promoted a "social approach to acting," committed to "an intelligent appraisal of the social forces at work in this particular political period . . . and as people who consider the preparation of democracy and democratic culture a matter of life or death."[92] They also supported the war effort by performing for soldiers in California.[93] But despite this service, their leftist political connections later made them one of the first targets of the postwar anticommunist investigation in the California State Senate (the Tenney Committee), leading to the company's closing in 1950.

"The Battle of the Warsaw Ghetto" most resembles the FTP's Living Newspaper plays in its deployment of "actualities" (reportage and found text), as well as in its reliance on recorded sound effects, voice-over narration, and direct-address commentary. In his stage directions, Hecht calls for "the rumble of [tank] wheels" and "the sounds of distant shooting and the cries of battle" (29). At two pivotal moments, a disembodied voice speaks over a loudspeaker. First, Joseph Goebbels is heard pronouncing: "The extermination of the Jewish race is of historic importance" (28). At the battle's end, Hecht interpolates the verbatim text of the ghetto's final radio dispatches: "Death sentence has been proclaimed on the last 35,000 Jews in Warsaw. Gun salvoes are echoing in the streets. Women and children are defending themselves with their bare hands. Help us" (30).[94] Thanks to a live broadcast of the Hollywood Bowl performance by the Los Angeles station KFWB, *We Will Never Die* could relay this brief transmission from the front lines of the Jewish struggle in Europe to many more people than originally heard it, even if too late to save the fighters themselves.

Such use of amplification and recorded sound was typical of the Living Newspapers, which, in turn, adapted the practice from the agitprop productions of Erwin Piscator, who originated the stagecraft of "Epic Theatre" in 1920s Berlin. Piscator's innovation, writes Attilio Favorini, "was to create a drama based on the principles of news reportage, constructed in an epic succession of tableaux and stations, and designed to promote direct social action . . . [by] bombarding the emotions with an arsenal of theater technology to achieve maximal audience manipulation."[95] "Bombarding" to "promote direct social action" is precisely what Hecht and his collaborators aimed for in "The Battle of the Warsaw Ghetto," a scene with dozens of actors vigorously simulating armed combat accompanied by impassioned narration, Waxman's dissonant musical score, and the percussive sounds of warfare. At various times, Hecht's narrators cheer the fighters on, crying "Rally, Jews!"—but instead of the already fallen fighters of Warsaw, they were really addressing the American Jews in the audience before them (29, 31).

## CONCLUSION: *WE WILL NEVER DIE* IN THE PUBLIC SPHERE

In his memoirs, Hecht tells of meeting with a disappointed Weill after the end of the pageant's tour to assess its success. "All we have done is make a lot of Jews cry," Weill joked sardonically, "which is not a unique accomplishment."[96] If its goals were to compel the U.S. government to take immediate action to rescue the Jews of Europe, then *We Will Never Die* could not claim such a clear victory, but not for lack of trying. The *We Will Never Die* performance in Washington's Constitution Hall certainly succeeded in capturing, at least for one night, the attention of the highest levels of government, including thirty-eight senators, seven supreme court justices, two cabinet secretaries, and First Lady Eleanor Roosevelt. (Washington was the only city where tickets were not sold to the public and seating was reserved for invited dignitaries only.)[97]

Hecht refused to tone down the pageant's confrontational rhetoric for the nation's leaders and even added an extra curtain speech for the narrators Muni and Robinson, who were reprising their New York roles. It begins in the spirit of many classical theatrical "epilogues," in which the lead actor removes the "mask" of their character to refocus attention on the spectators in direct address: "We, the actors who have performed for you tonight are nearly done. But there is another cast of actors involved in this tale whose performance is not done. This cast is our audience. . . . And tonight it is not as actors playing parts on a stage soon to be dismantled, but as the spokesmen of a people that is being exterminated, that we stand before you—the official, the accredited, the elected makers of history" (37–38). But this humble beginning soon leads to a direct accusation of hypocrisy: "In this city, not far away, are the halls from which Justice has sounded her loudest battle cries, the chambers from which have issued man's noblest promises to tomorrow. Stranger than the mass murder of the civilians of Europe is the silence of these halls today. Stranger than the brutality of the massacre is the quiet of its onlookers in these chambers" (38–39). The narrators even implicate the "quiet onlookers" in the U.S. government as "honorary members of the German posse."

Such confrontational tactics did not repel the First Lady, who, in her daily newspaper column, "My Day," called *We Will Never Die* "one of the most impressive and moving pageants I have ever seen," adding: "No one will ever forget those haunting words: 'Remember us.'"[98] And while no immediate change in political, diplomatic, or military policies ensued, Bergson himself believed that the pageant advanced his own lobbying campaign effectively enough to make a difference in swaying the Roosevelt administration to establish (in January 1944) the War Refugee Board, which ultimately resettled an estimated 100,000 European Jews in safe havens during the final year of the war.[99]

But whatever the pageant may have lacked in direct, policy-making efficacy, it made up for in consciousness raising. In addition to the 40,000 attendees in New York, approximately an additional 75,000 saw the pageant on tour.[100] The newspaper coverage in each city (all of them major media markets) was substantial, and while Hecht may have overstated his case in claiming, "The news and pictures of our pageant in the press were the first American newspaper reports on the Jewish massacre in Europe," these certainly were *among* the first articles referencing the Holocaust in those months after that first Associated Press item in November 1942.[101]

Expanding that impact even further was the occasional appearance of *We Will Never Die* in mass media. In the major media markets of New York, Los Angeles, and Washington, D.C., the performance was broadcast live on the radio, a significant exposure given that "radio coverage of the Holocaust was rare."[102] The broadcast of the Hollywood Bowl performance (on the Warner Brothers–owned station KFWB) might have been the first time, during the "Warsaw Ghetto" scene, the names Auschwitz and Treblinka were uttered on American radio.[103]

*We Will Never Die* even made its way into cinemas. A Fox Movietone crew filmed excerpts of the Madison Square Garden rehearsal for a newsreel package that was distributed to movie theatres nationwide the week of March 16, 1943. Entitled "Memorial Pageant to the Persecuted Jews of Europe," the ninety-eight-second segment contained several clips of words, music, and images from the performance, including Sidney reciting one of the "Remember Us" stories: "In Lublin five hundred of our women and children were led to the market place and stood against the vegetable stalls we knew so well. Here the Germans turned machine guns on us and killed us all. Remember us."[104] The newsreel's most striking moment is the thirty seconds given to Muni's delivery of a particularly blunt passage from Hecht's closing narration. Viewed today, the grainy black-and-white film of this prescient speech, effectively predicting the ominous number of "six million" (given the two million dead already alluded to), feels like a time warp into an "alternate history" where stopping the Holocaust still seems possible: "There are four million Jews surviving in Europe. The Germans have promised to deliver to the world by the end of the year a Christmas package of four million dead Jews. And this is not a Jewish problem. It is a problem that belongs

FROM "VANISHING" TO VISIBLE

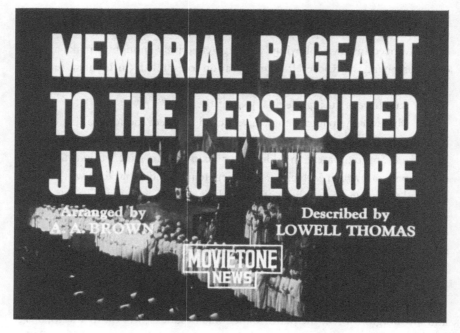

Figure 3. Fox Movietone News promotes *We Will Never Die* in a newsreel segment released in U.S. cinemas. Source: "Memorial pageant to the persecuted Jews of Europe," Fox Movietone News 25, no. 55 (Tuesday March 16, 1943). Moving Image Research Collections, University of South Carolina.

to humanity. It is a challenge to the soul of man." Muni, experienced film actor that he was, delivers the line directly to the camera, as if to broadcast his warning beyond Madison Square Garden into cinemas nationwide. *We Will Never Die* may not have spurred the kind of action its creators had hoped for, but its words were heard by over 100,000 Americans in person and countless more by radio or newsreel, which potentially had greater reach than small articles on the inside pages of elite newspapers.

## EPILOGUE: "CALL THE NEXT CASE"

Hecht's expectations for the politically efficacious impact of such a performance might have been overly optimistic to begin with. "Consider what would happen to the Germans if they were to hear that their crime was sickening the world!" he entreated his Broadway colleagues at George S. Kaufman's apartment back in early 1943.[105] He later conceded, "My theory had been wrong" in that "the Germans, made aware that the murder of the Jews was humanly distasteful to the

Figure 4. "The Germans have promised to deliver to the world by the end of the year a Christmas package of four million dead Jews." Paul Muni, flanked by actors representing the victims of Nazi massacres, speaks to American cinema audiences via newsreel. Source: "Memorial pageant to the persecuted Jews of Europe," Fox Movietone News 25, no. 55 (Tuesday March 16, 1943). Moving Image Research Collections, University of South Carolina.

world, had not stayed their reddened hands" and "continued killing Jews." But he consoled himself with the belief that "only half an outcry" had been achieved; he and his colleagues had done their part with *We Will Never Die* and other media campaigns, but it was the politicians who had failed—not the leaders of the enemy side, but his own: "The political outcry had been missing. With all our mass meetings and stinging propaganda we had managed to rouse no protest against the Jewish massacre from Roosevelt, Churchill, Stalin, or their official governments."[106] He emerged from the experience not just disheartened about the fate of the Jews but also embittered against the American and British governments.

Hecht's postwar propaganda work would focus his polemical sights on the latter as he took up the fight against Great Britain for a Jewish Palestine. But in the final days of the war, he considered one more Holocaust play to tell the world how much his own government had failed the Jews. In April 1945, Hecht was in California working on a State Department commission to write another kind of "pageant," one to commemorate the founding of the United Nations (the "San Francisco Conference"). But his grievance against the Roosevelt administration's failings got the best of him as he pondered a different, more subversive propaganda piece as a rebuttal to the assigned task:

> A grandiose propaganda stroke had occurred, simultaneously, to me. I would write and stage another show also while in San Francisco, one that would explode the Jewish issue in the face of the entire United Nations. This one would be put on in a theater and run as long as the delegates remained in session. . . .
>
> Preparing now my secret propaganda play to be played in San Francisco, I grinned at the thought of the State Department attending its opening. The show I was writing was going to be a long one-acter, titled, *Call the Next Case*. Its plot was: Franklin Delano Roosevelt being summoned before the Bar of History to state what he had done to save the Jews of Europe. The jury trying the case consisted of twelve dead Jews from the German crematoriums.[107]

In this new variation of the "Remember Us" scene from *We Will Never Die*, it would have been FDR in the dock, with the ghostly victims casting their judgment not against their Nazi murderers but their supposed American protector.

"Call the Next Case" would have been the most shocking and provocative of all Hecht's protest plays. But fate intervened on April 12, 1945: "I was writing the script in a Beverly Hills hotel with the radio playing soft music. The music stopped abruptly and a faltering voice announced that President Roosevelt had just died." After listening to the immediate outpouring of public mourning and worshipful eulogizing, Hecht "threw away the pages of *Call the Next Case*."[108] Indeed, no trace is to be found in Hecht's archives of what, in the face of FDR's civic canonization, could have been one of the most incendiary American plays ever staged.

As a frequent contributor to the Popular Front antifascist campaign and the U.S. war effort, Hecht had vocally supported Roosevelt on many occasions. (He even wrote a special short propaganda play, *The Common Man*, for his 1944 presidential campaign.)[109] In the ten years since his first public pronouncement against Nazi antisemitism, Hecht had not only found his Jewish voice, but he increasingly identified as a patriotic American as well. As he would later recall: "I was aware I was doing all these things as a Jew. My eloquence on behalf of democracy was inspired chiefly by my Jewish anger. I had been no partisan of democracy in my earlier years. Its sins had seemed to me more prominent than its virtues. But now that it was the potential enemy of the new German Police State I was its uncarping disciple. Thus, oddly, in addition to becoming a Jew in 1939 I became also an American—and remained one."[110] Once the war was over, however, Hecht turned away from domestic politics. After his disappointment in Roosevelt and the Washington political establishment, he felt no further need to subsume his personal cause to the national. In his next forays into political theatre, as he refocused his energies on Palestine, his underlying "Jewish anger" would now surface in unalloyed form.

# Part II

# Tevye and the Terrorists

## Plays for Palestine, 1944–1947

# 3

# The Assassination of "Lord Moisha"

*A Jewish Fairy Tale* and the Pivot to Palestine

IN MARCH 1943, the same month that *We Will Never Die* premiered in New York, Alfred A. Knopf published *The World of Sholom Aleichem*, the first book-length study of the Yiddish writer in English. Written by Romanian-born American Jewish scholar Maurice Samuel, it played a key role in introducing non-Yiddish speakers to an author whose notoriety had still not spilled into the American cultural mainstream three decades after his death in 1916. It helped spark a Sholem-Aleichem renaissance of new translations and performances that eventually led to the 1964 Broadway musical *Fiddler on the Roof*, based on the tales of his character Tevye the Dairyman. But unlike the heartwarming nostalgia offered by *Fiddler*, Samuel's 1943 take on Sholem-Aleichem was mournful. Writing amid the early revelations of Nazi Germany's planned extermination of European Jewry, Samuel stresses in his introduction that the land of Tevye and his ilk is "a world that is no more" now that "the fiery harrow of two world wars have passed closely across its soil," calling his book "an exercise in necromancy, or calling up of the dead."[1] This Holocaust-infused framing of Sholem-Aleichem's oeuvre set a new tone for the postwar American reappraisal of a writer known to previous generations of Jewish readers worldwide as a delightful ironist. As Alisa Solomon writes in her cultural history of *Fiddler*, the figure of Tevye in particular "emerges from Samuel's pages as the dominant exemplar, even the spokesperson, for the murdered Jews of Eastern Europe."[2]

One of the many readers of Samuel's book was Ben Hecht, already an avowed admirer of the Yiddish author. In a 1941 column for *PM*, he commemorated the twenty-fifth anniversary of his death and singled out "the immortal Tevya [sic]" as a favorite character.³ When *The World of Sholom Aleichem* was published on March 1, 1943, Hecht was in the final stages of preparing *We Will Never Die* for its March 9 premiere and, perhaps not coincidentally, the name "Shalemalechem" appears in a revised script of the pageant's "Roll Call of the Great Jews," after being absent from Hecht's original draft.⁴ He was still thinking about "Maurice Samuels' [sic] excellent book" three years later; in a July 1946 book review of Julius and Frances Butwin's *The Old Country*, a collection of Sholem-Aleichem stories in translation, Hecht begins his article with a virtual paraphrase of Samuel's elegiac thesis: "'The Old Country,' a collection of Sholom Aleichem's tales, is more than a book. It is the epitaph of a vanished people. The salty and hilarious folk of whom it tells—the Jews of Europe—are dead. All the Tevyas [sic] whose souls and sayings, whose bizarre and tender antics Sholom Aleichem immortalized in the richest Yiddish prose ever written—were massacred six million strong, by the Germans. And all the quaint and heartwarming villages in which the Jews of Europe lived are no longer on the map."⁵ Hecht shares with readers that, "I have been in love with the stories of Sholom Aleichem for a long time."⁶ But he does not mention that, at that very moment, he was currently working on his own homage to the Yiddish storyteller—a "translation" in the sense of transformation—bringing Tevye into the nightmare world of the 1940s. That play, *A Flag Is Born*, opened on Broadway two months later, in September 1946, and brought the current crisis of the Jewish people—the aftermath of the Holocaust, now compounded by the struggle for a postwar Jewish homeland—to the American stage for the first time.

It was not the only time Hecht utilized the Tevye character for this purpose. *A Flag Is Born* was one of three propaganda plays Hecht wrote for Bergson's Revisionist Zionist organization supporting their campaign for a Jewish state in British-controlled Palestine. Just as *We Will Never Die* juxtaposed the martyred villagers of Eastern Europe in the "Remember Us" scene with the young soldiers of "Jews in the War," Hecht continued to dramatize the rise of a new Jewish identity out of the ashes of the Holocaust. He now told that story from the perspective of a Tevye figure—a ghostly representative of the "vanished" Jewish generations of the past who ultimately gives his blessing to the militants of the Jewish future. Collectively, these plays dramatize a passing of the torch from a dying culture to an ascendant one—from the "Old Country" to the "New Jew" of Zionism.

For Hecht, the Jewish struggles in Europe and Palestine were part of a continuous narrative, as both conflicts overlapped in the war's final years and months. But some in his audience were shocked to see that the enemy in his new plays was no longer Germany but the United Kingdom, a popular wartime ally. The increasingly direct attacks Hecht made on the British government in these works and other propaganda writings made him new enemies and brought him new troubles in the postwar years, including a U.K. boycott of his films. The deeper Hecht dove into the Zionist cause, the more confrontational, contrarian, and provocative his theatre of Jewish protest became.

## "A PEOPLE TO WHOM I BELONGED"

Hecht's affinity for the world of Sholem-Aleichem, and his use of it to theatrically represent the tragedy of the Holocaust, reflects his personal identification with that world via his own heritage. "My family, including all the uncles, aunts, cousins, of whom I ever got wind, were all Jews, all immigrants from Russia, and all people of lowly origin," he wrote.[7] By "Russia," he meant the Eastern European Pale of Settlement that forms the setting of the Sholem-Aleichem tales.[8] Resettling in the Midwestern United States, his parents and extended family appear to have transplanted their old culture to even such an un-Jewish land as Racine, Wisconsin. "They were a noisy and impoverished lot and saltier than any people I have since encountered," he recalled, describing the atmosphere of his childhood as "a sort of Yiddish Canterbury Tales" of old-world memories and customs.[9] Hecht, who decamped for Chicago at age seventeen, left that culture behind and easily assimilated into mainstream American life as a popular writer. But as his Jewish identity reawakened in him with the rise of Nazism, it was the direct threat to the inhabitants of "The Old Country" that most stirred him to action. "A people to whom I belonged," he later wrote, "who had produced my mother, father and all the relatives I had loved, was being turned into an exterminator's quarry, and there was no outcry against the deed."[10] Or, as he would more bluntly put it: "Much of what I have done as a Jewish propagandist has been done because I loved my family."[11] It is not surprising, then, that as Hecht continued to dramatize the Holocaust and the fight for Palestine, older shtetl figures would continue to take center stage despite his sponsor's shift in focus away from Eastern Europe to the new generation of young Jewish soldiers in Palestine.

Hecht's adoption of the Tevye character is prefigured by his use of shtetl figures in *We Will Never Die* and in another wartime pageant he wrote in 1943, *A Tribute to Gallantry*, both of which recount the violent destruction of Sholem-Aleichem's "world that is no more." The "Remember Us" scene of *We Will Never Die* takes us to "The Old Country" as it had become in 1943, populated by the ghosts of pious villagers from an extinct culture unprepared for the ruthlessness of modern warfare. The reports Hecht had drawn on as his sources for "Remember Us" were from early in the war (prior to the full operation of extermination camps), and many of the massacres recounted occurred in towns in Ukraine, Latvia, and Poland—the landscape of Sholem-Aleichem's tales. One episode introduces us to "five bearded old men" from Włocławek, Poland—the site of a massacre by German *Einsatzgruppe* troops in the fall of 1939—who tell how "the Germans came when we were at prayer" and "tore the prayer shawls from our heads," then "made us use our prayer shawls as mops to clean out German latrines" before executing them.[12] The depicted desecration of religious ritual recalls how essential piety is to reception of Sholem-Aleichem's characters, something that, in the "rhetoric of [post-Holocaust] nostalgia, cloaked Tevye in the stylized role of the archetypical folk Jew who maintains his customs in the face of adversity."[13]

Hecht came closer to deploying the character of Tevye himself in *A Tribute to Gallantry*, a political "pageant" written not for Bergson's Jewish rescue efforts but for the war effort at large. The National War Fund had been founded in early 1943 as a private philanthropic project (at the direction of President Roosevelt) to subsume all existing war fundraising drives under one umbrella organization in order to streamline and maximize contributions. In preparation for the nationwide launch of the initiative in the fall, Hecht was commissioned by the New York Committee of the National War Fund (each state had its own branch) to produce a performance piece for a gala fundraising dinner at New York's Waldorf Astoria Hotel on October 5, 1943.[14] The headliner of the event was President Roosevelt himself, albeit by radio, addressing the nation on the purpose of the project, which would fund not only services for the armed forces but also relief efforts for populations suffering under Axis aggression in Europe and Asia. While the fate of European Jews in particular was not explicitly on the agenda of the National War Fund, Hecht, in his contribution to the evening, seized the opportunity to prominently feature their story.

"A Tribute to Gallantry" was the name of the fundraising event itself, drawing attention to the sacrifices of those in uniform fighting on Americans' behalf. Hecht's dramatic composition for the evening bears the same title, but apparently more by default than design, since he used this unique platform before the philanthropists of the National War Fund to shift their attention from selfless military valor to the suffering of noncombatants bearing the brunt of this war's unprecedented targeting of civilians. The narrator of his pageant, after paying due tribute to the fallen soldiers of the armed forces, turns to "the dead who had no chance to fight": "There is a fact about our war that we hold dim in our heads because it is too ugly a fact to look upon. Tonight we will look upon it. We will look on the fact that more unarmed human beings than soldiers have been killed in the war made by the Germans.... We will look on the fact that the killing off of innocent populations has been the new military weapon introduced into war by the Germans and the Japanese."[15] What ensues is a scene of the afterlife, represented archetypically on stage by "a gate in the sky" attended by a "Gate Keeper" (45). The action of the pageant (or "Tableau" as some press accounts referred to it) consists of different groups of war dead arriving at the gate, to which the Gate Keeper admits them. First, soldiers come from the battlefield and they willingly pass through. But then a succession of different groups of "men, women and children without guns, and dressed in ragged clothes" starts to arrive. The sympathetic Gate Keeper entreats them all to "pass inside the gate" and "find rest there," because "inside the gate all that happened on earth to you is forgotten. Pass inside—peace waits for you" (49). But one by one, unlike the enlisted soldiers, this diverse collection of innocent bystanders declines the Gate Keeper's invitation and, in a quiet protest, declares they are not yet ready for "peace," not ready to "forget" or disappear through the gate. Theatrically, this results in the bodies of these dead refusing to disappear from the audience's view as they remain and grow in numbers throughout the scene until they fill the stage, a visual admonition to the audience of National War Fund donors that not all war dead wear uniforms. The tableau also mirrors Hecht's vision in *We Will Never Die* of similarly murdered peoples calling on the audience—and all Americans—to "Remember Us."[16]

The ghosts of *A Tribute to Gallantry* hail from all corners of the world war—including the London Blitz, the Russian front, the Lidice massacre, and Chinese farmers slaughtered by Japanese invaders. But among these is also an "Old Jew," who enters "bearing a broken torah" as "a child clings to his coat" (49–50). The Gate Keeper greets him with a nod to a continuing history of persecution, saying, "Old Jew—you again," and asks what brings him here now.

GATE KEEPER: What is your story?
OLD JEW: Three million of us were murdered—we were slaughtered in lime kilns—in gas chambers—in fires—in front of guns. We had no weapons. We had only our old prayers. They were still burning us. They have vowed to kill all the Jews in Europe.
GATE KEEPER: Pass inside the gate and forget.
OLD JEW: No. We do not want to forget ... not yet.... We will wait. (50)

While most of the ghostly avatars in *Tribute to Gallantry* hail from very specific places, the "Old Jew" announces he is a representative of all "three million" of the dead Jews of Europe, reminding the audience of the larger story of the Jewish genocide, which Hecht considered distinct from the other war crimes. The character's story here echoes the massacres recounted in "Remember Us," but Hecht updated the details based on what had been learned in the seven months since March 1943. The "2,000,000 Jewish Dead of Europe" cited in *We Will Never Die* has been revised upward to 3,000,000. The methods of killing have now escalated from the brute force of firing squads and hangings to the "lime kilns" and "gas chambers" of the concentration camps. Hecht's "Old Jew" utters what to many was still an unthinkable prophecy in the fall of October 1943: "They have vowed to kill all the Jews in Europe." (The statement reached an even greater audience when *A Tribute to Gallantry* was performed a second time at a National War Fund rally at Madison Square Garden a few weeks later before an audience of "20,000 campaign workers.")[17]

While "Old Jew" is not identified with any particular location, the character's links to Sholem-Aleichem's world were conveyed onstage not just in Hecht's written description but by the actor he cast in the role: Maurice Schwartz. Schwartz had been a leading Yiddish Theatre actor in New York since 1918, and one of his greatest triumphs was the world premiere stage adaptation of *Tevye the Dairyman*. He continued to play the title role in repertory for many years and even starred in his own widely distributed film of the play in 1939 (released in English-speaking cinemas as *Tevya*). So identified did he become with the character that, as one of his colleagues joked, "It was hard to tell if Schwartz created Tevye or Tevye created Schwartz."[18] Schwartz had by now put his personal stamp on the role, portraying Tevye not as the jovial figure he would later become in *Fiddler on the Roof* but as "an older, broken man held together and aloft by the wisdom and unyielding practice of Judaism."[19] Clearly, it was this Tevye that Hecht wanted to bring onstage in *A Tribute to Gallantry* to embody the vanishing Jews of Europe, and this is the Tevye (or "Tevya") he would continue to develop as his own dramatic character in three more propaganda plays devoted to the Jewish cause in Palestine.

## PIVOTING TO PALESTINE

When Hecht first met Bergson in 1941, he had agreed to work with him on the rescue of European Jews, but not on the fight for Palestine. Like most American Jews of his generation, he had viewed Zionism as a relatively obscure and recent movement, irrelevant to those already assimilated into mainstream American life. "I felt sorry for my visitors and their cause," he recalled of their first meeting. "They could have selected no more unqualified and uninformed and un-

## THE ASSASSINATION OF "LORD MOISHA"

Palestine-minded man in the entire land. . . . I had no interest in Palestine and had always bolted any conversation about a Jewish homeland."[20] He expressed to Bergson his concern that, for the American public, focus on the Palestine conflict "confused the issue" of the more immediate crisis of Jews in Europe and would also "frighten off large sections of important Jews who don't care to get involved in a Palestine-anti-British row."[21] Bergson agreed on a "one thing at a time" strategy.

By early 1944, Bergson had convinced Hecht that the time had come for the next step and that Jewish rescue and the fate of Palestine had become inexorably linked. When Britain acquired Palestine from the defeated Ottoman Empire at the close of World War I, it was granted a Mandate by the League of Nations to shepherd the land's transition to eventual independence. Part of this charge was to follow through on its 1917 pledge to establish a "national home for the Jewish people" in the territory (made in what became known as the Balfour Declaration). But after thousands of Jews had immigrated there encouraged by that prospect, no concrete steps had yet been taken by the outbreak of World War II. And just when European Jews were in desperate need of safe havens after the rise of Nazism, the British, concerned about civil unrest between Jews and Palestinian Arabs, started severely limiting Jewish immigration in 1939. With Western Allied nations like the United States still enforcing strict immigration quotas of their own, Palestine became the last, best hope for activists trying to smuggle Jewish refugees out of Europe. Bergson and other Zionist leaders no longer saw Britain as a reliable partner in either their short-term goal of resettlement or their long-term goal of a Jewish state—and they were no longer willing to wait for the end of World War II before taking action themselves.

Bergson made Hecht a co-chairman of his new committee, the American League for a Free Palestine, which despite its generalized name was actually a lobbying group for one particular faction of the Palestine struggle—the *Irgun Zvai Leumi*, the military wing of the Revisionist Zionist movement of which Bergson was the chief American representative. Like other such similar underground forces, the *Irgun* was working outside of the official Jewish Agency leadership in Palestine to pursue a more aggressive strategy to resettle refugees, even to the point of undermining British rule by violence. Such acts branded them "Palestinian [i.e., Jewish] terrorists" in the British and Western press, but Hecht was undeterred from associating with them. In fact, it soon became evident in his work for them that he considered the term a badge of honor.

Tensions in Palestine ratcheted up exponentially after November 6, 1944, when the top British colonial official in the Middle East, Walter Guinness (aka Lord Moyne), was assassinated in Cairo by two members of a different underground, the *Lehi*, or "Stern Gang." In an angry speech before Parliament eleven days later, Winston Churchill condemned such "terrorism" and its sponsors, calling all such fighters "gangsters worthy of Nazi Germany" and holding all Jewish leaders in Palestine responsible for policing their own extremists.[22] Claiming he had so far been among the most "consistent friends of the Jews" in his support of Zionism, Churchill now warned that "many like myself will have to reconsider the position we have maintained so consistently" in support of a Jewish homeland. "His Majesty's Government is entitled to demand and to receive," he added, "the wholehearted co-operation of the entire Jewish community."

While the official Jewish authorities in Palestine (the Jewish Agency led by the future Israeli prime minister David Ben-Gurion) agreed to cooperate with the British by purging extremists, the more radical underground organizations were outraged at Churchill's comparison of their fighters to the very German soldiers currently killing the Jews of Europe. Bergson condemned Churchill for choosing to "castigate and threaten the entire Hebrew people in connection with the assassination of Lord Moyne by two Hebrew fanatics from Palestine" but "not [to] touch upon the horrifying fact of the extermination of the vast majority of the Jewish people of Europe . . . [and] the slaughter which continues unabated."[23] As an answer to Churchill, Bergson made a special addition to his upcoming rally on December 4: a new play about the Moyne assassination by Ben Hecht.

## *A JEWISH FAIRY TALE* (1944)

At seventeen pages, Hecht's one-act *A Jewish Fairy Tale* reads more like a satirical revue sketch than a dramatic play. (Given the time between the assassination and the performance, he clearly wrote it very quickly.) Rather than dramatize the violent event itself, Hecht wanted to decry the British reaction and its ramification for Jews at such a dangerous time, when the war—and the Holocaust—still raged on. His method of doing so was to ridicule Churchill as a hypocrite by pitting him against the sympathetic and commonsense wisdom of "a dead Jew by the name of Tevya."[24]

Like *A Tribute to Gallantry*, *A Jewish Fairy Tale* takes place in an abstract afterlife setting, where an old Jewish man arrives directly from his death in a concentration camp. A "Narrator" describes his entrance: "Once upon a time there was a dead Jew by the name of Tevya who sat on a cloud and hummed to himself as he drifted slowly on his last journey toward the gates of Heaven and the Almighty God waiting to receive him . . . afloat on his cloud and talking a little wistfully to himself as he travels upward among the stars" (2). The image strikingly recalls Sholem-Aleichem's final Tevye story, "Get Thee Out," in which the protagonist has been evicted from his home during a pogrom and finds himself a lonely Wandering Jew, "suspended somewhere in time and space on a train."[25] Hecht's Narrator identifies him as "Tevya from Lublin" (in Poland), and when Tevya first speaks, "a folk song" plays in the background—composed by Sholom Secunda, who also wrote the score for Schwartz's 1939 *Tevya* film (2).[26]

Befitting a fairy tale, Hecht begins the action in a whimsical tone. The Narrator speaks in the style of a radio announcer ("Come in, Tevya from Lublin"), and Tevya's opening monologue echoes the Sholem-Aleichem style as he puts the best possible face on an ominous situation:

> What is there to worry about? I feel good. Nothing hurts me. I am riding on a fine cloud. And, everything considered, it's altogether a fine thing to be going at last to Heaven. And to see God and find out what is the meaning of everything. Why He made Jews and Gentiles. Why he sends a wind to blow down houses. . . . And if it is true that a piece of bread brought into a room by a mouse on the Passover makes the whole house trafe and we must clean everything from top to bottom again. I will find everything out and become wiser than the biggest and holiest rabbi. (2)

But Hecht soon punctures such Old Country nostalgia with reminders that we are not in the past anymore. The Narrator interrupts Tevya's happy heavenly musings to remind us how, on earth, he "died naked, without a rag on his back—and standing up in a lime pit full of burning lime—with ten thousand Jews standing crowded in the same lime pit and all burning with him" (3). Tevya, too, suddenly remembers the circumstances that brought him here: "How they killed us. How they burned us. How they butchered the little ones, the old ones." But, being no troublemaker, he tells himself, "What kind of talk is that to bring into Heaven? . . . It's much better for everybody, if I arrive relaxed, rested, and remembering nothing of what happened down below" (4). Wary of offending God or drawing attention to himself, he says, "The Almighty doesn't want somebody to come hollering into Heaven with all his troubles hot on his tongue." But while Tevya initially succumbs to the same pressure the Gate Keeper in *A Tribute to Gallantry* puts on the dead to "pass inside the gate and forget," he persists in testifying to the audience of his suffering.

Soon Tevya meets God—or at least a character named "God." Amid a fanfare of "fiddles playing," "angel voices," and "hallelujahs," Tevya senses the presence of the "Ruler of the Universe" and rejoices with "tears of gladness that ran down his beard" (5–6). But a sudden silence descends when "an ominous note in the Almighty's voice froze Tevya's soul":

GOD (*Sternly*): Tevya, you have displeased me. You have angered me. You have made My face dark against you!
TEVYA: Forgive me, blessed Ruler of the Universe. Forgive my sins which are many as the trees in the wilderness. Shed thy mercy on me
[. . .]
GOD: Shame on you, Tevya, to come here singing and chanting My name—with a crime on your hands. (6–7)

It takes a few moments for Tevya to realize that he is not simply being admonished to atone for everyday sins. The "crime" God speaks of turns out to be very specific, that "an Englishman has been killed" (8). Then the figure behind the disembodied voice is fully revealed: "Tevya looks for the first time at God and is surprised to see that God is smoking a cigar and wears a yachting cap." The audience has probably already identified this "God" from the signature British accent of a voice heard often on American radio: that of Winston Churchill.

Unmasked to the audience (if not to Tevya) as a false deity, this God then arraigns Tevya before his "Bar of Judgment" (6) for the assassination of Lord Moyne—a dramatic enactment of Churchill's stated promise to hold "every man, woman, and child of the Jewish community" responsible for "bring[ing] this terrorism to a speedy end."[27] Undeterred by the gravity of the assassination and severe political tensions surrounding it, Hecht mines the extremity of Churchill's response for bitter comedy, mocking it in a distinctly Yiddish vein. When first told the name of the murder victim is Lord Moyne, Tevya mishears it as "Lord Moisha" (9). (He later calls him "Lord Shmoyne" [16]). Hearing of "a crime in Palestine," he responds quizzically, "You mean when Solomon married the Egyptian Queen?" (9). Tevya's circumstances during the war have obviously kept him in the dark about the latest news headlines. "Excuse me, O Light of the Universe, I am an ignorant man," he pleads, reminding God, in a jarringly sardonic line, that he is only "a Jew from the cremation furnace—if you will forgive me mentioning it again" (9). While pleading ignorance, Hecht's Tevya (echoing Sholem-Aleichem's original) is also sly, his seeming digressions and evasions drawing attention away from the murder of one Lord Moyne and back to the assassination of millions of "Lord Moishas" like himself.

Hecht sets up an elaborate allegory in *A Jewish Fairy Tale* wherein the "Heaven" of the play stands in for Palestine and God/Churchill is the gatekeeper, blocking Tevya's entrance (i.e., immigration of Jewish refugees) until he and his people have properly repented for the "bloody crime on your hands" (7). The way God halts Tevya's "cloud" midair without admitting him to heaven and later (at the play's conclusion) sends him back down to earth mirrors how ships of Jewish refugees approaching Palestine were regularly intercepted by British guards and either detained or turned around. (Just as Tevya never enters the "Gates of Heaven," God refers to "the gates of Palestine" being "closed against all Jews by British policy" [3, 10].) Tevya—still believing he is talking to a politically disinterested party—even wonders if the reason God is displeased with him is for not making a pilgrimage to the Land of Israel (aliyah), as is expected of all Jews, something Sholem-Aleichem's Tevye also yearns to fulfill but cannot. He begs forgiveness for not being able to "go to Palestine and sing your praises" and reassures God that he and his fellow Jews "sang them in the furnace" (10). ("Tevya, your furnace arias are beside the point," God/Churchill dismissively replies.) Again not realizing with whom he is pleading, Tevya continues to press his case and essentially blames not Germany but the Allied nations (and implicitly England most of all) for his failure to live a full Jewish life:

> Two million Jews . . . wanted with all of their hearts to go to Jerusalem. We did everything. We gave bribes. We hid in the forests. We sent letters. We hollered on the radio. We prayed—all the time. Very loud. But nothing came of it—if you don't mind my saying so. O Blessed Lord of Israel—our enemies locked the doors of Palestine. Not the Germans or the Hungarians. But other enemies. . . . And the Jews who got as far as the Holy shores were sent back to drown in the sea and to burn in the furnaces . . . hundreds of thousands of them. (10–11)

Tevya speaking in the plural ("We did everything") makes him the voice at this moment for all "two million" of the murdered Jews, providing the kind of "testimony" Hecht's ghosts in *We Will Never Die* and *A Tribute to Gallantry* give of their suffering and their struggles against Western indifference. The "letters" and "radio" speeches invoked also recall Hecht's own propaganda writings continually pleading and warning the American public of what was to come if the peril of the Jews were ignored.

But unlike in those previous testimony scenes, here one of those victims directly addresses, albeit unwittingly, one of the world leaders responsible (in Hecht's view) for the continuation of that suffering. To pit Tevya against Churchill, onstage, during wartime in 1944, when Britain was still America's most steadfast and popular ally, was a bold theatrical gesture. The confrontation reaches its highest tension when Tevya all but calls out England by name as the "other enemy" ("not the Germans or the Hungarians") contributing to the horrors of the

Holocaust. (In response to Tevya's veiled accusation, God immediately engages in a cover-up: "He gestures to the Heavenly scribes to strike Tevya's remarks out of the Book of Fate, which bears the curious title 10 Downing Street" [11].)[28] This marks Hecht's first reference in his political writing to England being an enemy of the Jews nearly equal to Germany, a charge that would increasingly dominate his postwar propaganda.

(Hecht was not only willing to put his name to this minority view but, in the first performance, actually appeared onstage in the play as the Narrator. An advertisement for the evening announced: "Ben Hecht in Person Will Answer Prime Minister's Threat to All the Jews.")[29]

The play's resolution is that God gives Tevya a chance to redeem himself by sending him back to earth to convey his message that "all Jews, dead or alive, must beat their bosoms and cry shame on themselves" and "enter their synagogues and pray to Me to forgive them" for the sin of the Moyne assassination (13, 15). When Tevya counters, "They have no synagogues left, O Glory of Israel. They have been destroyed," God responds in a satirical outburst of mock-Churchillian tones: "This must not stop them. Then they must pray in the streets, in the fields. On the beaches. They must pray that My heart will be softened toward them once more" (15).[30] The parallels between this presumption of collective Jewish guilt and the ancient accusation that Jews bore responsibility for the death of Christ are not lost on Hecht, who mines much irony out of God designating Tevya not just his "messenger" but his "Savior for the Jews." ("Another one," Tevya jokes in a Yiddish-inflected aside.)[31] The scene thus returns us to the very origins of antisemitism, perhaps explaining why Hecht's curiously Christian-specific vision of "Heaven"—replete with "Pearly Gates"—has seemed so unwelcoming to "Tevya from Lublin" from the outset. In a comical yet humiliating image, Tevya becomes a mock messiah, a travesty of a figure that, in its original Jewish meaning, was to redeem the Jewish people and return them to their homeland. Instead of a message of hope, this savior brings more punishment and suffering—not for their rejection of Christ but of Churchill.

Tevya is not stupid; after God dismisses him, he suspects something is not as it seems in what he just experienced. As he floats back to earth, he wonders: "How do I know it was God who spoke to me. A beard, he didn't have. And does it say anything in the Holy Books that God wears a cap? No, not one word. What if it wasn't God—but just somebody with a big cigar. Who maybe thinks he's god" (17). He grumbles to himself about making all Jews "put on a tallis and apologize because somebody else got killed—for a change" (17), and he wishes "the Almighty" had given him "a different kind of message to the Jews. Maybe that He was a little sorry they had all been killed" rather than "so much excitement over one Englishman" (16). And yet, just as Sholem-Aleichem's Tevye responds to his banishment from his village by accepting it as God's will (saying, "You don't argue with God" and "Tevye asks no questions. When he is told to go, he goes"), Hecht's version ultimately rationalizes: "Tevya, you mustn't argue. This was God. And you must do what he says" (17).[32]

Hecht's Narrator facetiously concludes the play by saying, "We hope, good listeners, that our fairy tale has not carried too depressing a moral" (17). But the image he leaves us with of Jewish powerlessness versus global indifference is not just depressing but demoralizing. The Tevyas of the world will never be able to save themselves, we are shown. Hecht's affection for both the original Tevye and his own Tevya is as genuine as his love for his "Old Country" ancestors, but he also reinforces a fundamental Zionist tenet that "diaspora" Jews (especially those stuck in Eastern Europe) could muster neither the physical strength to fight back with force nor the courageous spirit to disobey authority. As Paul Breines summarizes in *Tough Jews*: "Statelessness, according to Zionism, is the cause of meekness, frailty, passivity, humiliation, pogroms, futile appeals to reason and dialogue."[33] Or, in the words of David Raziel, an early commander of the *Irgun* army and hero of the Revisionist movement with which Hecht was now aligned: "Bent backs [are] the inheritance of the Diaspora."[34]

Hecht's choice to place Sholem-Aleichem's beloved shtetl dweller at the center of a play about the Moyne assassination is an odd one. There were no Tevyas involved in the shooting. The only old Russian Jews in the vicinity would have been on boats currently being turned away or those already safely immigrated. The "heroes" of the story (from the militant Zionist perspective, at least) are Moyne's assassins—who remain offstage and unnamed. Tevya's role is to bear witness to what has brought the Jews to this point and to implicitly justify the actions the "terrorists" have taken on his behalf. In his following Palestine plays, Hecht would bring his Tevya and the terrorists into more direct contact onstage to show how the "New Jew" will be the savior and redeemer of the old.

This dynamic between the two figures recalls the drawing by the Polish Jewish émigré illustrator Arthur Szyk that became the official poster for *We Will Never Die*.[35] The drawing shows a young Jewish soldier, identified by a Star of David on his helmet, carrying the seemingly lifeless body of a white-bearded man holding a torah. As the soldier cradles the old man with his left arm, he raises his other hand high, brandishing a machine gun, as his face bellows forth a war cry. As if inspired by this drawing, Hecht's Palestine plays all feature a dramatic tension between a dead or dying shtetl elder and a vigorous young Jewish male, a tension that resolves with an act of heroism or sacrifice the younger man takes on the old one's behalf.

Figure 5. Program cover for *We Will Never Die* performance in Constitution Hall in Washington, D.C., featuring the drawing "Tears of Rage" by Arthur Szyk. Source: The Taube Family Arthur Szyk Collection at the Magnes Collection of Jewish Art and Life, University of California, Berkeley.

These dueling lead characters remarkably prefigure the protagonists of two iconic postwar Jewish American dramas: the new incarnation of Tevye created for the 1964 Broadway musical *Fiddler on the Roof* and the Zionist soldier Ari Ben Canaan in the 1960 Hollywood epic *Exodus*. To see these figures already confronting each other in Hecht's plays of the 1940s reveals how much those two popular culture milestones owed to artists like Hecht who paved the way for a postwar reexamination of Jewish identity.

## PRODUCTION HISTORY

*A Jewish Fairy Tale* was only performed twice and was not reviewed by the press, but the production was a star-studded effort, bringing together Luther and Stella Adler, two children of the onetime king of New York Yiddish Theatre, Jacob Adler. With Stella directing her brother playing Tevya, they might have recalled how Sholem-Aleichem himself had once, to no avail, offered Jacob the role in his own stage adaptation of the character's stories. "God" was played by the popular film comedy star Ralph Bellamy, presumably in the style of a Churchill impersonation, a role rife with comic opportunities. But as part of a longer Bergson fundraising evening at New York's Carnegie Hall on December 4, 1944 ("What's to Become of the Jews of Europe?"), the thirty-minute play did not merit even a mention in the next day's *New York Times* article about the event.[36] It had one more performance in Philadelphia, where Bergson remounted the complete program two months later, but it was never published, and no trace of any further performances survive.[37]

Such "occasional pieces" underline the ephemerality of political protest theatre in general, especially when it addresses historical events with immediacy. Just twenty-eight days passed between the Lord Moyne assassination and the staging of Hecht's theatrical response. Sometimes transience is part of the trade an artist makes in exchange for staging an urgent intervention. Hecht had set his sights on the audience of the day, not posterity, because action was needed right then, not later. Fortunately, the text of *A Jewish Fairy Tale* survives, but so much other political theatre of the moment is quickly lost to history.

# 4

# The Death of Tevye and the Birth of Israel

## *A Flag Is Born* on Broadway

ON SEPTEMBER 5, 1946, armed Zionist soldiers stormed the stage of New York's Alvin Theatre. "The past is dead," one proclaimed, "the whole black past of the Jews." "We speak," declared another, "in a new Jewish language. The language of guns." "Come," they said to the play's wayward young hero, a Holocaust survivor, "help us give birth to a flag."[1] Marching to the Zionist anthem "Hatikvah," they exited waving a banner resembling what would become the flag of the State of Israel nearly two years before such a country existed. Broadway audiences had never seen Jews such as these.

This was the spectacular ending of Ben Hecht's *A Flag Is Born*. Not only was it the first Zionist play on Broadway but, predating the dramatization of *The Diary of Anne Frank* by nine years, it was also its first Holocaust drama, addressing as it did the aftermath of World War II from the perspective of Jewish survivors. Even more unusual for Broadway was its overt propagandizing, onstage and off, for a then controversial political cause: the immediate recognition of a Jewish homeland in Palestine and the ousting of British rule there by force. While Zionism per se was rapidly gaining support in the United States after the war, Hecht and his colleagues were championing its most strident and, some even said, "terrorist" faction. Moreover, they were waging a war against Great Britain, the United States' popular wartime ally, whom they accused of imperialism and even Nazi-comparable racism. While such confrontational stances are not the usual makings of a "hit," the play found a sizable audience and ran four months on Broadway before touring several other cities.

THE DEATH OF TEVYE AND THE BIRTH OF ISRAEL

Figure 6. Broadway's Alvin Theatre during the run of *A Flag Is Born*. Source: Ben Hecht, *A Flag Is Born* (published script), New York: American League for a Free Palestine, 1946. Newberry Library, Ben Hecht Papers.

At a time when popular culture had not yet absorbed the shock of the Holocaust and when the entertainment industry was still cautious in approaching Jewish subject matter of any kind, the mounting of *A Flag Is Born* on Broadway was part of an important cultural moment in postwar Jewish American identity. The aftermath of the war opened up an opportunity in the American public sphere to finally address issues onstage not just of Jewish persecution but of cultural identity—which was about to change drastically for the wartime generation of American Jews compared to that of their immigrant parents and grandparents. As an almost classically styled tragedy of death and rebirth, *A Flag Is Born* addressed those crises of identity through a variety of theatrical forms, each a theatrical analog to a different aspect of the Jewish experience. The vanishing of the Jewish diaspora was communicated through the dying art of the Yiddish Theatre, the ideals of Zionism through the spectacle of biblical pageantry, and the case for Jewish armed resistance via the agitprop staging that once rallied support for labor and antifascist "partisans." Undergirding all this multilayered stagecraft was the symbolic narrative of a confrontation between two competing Jewish identities—the old "wandering Jew" of the diaspora and the young "Tough Jew" of the new Zion. The fact that these figures were embodied onstage by the aging Paul Muni and a rising star named Marlon Brando added yet more theatrical resonance to the cultural, generational, and epochal shift the play depicted.

## "DISPLACED PERSONS"

Since the end of the European war in the summer of 1945, the conflict between ruler and ruled in Palestine had grown even more intractable. The demands for more Jewish immigration to Palestine became more desperate due to the millions of stranded and homeless European Jewish survivors, referred to as "Displaced Persons." Jewish underground armies like Bergson's *Irgun* had resumed and intensified their efforts to smuggle Jews into Palestine in defiance of British blockades. Therefore, at issue after the war was not only the larger question of an independent Jewish state but the more immediate problem of what was to become of the Displaced Persons. It was this crisis that *A Flag Is Born*—with its narrative of a trio of Holocaust survivors seeking refuge in the Holy Land—addressed most directly.

The very weeks preceding the play's September 5 opening marked an especially sharp escalation in the Jewish-British conflict. In July the *Irgun* bombed Jerusalem's King David Hotel (the site of the British Mandate's administrative offices); Hecht told a reporter that he only regretted that "there were four other hotels housing the illegal British occupation troops that they didn't blow up."[2] For Hecht, such violence was justified by the same motives that drove other "resistance" fighters in World War II and populist revolutionaries throughout history. The *Irgun*, he claimed, was "making history in the same way as the *Maquis* [i.e., French resistance], the Partisans, the Irish rebels and the American revolutionists."[3]

Hecht had stepped into a prominent role for Bergson in April 1946 by co-chairing a "repatriation" committee to aid the (still illegal) resettlement of Jews in Palestine, writing many newspaper advertisements drawing on the imagery of the American Civil War by calling for an "underground railway" for the Displaced Persons.[4] But when the fundraising effort fell short of goals, Bergson knew that angry editorials alone would not bring in enough contributions to purchase the ships necessary to transport the hundreds of thousands of refugees that he was promising. Hecht therefore proposed repeating their success with *We Will Never Die* with another staged protest, counting on the unique potential of performance as a powerful platform for the disenfranchised and voiceless. "There is no Parliament or Congress or World Court from which the Hebrews can speak," he wrote in a statement printed in the *A Flag Is Born* program. "Here, then, on the Stage in front of you is the Hebrew and his only Parliament."[5]

## "A WORLD THAT HAS DISAPPEARED"

Hecht's vision for *A Flag Is Born* was to dramatize the birth of a Jewish state out of the ashes of the Holocaust. This is instantly clear in the play's opening desolate tableau, which one reviewer described as "Goya-like."[6] In his stage directions, Hecht describes a "battered graveyard" into which arrives an old couple recently liberated from Treblinka. The man is, once again, Sholem-Aleichem's Tevye (again spelled "Tevya"), whom Hecht had introduced in *A Jewish Fairy Tale*. The woman, his wife, is called Zelda—but Hecht had originally named her Goldie, the name of Tevye's wife in Sholem-Aleichem's original stories.[7] In the script's opening narration, Hecht again channels the lachrymose tone of Maurice Samuel's *The World of Sholom Aleichem*. "This is a tale of a world that has disappeared," announces the play's onstage "Speaker" (played in the premiere by the noted antifascist, and non-Jewish, war correspondent Quentin Reynolds), reminding the audience that amid postwar jubilation, the world had still not reckoned with, or even acknowledged, how close Hitler's Final Solution came to achieving its genocidal goals: "History will say, 'of all the things that happened in that time—our time—the slaughter of the Jews of Europe was the only thing that counted forever in the annals of man. The proud orations of heroes and conquerors will be a footnote in history beside the great silence that watched this slaughter.' Yes, in the history books it will not be victories—it will be this silence that identifies and condemns our era" (1–2). Long before the significance of the Holocaust was clearly marked in mainstream American culture, *A Flag Is Born* was prescient in identifying it as one of the war's primary legacies. Such a call to conscience ran counter to the prevailing optimism of postwar American discourse.

While the play never visually represents or enacts the horrors of the concentration camps, the constant description from the stage constituted a kind of bearing witness at a time when such stories—especially as told by survivors themselves—were still shockingly new to the public. Hecht describes the tragedy with a specificity that was still unfamiliar to the general American public. The Speaker tells of the "six millions [who] were murdered in the furnaces" (2); Tevya calls the entire European Jewish heritage "a dream that died in a gas chamber" (38); another character—a younger survivor named David—describes victims "walking naked—two by two—to the furnaces" (7) and curses the world for making "a garbage pile of my people" (45).

To appreciate the potential impact of such testimony upon a 1946 audience, one must take into account what Jeffrey Shandler calls the "inchoate status of the Holocaust as a historical concept during the first postwar years."[8] Newsreels about the liberation of the concentration camps—exhibited in movie theatres in April and May of 1945—clearly moved those who saw them, but these images were only publicly screened for a few weeks and were not as ubiquitous as they would later become via television and other media. Also, while Hitler's persecution of Jews was common knowledge, much of the early postwar coverage of the camps framed the tragedy as one among many of the war's gruesome horrors, without foregrounding the predominantly Jewish identity of the victims and survivors. As Shandler argues, "What would later be distinguished as a separate 'war against the Jews' was not yet codified as a discrete unit of human experience with its own authoritative sources, narrative boundaries, vocabulary, historiography, and scholarly apparatus. Jews were not singled out as the quintessential victims of Nazi persecution, *nor were Jewish responses regarded as central to the postwar understanding of this chapter of history*."[9] *A Flag Is Born* forcefully claimed the unfolding story of the Holocaust as a Jewish story, framing it as a "discrete" and exceptional event, and it did so from an expressly Jewish perspective—a rare "Jewish response" in the public sphere at that moment.

Yet while insisting on its uniqueness, the play does not treat the Holocaust as an isolated problem. The motif of a "disappearing" world echoed the foundational Zionist premise that Jewish life in the diaspora had always been precarious and was destined to fail, a failure whose inevitability the Holocaust only confirmed. Hecht gives voice to this belief through the character of David, another survivor, whom Tevya and Zelda encounter on their journey to Palestine. David, only eighteen but already hopelessly cynical, recites the succession of migrations and expulsions from one host country to another that constitutes the history of Jewish "wandering": "Jewish prayers can't get to God, Tevya, without an English visa. This is the new law. Yesterday our prayers needed a German visa. And the day before yesterday they required a Spanish visa. You see, our trouble is, Tevya, we have been praying in the wrong countries . . . My father taught me that I belonged in the land where I was born. Then, one day, all the Jews in that land were gathered together like a pile of garbage and burned up. From this I learned that the teachings of my father were wrong (9)" Tevya, too, eventually gives up hope for the diaspora:

> In the old days the Jews did not need Palestine because they had many fine homelands in Europe. . . . And in the old days when somebody said to me, "Tevya, go to Palestine and live in the Holy Land like a good Jew,"

I answered them back, "Why do I have to go anywhere? I am through going. Name me a place in the world, and I have gone in, gone out. Now I have a home. Europe." . . . Then it turns out this was only a dream about a home. A dream that died in a gas chamber. (38)

That "dream"—the utopian promise of a "melting pot" as extolled in Israel Zangwill's landmark 1908 play of that name—has now gone up in flames, says Hecht.

As he did in *A Jewish Fairy Tale*, Hecht uses the Tevye figure (and now his wife) as an avatar for the old culture of the Eastern European shtetl. This Tevya says he is from "Dubinky" (i.e., Dubienka in Poland) (7). The stage directions note that Zelda's "fifty-five years have the look of fifty-five centuries," close to the approximately 5,700 years of the Jewish calendar. These characters embody not only the recent European experience but the whole history of the Jewish people. It is no coincidence that they find themselves in a cemetery, for even though they still aspire to get to Palestine, the graveyard is their own. As Hecht stated outright in an early draft of the play, "Here lie the dead Jews of Europe."[10]

*A Flag Is Born* conjures up ghosts of another "disappearing world" as well—the Yiddish Theatre. By the late forties, Yiddish Theatre was going the way of Tevya and Zelda themselves. Hasia Diner poetically cites the closing of the legendary Lower East Side actors' hangout Café Royale in 1945 as the form's symbolic death knell.[11] When Maurice Schwartz's Yiddish Art Theatre closed in 1950, it was the last major company of its kind active in New York. Not only was the Eastern European Jewish culture from which the art form came now extinguished but, among American Jews, the Yiddish language was disappearing as the original immigrant generations passed on and their children (and grandchildren) increasingly took to English as their new *mamaloshen*.

Hecht uses the form and conventions of the Yiddish Theatre as a theatrical analog to the dying culture of the Jewish diaspora at large. This was most evident in the casting of many famous Second Avenue performers in the lead roles. Tevya was played by Paul Muni, the American Yiddish stage's most famous alumnus. As the play's program reminded audiences: "Long before Broadway began to cheer Paul Muni, the name of Muni Weisenfreund was a familiar one to Second Avenue audiences. For eighteen years his world was the Yiddish-language theatre of New York."[12] The program also identified director Luther Adler as "the son of the late Jacob P. Adler, founder of the Yiddish stage in America." Playing Zelda was Celia Adler (Jacob's daughter by a different marriage), who is hailed as not only "the reigning member of the Royal Family of the Yiddish Theatre" but also its "First Lady." (Before *Flag* she had appeared in only two English-speaking stage roles in her entire four-decade career.) Many reviewers made note of these lineages: from the complimentary ("Paul Muni gave an ardent downtown performance," said the *New York Journal-American*) to the critical (Celia Adler acted in "a broader style of the older Yiddish persuasion," according to the *Chicago Tribune*).[13] These connections were further reinforced when, after Muni's four-week contract expired, Luther Adler himself stepped into the role of Tevya. For the national tour, Adler turned the part over to yet another Second Avenue icon, Jacob Ben-Ami—thereby offering the audience two lead actors whose careers had almost entirely been in Yiddish Theatre.[14] So obvious were the Yiddish Theatre connections to one critic that he felt it imperative to reassure readers that the play "is, of course, in English."[15]

The character of Tevya's wife Zelda provided another direct link to the Yiddish Theatre tradition. Celia's performance was, by many accounts, as "downtown" in style as Muni's, especially when she channeled the form's sentimental strain in a scene that interpolated the famous lullaby "*Rozhinkes mit Mandlen*" ("Raisins and Almonds"), a perennial favorite of the Second Avenue stage ever since Abraham Goldfaden wrote it for his operetta *Shulamith* in 1881. Nibbling whatever scraps of stale bread she and Tevya have left, Zelda has a flashback to Friday Shabbos dinners with her now dead children. "Glowing with memories," Hecht tells us, she envisions her five children before her and begins talking to them (19). When she hears her youngest crying, she is completely lost in her memories amid the stark reality of the graveyard, and "for several moments the stage is motionless as Zelda sits singing and rocking and looking into the lighted place in front of her" (20). Zelda's singing of this beloved melody to her (now dead) baby exploits the great sentimental appeal of the Yiddish Theatre to American Jewish audiences—an appeal only heightened by the presence of an actress whose most famous Yiddish film, *Where Is My Child?* (1937), cemented her persona in the genre as a forlorn mother.

"Homesickness," writes Nahma Sandrow, "was a recurrent theme" in the Yiddish Theatre, especially via music.[16] The lilting, minor-key melody of "Raisins and Almonds" must have made for a moment of great pathos and nostalgia in its longing for happier times. But the play had already worked to disenchant any notion of an idealized "old country" by framing its story with the harsh diaspora negation of its opening. By framing Zelda's reminiscence not as a fond flashback but as a desperate delusion (the stage directions say that "her mind has grown vague" and her suddenly "strong voice . . . belongs to another long ago"), Hecht conveys to the largely Jewish American audience that they can't go home again, in this case to the world of their parents and grandparents (19). As he does repeatedly throughout the play, Hecht resurrects the Yiddish Theatre form only to dismantle it.

## PAST AS PRESENT

At the play's midpoint, Tevya experiences a series of visions from the Hebrew Bible. These reference the Yiddish Theatre as well, since "reenactments of events out of Jewish history served to preserve and reinforce communal identity in the face of isolation and assimilation."[17] With Kurt Weill again repurposing music for Hecht from his 1937 opera *The Eternal Road*, these scenes also recall that work's grand tableaus of ancient glories as a "road of promise" for Zionist aspirations. (*The Eternal Road*'s original German title was *Der Weg der Verheissung*.) Hecht's less pious and more bellicose postwar pageantry in *A Flag Is Born* reflects the catastrophic events of the decade between the two works, taking more liberties with scripture to emphasize modern parallels so that past and present interact more dynamically. He enables Tevya, the beleaguered modern Jew, to traverse time and space and learn directly from his forebears—as if the spectacle of earlier Zionist pageants were too remote to achieve the goal of efficacy. If in *The Eternal Road* past is prologue, in *A Flag Is Born* it is the immediate present.

King Saul, for instance, is shown in *The Eternal Road* as cowardly and weak, but Hecht portrays him as a proto-Maccabee, saving villagers from the invading Ammonites. The narrative of aiding an endangered population against a tyrant not only parallels Hecht's view of the Palestine struggle but allegorizes the appeasement debates of the 1930s. In Hecht's telling, three citizens of Jabesh-Gilead approach Saul and argue over whether or not to surrender to the enemy's demands: an "Old One" represents the most vulnerable of the Jewish inhabitants; a "Young One" in armor takes the militant stance of fighting and resisting; and, in between, stands a "Middle Aged One," who is "richly dressed" and full of excuses for why not to go to war (13). Echoing isolationists in America and Europe who sought peace or neutrality with Hitler, this interpolated, nonscriptural character of Hecht's argues that he and his brethren are "powerless against the enemy" who is a "great and powerful king," and that it is Saul "who will destroy Israel, not Nahash," if he does not capitulate. When the Young One reminds him the Ammonites mean to enslave them, the Middle Aged One—"his voice unctuous and appeasing"—shrugs off the possibility: "Perhaps not slavery. Who knows? Perhaps we can make friends with the Amonite . . . do nothing to anger him . . . show how learned and law abiding we are . . . woo him by turning a kindly face to him. . . . Nahash the Amonite will take what he wants. But he is only a man. He cannot devour us. The quicker we surrender the less he will take away from us (14)." In so closely echoing the early reassurances of prewar politicians and intellectuals about the supposed difference between Hitler's rhetoric and intentions, Hecht disrupts the conventionally reverent nature of pageantry, reframing the biblical reenactment with a disturbing contemporary parallel.

Tevya's next vision, of King Solomon, stands out in its naked appeal to Jewish masculinity and the need to physically revitalize the perceived impotence of the old wandering Jew. "The motif of the Jew as bridegroom and the Land of Israel as bride," writes Amos Oz, "is common in ancient writings, as well as in modern literature and Zionist slogans."[18] Hecht brings this metaphor to life onstage when Solomon enters with an ensemble of "sandaled women, garlanded and lovely," who "dance slowly" as he sings lines from that erotic poem of scripture, the Song of Solomon (24). On the surface, the scene may appear to be a digression, a typical Broadway production number (replete with chorus girls). But one common reading of the Song of Solomon text throughout Jewish history is as a paean not just to the love between man and woman but between God and Israel. Hecht has already had King Saul announce this theme in his call to battle the Amorites: "Out of the whole world we have married only this land—and it is our bride. . . . [A] stranger has come for our bride—the fair Hebrew bride of Israel . . . who wishes to despoil her and use her basely" (16). And his onstage narrator explicitly describes Tevya's response to Solomon's Temple as an awakening of his "manhood": "This is Tevya's last secret in the graveyard—that he dreams of the glory of being a man. His soul has not accepted the lower levels designed for it by the hate and villainy of a world. It will not bow to contempt or murder. Condemned to survive as human rubbish, it will lift itself up out of the dust and move bewilderedly toward its destiny—manhood. Such is the reason of Tevya's journey to Palestine. There his manhood lies" (23). The modern-day warriors who take the stage at the end of the play also reinforce the sentiment: "Saul and the Maccabees live again in Palestine. Their strong arms are bared again . . . The manhood the world took from us roars again in Palestine" (47).

## "THE COUNCIL OF THE MIGHTY"

When Tevya pleads with King Solomon that his people have been "scattered . . . from our house" and left to build new houses in lands that did not want them, Solomon decrees: "This is my judgment, Tevya—go to the world, speak to it, be not afraid of its mighty councils. For in you is my own wisdom" (29). This command suddenly places Tevya, via the play's fantastic and free-form dramaturgy, before the assembly of world leaders at the "Council of the Mighty,"

Hecht's stand-in for the United Nations. The UN had been founded the year before *A Flag Is Born*, with the lofty mission of healing the postwar world with peacekeeping and guaranteeing human rights globally. It would soon become very involved in the Palestine conflict (especially in its failed 1947 "partition" plan), but had yet to formally support a Jewish state in the fall of 1946. Hecht and his Zionist colleagues saw the UN's inaction as furthering the suffering of Jews, which made it yet another target of Hecht's polemic in his play. And his portrayal of its diplomats as petty, elitist bureaucrats moves *A Flag Is Born* into yet another theatrical mode: political satire.

Hecht's comic depiction of a "Council of the Mighty" (specifically a committee modeled on the UN Security Council) hearkens back to earlier Popular Front satires of imperialist "Great Powers," such as the "Four Little Angels of Peace" song from *Pins and Needles* (1937–1940). As in that revue, the tone is set musically at first, with the stage directions calling for "a medley of satyrically [sic] patriotic themes—'The Punishment To Fit the Crime,' 'Give My Regards to Broadway,' 'The Marseillaise,' the 'Russian March,' etc." (29). (The Mikado reference resonated with one critic, who praised the scene's "bitter Gilbert and Sullivan irony.")[19] So jarring was the tonal shift into the scene that one critic lamented that, after the "profoundly moving" Saul and Solomon scenes, "suddenly Mr. Hecht descends to sarcastic invective, and 'A Flag is Born' turns into hysterical anti-British propaganda with a cynical court of diplomats."[20] The music anticipates what was described as a "flippant" and "burlesque" characterization of world leaders (those who hold the fate of the Jews in their hands) as grotesque buffoons.[21]

The "Council of the Mighty" scene announces *A Flag Is Born* as an anti-imperialist as well as Zionist project—at a moment when those two agendas converged for what remained of the old Popular Front, for which the "politics of antifascist and anti-imperialist solidarity" had always been a pillar.[22] Opposition to the British Empire on the left, however, had been complicated by England's wartime alliance against fascism. Now, with the war over, Hecht revived popular prewar stereotypes of British imperial haughtiness. The English delegates on the council, for instance, dismiss Tevya as an "illegal interloper" (32) guilty of a "breach of international courtesy" (31). Their unvarnished racism and antisemitism are also on display when they accuse this "bold and mocking Semite" (35) of "oriental evasion" and Jews in general of "always push[ing] themselves to the head of the line" (31). For Hecht, the British are not only the new enemy but the new Germany; when Tevya tries to engage the Council in debate about Palestine, the "English Statesman" refuses even to recognize him because "we're at war with the Jews." Tevya fires back with jarringly impolitic sarcasm:

TEVYA: Excuse me—but I would like to ask what you are doing here, sitting in a front seat! You Germans were already defeated. So what is Germany doing in a front seat again?
ENGLISH STATESMAN: I am not Germany. I am England.
TEVYA: England! England is having a war with the Jews! Who can believe such a thing! (34)

When the Englishman accuses Jews in Palestine of "tak[ing] up arms against British law and order," Tevya retorts: "Is it the law and order left over by Buchenwald and Dachau, maybe?" (35). As shocking as the conflation of wartime Germany and postwar England would have seemed to a postwar American audience, Popular Front followers would have recognized the overlap in antifascist and anti-imperialist discourses of prewar progressive politics.

In contrast to the imperial and amoral bureaucrats on the council, Tevya emerges as the only noble "statesman" in the room. As in *A Jewish Fairy Tale*—where Hecht's Tevya holds his own in a private audience with Winston Churchill—Hecht sets up a momentary carnivalesque inversion of power, where the lowly man can school his rulers. The eloquent three-page oration that Tevya delivers provides Hecht with an unfiltered platform for his polemic through direct address to the audience. In the persona of Muni, the moment also recalled the numerous "closing arguments" the actor had given in many Warner Brothers social conscience films of the thirties, most notably his final courtroom summation in defense of Alfred Dreyfus in *The Life of Emil Zola*. While some critics complained of the patently propagandistic technique of having Muni effectively step outside the frame of the play, exploiting the stage as "the Hebrew's only parliament" was Hecht's expressed intention.

The delegates' initial favorable response to Tevya's speech suggests that he has won the day, but satire brings the proceedings back to "reality" when they then bicker over protocol and only agree to postpone the Palestine question to next meeting's "agenda"—a word that mocks Tevya with its dismissiveness. It was, after all, a long series of well-intentioned "agendas" and diplomatic conferences that failed to save the Jews during the war and now continued to impede action in Palestine. As Hecht describes the scene, "Each Statesman in turn repeats 'agenda' to the next and begins to chuckle," leaving Tevya alone onstage crying, "No, No! An agenda again!" as the scene dissolves back into the graveyard (42). Having abandoned the Jews before to an "agenda" at countless conferences during the tragedy of the Holocaust, history has now repeated itself, as Marx would have it, as farce.

Figure 7. "Here, then, on the Stage in front of you is the Hebrew and his only Parliament." Paul Muni as Tevya addresses the "Council of the Mighty," the play's satire on the United Nations. Source: Ben Hecht, *A Flag Is Born* (published script), New York: American League for a Free Palestine, 1946. Newberry Library, Ben Hecht Papers.

For all the comical yet substantive dialogue over policy in Tevya's clash with the council, one issue gets surprisingly short shrift, given what the real United Nations would soon be most occupied with when it confronted the Palestine question. The British ambassador brings up the Arab population and argues that Britain must stay in Palestine to keep peace between rival Jewish and Arab factions. Tevya's rebuttal is to accuse Britain of hollow hypocrisy: "You don't want to do wrong by the Arabs? Since when does England worry about doing wrong to people whose land it steals?" He even goes further to assert Jewish solidarity with Palestinian Arabs against the nation that is their common enemy: "Who would treat the Arabs better, Jews who are their brothers, or Englishmen who are their masters?" (39). Remarkably, these are the only words in the entire play (or any of Hecht's Palestine plays) spoken about Arab-Jewish relations. Tevya's seemingly conciliatory tone echoes the Bergson group's official public position on the issue that the new state should be both democratic and "secular" for both peoples. But the political party that Bergson and the *Irgun* leadership eventually formed in the new Israeli parliament—first as *Herut*, later as *Likud*—

quickly became the most bellicose faction in the new state's relationship with Arabs and the Arab world, starting with the Arab-Israeli war of 1948.

Hecht's attempt to diminish the Arab role in the Palestine story appears carefully calculated to avoid a racial animus that would violate Popular Front tenets of racial and religious tolerance. Tevya describes Jews and Arabs as "brothers," fellow oppressed peoples, then notably pivots to refocus the debate on British imperialism (their common English "masters"). But as early drafts reveal, Hecht envisioned no co-ownership of the new state—the play's original title was "Palestine is Ours!"[23]

## THE ZIONIST AS PROLETARIAN HERO

Tevya's day in court ultimately fails, we learn, because Jews cannot rely on others to address their problems and must take their future into their own hands. He will not live long enough to heed that lesson, but the mission will be taken up by the other survivor he has met along the way, the nihilistic youth, David. "Muscular Judaism," the half-century-old Zionist project to transform the perception of Jewish identity, had finally come to Broadway—and in the person, no less, of a young unknown actor who was about to redefine masculinity in American popular culture: Marlon Brando.

If Tevya and Zelda embody the decline of life in the diaspora, then David exudes the physical renewal promised by Zionism. He is first seen rising, golem-like, from the dirt of the graveyard, and while he has only been resting, the sight is enough to frighten Tevya and Zelda into asking if he is a ghost (6–7). While the older couple have been depleted by Treblinka, David is radicalized. Exemplifying Bergson's motto, "action, not pity," he casts a ruthlessly unsentimental eye on his own trauma. Recalling those he watched die in the camps, he mocks their desperate prayers and holds God responsible for their suffering:

YOUTH [David]: . . . I heard you praying before. I don't like to hear a man praying. I heard prayers in Treblinka.
ZELDA (*wailing*): Treblinka! Treblinka . . . Ai—my sons and daughters—
YOUTH (*coldly*): Did they die in Treblinka, mama? (*Zelda and Tevya cover their faces with their hands.*) Maybe I saw them. I saw a million Jews die. I used to hide in a tree at night and count them—when they were walking naked—two by two—to the furnaces. And praying. (*His voice grows mocking as he chants the prayer.*) Shmai Yisrael, Adonai Elahanu—(*Tevya picks up the prayer and continues it, mumbling the words. Zelda holds her hands over her face. The*

*youth listens to Tevya for a moment and then continues coldly.*) My father's God suffered a great misfortune. The earth was His face—but vermin overran it and ate out its eyes, so He couldn't see. One doesn't pray to such a God. One pities Him. And tries to forget Him—like a poor relation. (7–8)

In contrast to Tevya and Zelda's "wailing" piety, David's cynical outlook sounds blasphemous. But it is not his lack of faith that marks him as a radical as much as his refusal to accept suffering as a given for the Jewish people.

The tension between David and his elders in the play is not just religious and generational but dramaturgical as well. While Tevya and Zelda appear to have come straight from a Sholem-Aleichem play on Second Avenue, David—a "gaunt and grim" eighteen-year-old in "dungarees, a black turtle-necked sweater, a torn cap and shoes"—recalls the proletarian hero of 1930s agitprop (6).[24] "Agitating" is indeed his main function in the play, whether it is goading Tevya and Zelda out of their pious submission or provoking the audience to ponder its own culpability in the characters' predicament. No subject could have been more sensitive (or even taboo) in postwar Jewish American culture than the question of whether American Jews could have done more to stop the Holocaust—and yet, halfway through the play, David stops the action, marches downstage, and accuses his audience of exactly that.

The force of its confrontational staging made this speech one of the most controversial—and most remembered—moments in the play. The element of disruption was heightened in performance by directly following Zelda's sentimental, Yiddish Theatre–style singing of "Raisins and Almonds" with a sudden change in modes from melancholic empathy to stark alienation.[25] As Zelda's singing fades, David suddenly "rises and turns away from them" and "raises his face and remains looking wildly into the night that is over the audience" (20). The framing of the monologue being delivered "into the night" notwithstanding, the very first words reveal a very clear and specific use of direct address from the stage: "Where were you—Jews? Where were you when the killing was going on? When the six million were being burned and buried alive in the lime pits, where were you? Where was your voice crying out against the slaughter? We didn't hear any voice. There was no voice. You Jews of America! You Jews of England! Strong Jews, rich Jews, high-up Jews; Jews of power and genius! Where was your cry of rage that could have filled the world and stopped the fires? Nowhere! Because you were ashamed to cry out as Jews" (20–21). In Brando's own account, the moment was apparently so charged that, on some nights, "Jewish girls got out of their seats and screamed and cried from the aisles out of sadness."[26] One spectator later recalled, "The whole audience sort of rose up en masse. You

Figures 8 and 9. Tevya vs. David: *A Flag Is Born*'s clash of Jewish generations. Top photo: Marlon Brando and Paul Muni. Bottom: (from the replacement cast), Sidney Lumet and Luther Adler. Celia Adler, as Tevya's wife Zelda, looks on in both. Sources: (fig. 8) Ben Hecht, *A Flag Is Born* (published script), New York: American League for a Free Palestine, 1946. Newberry Library, Ben Hecht Papers; (fig. 9) Lucas-Pritchard, "Sidney Lumet as David, Luther Adler as Tevya and Celia Adler as Zelda in 'A Flag Is Born,'" accession number 80.103.891, Museum of the City of New York.

could feel them reacting."[27] Not all reactions were affirmative, however; at one performance, after Brando asked, "Where were you, Jews?" an older woman in the audience yelled back, "Where were *you*?"[28] On such occasions, the "agitation" aspect of this agitprop gesture became evident—rather than refute the actor's speech, the audience's response reinforced its political potency through the breaking down of the fourth wall. Such a call-and-response interaction between an actor and a "rising en masse" audience might have recalled, for some, another famous Broadway agitprop moment a decade earlier—the final call of "Strike!" from Clifford Odets's *Waiting for Lefty* (1935). It was a play *Flag*'s director, Luther Adler, knew well as a member of the original cast.

The play's final scene combines a multitude of agitprop techniques with a more mystical evocation of Jewish pageantry and symbolism. When Tevya wakes up from his United Nations dream, he finds himself back in the graveyard and realizes that Zelda has died. Tevya says the Kaddish for her, an action that doubly serves onstage as a speech act memorializing all the Jewish dead of the war—exactly as *We Will Never Die* had done in its final moments. In addition to a lament, it serves also as a catalyst for action; the Kaddish must be said for that "world that has disappeared" before it can finally be left behind and a new world be born. A moment of historical transformation is at hand.

In this narrative logic, not even Tevya is permitted to survive into the new Jewish future. After Zelda dies, he appears ready to join David on the journey, but he is summoned by an "Angel of Death."[29] David's initial reaction to losing Tevya is fatalistic: "You—World, who made a garbage pile of my people, you didn't kill me. An oversight—to be corrected" (45). He takes out a knife, but before he can plunge it into his own heart, he is stopped by three "Palestinian soldiers" beckoning him: "We're waiting for you, David."[30] (In a gesture of cross-Zionist solidarity, the soldiers are identified as not just from the *Irgun* but a "Hebrew army of Palestine" made up of all the major guerrilla forces.)[31] The summoning of the angry but directionless David resembles the kind of "conversion" narrative that dominated much of 1930s proletarian fiction, where an adrift protagonist is corralled by dire circumstances—and by his "comrades"—into an epiphany of new consciousness leading to direct action. To amplify the call of the soldiers, Adler drew on a familiar "Epic Theatre" device of projecting film onto the back wall of the stage—in this case documentary footage of actual *Irgun* troops.[32]

David's full conversion to the cause is signified by his brandishing of the flag that gives the play its title. Constructing the symbol of the new Jewish state by grafting a Star of David on Tevya's worn *talis*, David merges old and new

## TEVYE AND THE TERRORISTS

in a dialectical synthesis, bidding farewell to the "disappeared world" while simultaneously bearing its legacy onto a new "road of promise." Hecht's closing stage directions read:

> David turns to the dead Tevya. He takes the talis from him. He takes a blue star from his own pocket. He puts the star on the talis, cutting away the talis fringes with his knife. From beyond the lighted bridge comes a chorus of soldiers singing the Hatikvah—in the distance beyond the bridge. . . . David tacks his talis-flag to a branch. He pauses and through the singing he hears the sound of guns, distant guns growing louder. He looks at Tevya. David turns toward the shining bridge. Holding his flag high, he walks toward the light, the singing and the sound of guns. (48)

Figure 10. "We speak in a new Jewish language, the language of guns." Soldiers of the *Irgun*, Haganah, and Stern armies unite to beckon David (Sidney Lumet) to Palestine. (Future famous Jewish American actors in the scene include "First Soldier" Jonathan Harris, directly facing David, and, behind him, "Second Soldier" Steven Hill.) Source: Lucas-Pritchard, "A Flag Is Born theater still," accession Number 80.103.888, Museum of the City of New York.

In describing 1930s proletarian literature, Malcolm Cowley notes a narrative pattern: "The older man dies for the cause, like John the Baptist, but the young hero takes over his faith and mission."[33] Perhaps this evocation is what Brooks Atkinson had in mind when he faulted the ending of *A Flag Is Born* as "an episode of flag waving that, from the point of view of stage craftsmanship, comes straight out of the rummage basket."[34]

## FROM SECOND AVENUE TO ACTORS STUDIO

Just as the meeting between Tevya and David in *A Flag Is Born* is a clash of opposites, so was the one onstage between the actors Muni and Brando. Muni was nearing the end of his career at the time, his film stardom having peaked by the late 1930s. (He would only appear in two more feature films after *Flag* before his death in 1967.) Brando, then twenty-two, had made his Broadway debut one year earlier, but was still one year away from his catapulting success in the stage premiere of *A Streetcar Named Desire* (1947). Brando was not Jewish himself—although, given how unknown he was at the time, a Broadway audience had no reason to assume otherwise. His casting in *Flag* was a direct result of his mentor, Stella Adler, and the Adler family, who, Brando felt, "virtually adopted me."[35] He would later write that despite being an outsider to their religion, he quickly took on the Zionist cause as his own: "I wanted to act in the play because of what we were beginning to learn about the true nature of the killing of the Jews and because of the empathy I felt for the Adlers. . . . I was beginning to hear a voice in my head that said I had a responsibility to do something about it and that acting was not an important vocation in life when the world was still facing so many problems."[36] Considering how much Brando went on to publicly campaign throughout his life for the rights of African Americans and Native Americans, *Flag* effectively launched his career as an actor-activist, very much in the mold of those prominent in the Depression-era "cultural front" such as Muni and the Adlers.

Brando's suitability for the role of David was due less to his credibility as a Jew than as a Popular Front-style proletarian hero in the mold of John Garfield. Just as Garfield had once been hailed as the new Muni, now Brando was poised to become the next Garfield. (Likewise, Garfield would later be described, in retrospect, as "the precursor to Brando.")[37] So natural was the comparison early on in Brando's career that the two actors were sometimes treated interchangeably. It was Garfield who was first offered the role of the working-class Polish American Stanley Kowalski in *A Streetcar Named Desire*, for instance.[38] Simultaneously, when *Streetcar*'s director, Elia Kazan, was casting his next film, *Gentleman's Agreement* (1947), he wanted Garfield for the role of "Dave," a Jewish American U.S. Army veteran.

When Garfield's availability became uncertain, he asked Luther Adler to recommend other actors, and Adler recommended Brando. Garfield did end up playing the role (his first on-screen performance as an explicitly Jewish character), but, had he not, Brando's film debut would have been as another fighting Jew named David.

The figure of John Garfield continued to haunt the role of David even when Brando left the cast and was replaced by another up-and-coming young actor raised in the tradition of the Group Theatre and Popular Front: Sidney Lumet. Lumet also grew up under the direct influence of the Yiddish Theatre. (His father, Baruch Lumet, was a Second Avenue veteran.) As a boy, he appeared as a child actor in Group Theatre productions and in *The Eternal Road*. When Lumet took over the role of David in *A Flag Is Born* on tour, critics explicitly compared him to "a younger John Garfield" and "straight from the Group Theatre school of acting" (by which was meant "tense, quick thrusting, sharply alert").[39] Shortly after *Flag*, Lumet began directing for television and film in a body of work that projected the legacy of both the Group's progressive Popular Front politics and its acting tradition into the second half of the twentieth century.[40]

Also linking Brando to Jewish American culture was his association with the new "method acting" movement in acting training. "Method acting from its inception," argues Henry Bial in his study *Acting Jewish*, "has been a cultural process for which Jewish American artists can claim a birthright, much as African Americans can claim jazz music. Its arrival and subsequent level of acceptance in the United States coincides with their own."[41] The Method began in the 1930s, when Lee Strasberg, the Group Theatre's co-director, began to train the company's actors in his own interpretation of Konstantin Stanislavsky's teachings.[42] Luther and Stella Adler, as well as Garfield, all went through this training. When Stella later disputed Strasberg's approach and began teaching her own version of Stanislavsky, one of her first students was Brando.[43]

But Russian realism was not the only influence on the Group's aesthetic. While the Group was not an all-Jewish company, many of its leading figures had either firsthand experience performing in Yiddish theatre (Stella and Luther Adler, as well as Morris Carnovsky) or grew up avidly attending performances (Strasberg and Harold Clurman). Thus, as Bial argues, "the American Method differs from 'pure Stanislavsky,' because (at least in part) the [Stanislavsky] 'system' arrived in the United States filtered through the emotionally and politically charged Yiddish Theatre."[44] This cultural crossbreeding of Stanislavsky and Second Avenue came to fruition after the war, when a new generation of actors trained by Strasberg and Adler brought it to their film work in Hollywood, often in films directed by Kazan, another former Group Theatre actor.[45] Unlike earlier American acting schools that aspired to class- and race-based, British-inspired standards of elocution and comportment, the Actors Studio (founded in 1947 by ex-Group members) extended the Group's Popular Front–inflected mission to promote a pluralist vision of America where ethnic markers—such as "Brooklyn" accents and foreign-sounding names—need not be erased in the name of good acting.[46]

Muni's schooling in the Yiddish Theatre predated any influence from the Method. But in his early Warner Brothers "ethnic" film roles (like the Al Capone figure in *Scarface* and the Polish coal miner in *Black Fury*), Muni excelled in the kinds of emotionally unrestrained performances Brando would later become known for. Muni, however, was, by many accounts, an "external" actor, learning dialogue and gesture by rote, leaving little room for spontaneity, and relying heavily on physical appearance and makeup to create a character—as opposed to the Method's shunning of such surface details in favor of an "inside-out" approach. The two actors' opposite "methods" were bound to clash in *A Flag Is Born*. Brando tells a story of when, at the end of the play, David lays the deceased Tevya to rest by covering him with a *talis* shawl, the older actor sometimes seemed reluctant to cede his place: "[I] covered him completely, face and all. I began my big speech, and when I looked down I saw the flag crawl down his forehead, slip away from his eyes along the bridge of his nose, slowly exposing his face inch by inch. It was like magic. I saw Muni's upstage hand, the one hidden from the audience, pulling down the flag by gathering folds in his fist. The old hambone couldn't stand not having his face in the final scene."[47] Zionist text and American-theatrical subtext interact in this moment as Oedipal drama: for the Jews and a Jewish state to survive, the young Muscle Jew must honor, yet bury, the weaker, victimized diasporic father figure—just as the young Method Actor seeks to honor his craft's Yiddish Theatre heritage while leaving behind its reliance on masks, disguise, and "old-world" melodramatic acting.

## "THE MURDER OF SIX MILLION PEOPLE IS NOT AN ENTERTAINING SUBJECT"

*A Flag Is Born* was a surprise Broadway success, especially for a propaganda play about foreign affairs and genocidal horrors. (It also ran nearly two hours without an intermission.) Its initial run at the Alvin Theatre was initially scheduled for only four weeks, but it was extended repeatedly for a total of 120 performances, moving to three other theatres before closing on December 14. It then toured major American cities during January and February 1947, playing in Chicago, Detroit, Philadelphia, Boston, and Baltimore. Total revenue from ticket sales and additional audience donations grossed close to $1 million.[48] Muni and Brando had left the cast after the play's first month, replaced by Luther

Adler and Sidney Lumet. Lumet continued as David on tour with Jacob Ben-Ami as Tevya. Stella Adler joined the cast as the Speaker for select performances in Philadelphia and Baltimore.[49] And Detroit audiences would have seen a guest appearance by Humphrey Bogart in that role had the movie star not canceled at the last minute.[50]

Critical reception, however, was mixed. As the first of Hecht's Jewish political plays to perform on Broadway, *Flag* was the first to be reviewed in newspaper theatre pages, and many critics were openly ambivalent (if not hostile) engaging with drama that was also advocacy.[51] The terms "propaganda" and even "pageantry" were used freely as pejoratives. The *New York Times*' Brooks Atkinson described Hecht's dramaturgy as "after the fashion of pageants, which at best are untalented theatre."[52] George Jean Nathan mocked "the tedium of its pageantry, the overemphasis of its documentary propaganda."[53] The *Boston Herald* critic complained the play poses "some pretty problems for the reviewer, whose task it is not to take sides but to tell you what went on and what sort of entertainment this is."[54] Irked by a "clarion quality of a soapbox harangue," the *Herald Tribune*'s Howard Barnes insisted international politics—perhaps especially those related to foreign Jews—was not dramatic criticism's concern: "[The play's] value as an instrument to open the doors of Palestine to Jewish refugees is not the business of this reviewer. As a show it is distinctly dubious."[55]

Critics who accepted the performance on its own formal terms, however, tended to be more favorable. Sidney J. Harris of the *Chicago Daily News* wrote, "Naturally, a play of this type cannot be judged by the ordinary standards of stagecraft," cautioning readers not to expect "amusement and escapism" since "the murder of six million people is not an entertaining subject."[56] Harriett Johnson in the *New York Post* argued that "Hecht obviously didn't set out to write a play," and that "to dismiss his pageant as propaganda, which it admittedly is, doesn't suffice."[57] Elliot Norton in the *Boston Post*, while wary of some of the play's more "hysterical" polemics, admitted to ultimately succumbing to its rhetorical and performative power: "Though it lapses into doubtful conversation at times, there is anguish and heartbreak as well as passionate pleading in this pageant play. Parts of it, as when the old man shouts his challenge to the World Court to give justice to the Jews, are electrifying. None of it is less than fascinating. That Mr. Hecht is justified in some of his statements is dubious. He oversimplifies. He brushes reason aside. But he believes and he fights like a tiger for what he believes. His uncompromising courage, which breathes in every scene of the show, is exhilarating in itself."[58] John Chapman in the *New York Daily News* likewise welcomed something more challenging than the usual Broadway fare: "Mr. Hecht and all those who have worked with him have reminded a rather sleepy commercial theatre that the stage still can be a forum, a pulpit and a platform."[59] Robert Garland in the *New York Journal American* sounded a similar note in writing, "If the Broadway stage is the proper place for propaganda, then 'A Flag is Born' is undoubtedly the proper propaganda for the Broadway stage."[60]

The most significant reviews may have been those most willing to engage with the play's politics and, as a result, raise awareness among readers of the international Jewish plight, both during the war and after. "*A Flag is Born* Has Message for Jews, Non-Jews Alike, Which Must Be Heard," proclaimed the headline of the *New York Morning Telegram*'s review.[61] The *Detroit Free Press* critic opined that David's speech "vehemently chiding the silence of American and British Jews whilst the Jews of Europe went to death in the Nazi gas chambers will not soon be forgotten by those who heard it in silence."[62] Others shared Hecht's own comparisons of the embattled Jewish resistance fighters to other popular insurrectionists. Claudia Cassidy in the *Chicago Tribune* claimed "no desire to talk of things I know little about, such as . . . this passionate conviction that the Jews must drive the British out of Palestine," but then quipped, "Who are the Irish to say you must not fight for freedom?"[63] *Variety*'s Nat Kahn was more strident: "[*A Flag Is Born*] depicts with vivid imagination, backed by documentary evidence, that here is a story that must be told not only to Jews but those of other creeds as well. It is a lesson in a fight for freedom, in very much the same manner of Parnell's Irish fight against the British, Lenin's against the Czarists, the Hebrews against the Pharaohs."[64] As the Lenin reference suggests (in spite of the coming chill of the Cold War), such reception indicated the potential appeal of *A Flag Is Born* to the old Popular Front coalition.

## "NOT JUST GREAT THEATRE—A CALL TO ACTION!"

*A Flag Is Born* also stood out from the rest of Broadway by doing its political work outside of the narrative of the play itself. After each performance, a fundraising appeal scripted by Hecht was given from the stage. Hecht himself delivered the speech on opening night: "You—out front—are not in a theater tonight. You're on a battlefield. We blow bugles at you. And of your applause of our bugle blowings, well and good. Applause can put a show over—but it's not enough to win a war. You have better weapons than applause. We need those weapons."[65] Patrons found inserts in their programs which included mock checks made out to the American League for a Free Palestine in envelopes pre-addressed to "Ben Hecht, Co-Chairman." An enclosed note declared, "'A FLAG IS BORN' is not just great theatre—it is a call to action! . . . Don't delay. Write your check at this performance and please turn it in at the theatre tonight. Join, work, and organize."[66] The tactic was apparently so effective that, according to one reporter, "members of the audience are contributing from five to thirty thousand dollars above the ticket expenditures via the blank checks enclosed in every program."[67]

Hecht's post-show speech also worked to Americanize the Palestine struggle as not just a Jewish cause (or an obscure foreign policy issue) but yet another Popular Front–style "fight for freedom." Echoing the same kind of rhetoric he had employed in 1941 for his "Fun to Be Free" rally advocating for U.S. war intervention, Hecht spoke in the language of progressive internationalism: "Who calls it a Palestinian front or a Jewish front? It's a bigger front than that. It's a front where the rights of man are battling for survival again. Always again. That is, and always has been, an American front. When the rights of man were imperiled in Europe—that was an American front, for America has large and sacred boundaries. Wherever oppression strikes at the soul of man, there the U.S.A. raises its flag." Hecht even appealed to the cherished memory of Franklin Roosevelt: "He—the president who led us in the war days—pronounced us the arsenal of democracy. We were—and still are—and we always will be." Even though Hecht had personally turned against Roosevelt by the end of the war for failing to do enough for European Jews, that did not stop him from invoking his name in order to rekindle the solidarity of the prewar Popular Front.

Such proselytizing even extended beyond the auditorium in a series of outreach events and demonstrations. Bergson's American League for a Free Palestine trained actors—including Brando and Lumet—in agitprop and rhetorical techniques to engage Jewish audiences in synagogues, community centers, and even on the streets. According to Atay Citron, "The idea was to take advantage of the actors' oratory skills and of their eagerness to perform, in order to attract the attention of passers-by. Once a crowd was gathered and the speech came to an end, a member of the League would step up to answer questions and to debate the issue."[68]

For Bergson's American League for a Free Palestine—the de facto producers of *A Flag Is Born*—the ultimate measure of the play's efficacy was the impact it made in Palestine.[69] "The first of a fleet of *A Flag is Born* ships sailed from an American port," the League proudly announced to supporters in December 1946, referring to a refurbished yacht bought from U.S. government surplus with proceeds from the play.[70] That month, the vessel left New York with a mostly American crew, bound for France, where 600 Holocaust survivors awaited transport to Palestine.[71] Once they boarded, the crew decided to honor the play's role in the operation by officially rechristening the ship the SS *Ben Hecht*. Through his play and his namesake vessel, Hecht had now stepped off the stage, outside the theatre, and into international politics.[72]

## THE DEATH OF TEVYE AND THE BIRTH OF ISRAEL

At home, though, *A Flag Is Born* stoked protest from fellow American Jews and other Zionist organizations. Tensions between Bergson's followers and those of larger organizations, like Rabbi Stephen Wise's American Jewish Congress, had been brewing ever since the wartime campaigns to rescue the European Jews—and stretching back further to the original schism between Vladimir Jabotinsky's Revisionist Zionists and the World Zionist Congress in 1925. During *Flag*'s Broadway run, the American rabbi Judah Magnes, then president of Hebrew University in Jerusalem, issued an open letter addressed to Eleanor Roosevelt calling on her to disassociate from the American League for a Free Palestine and withdraw as an official "sponsor" of *A Flag Is Born* due to its "appeal to terror." Magnes specifically protested the play's militant ending: "The climax of the play is the appearance of young Palestinians with rifles who declare: 'The new Jewish voice speaks from out of these guns'. . . . This is indeed a new Jewish voice, a voice which is opposed to the whole tradition of the Jewish religion."[73] When *A Flag Is Born* came to Philadelphia in January 1947, the Zionist Organization of America—the largest and oldest such group in the United States—organized a picketing of the play's opening to discourage audiences from donating money to the ALFP, which they characterized as an untrustworthy fringe group.[74]

While the Bergson/*Irgun* brand of militarism may have repelled other Jews, its outward celebration of brute force and "the language of guns" bore a special potential appeal in the militarized and victorious postwar culture of America at large. Whenever embroiled in conflicts with other Jewish organizations, Bergson always aimed his message at the broader non-Jewish American populace, appealing to public sentiments of fairness and tolerance, but also to military heroism and righteous vengeance. What Alan Wald has called "the intersection of radical secular Jewish identity and masculinity during the era of the Popular Front in arms," therefore, suited Bergson's purposes perfectly—especially after the war, when he could draw parallels between Jews taking up arms in Palestine and the average GI fighting German and Japanese tyranny.[75]

An even deeper connection to American mythology was made by stressing comparisons between the *Irgun*'s fight against Great Britain and the American Revolution. The slogan, "It's 1776 in Palestine," was used extensively in promoting *A Flag Is Born* and in all other Bergson publicity campaigns. The parallel was reinforced with a charcoal drawing that appeared in advertisements and became the official poster for the play. In the foreground, three muscular young men carry a rifle, a shovel, and a Star of David flag; behind them (as their mirror images) march the "fife and drums" trio of American Revolution iconography.

Such patriotic double flag waving also appears in the text of the play itself. In his oration before the UN Tevya reminds Great Britain, "you have never won a

Figure 11. Cover art for *A Flag Is Born*'s souvenir program. Source: Billy Rose Theatre Division, the New York Public Library. "American League for a Free Palestine presents A Flag is Born," New York Public Library Digital Collections, accessed March 10, 2024, https://digitalcollections.nypl.org/items/9927f0c0-fbbe-0130-dfeb-58d385a7bbd0.

war against a people that wanted to be free," adding, "how nice it would have been if you had acted a little different toward America long ago" (39). (The British ambassador agrees with "that point about the American Colonies," but further antagonizes the play's American audience by adding, "We should never have lost those, you know.") The soldiers at the end promise David that together they will "wrest our homeland out of British claws—as the Americans once did" (47).

Hecht made the parallel between the two rebellions even more explicit when he later adapted excerpts from *Flag* for a 1948 Bergson event at Madison Square Garden called "Colors of Hebrew Freedom" saluting a brigade of American veterans planning to fight in Palestine under the banner of the "George Washington Legion."[76] Hecht adapted the final two scenes of his play into a thirteen-page piece he called "An End to Silence," with an expanded musical cue accompanying the hoisting of the flag: "The music breaks into the strains of the *Hatikvah*, with strains of 'Yankee Doodle' and 'Over There' running through it."[77] And instead of screen-projected *Irgun* fighters, David and his cohorts were now joined onstage by the real-life George Washington Legion itself. A *New York Times* report the next day noted that "a newly designed standard was presented to the legion," suggesting that the actors may have actually handed the soldiers their "flag" prop from the play, seamlessly fusing the play with the brigade's real-life crusade.[78]

## BRIDGING JEWISH IDENTITIES

In a gesture out of symbolist drama, *A Flag Is Born* is structured around the image of a bridge. David tells Tevya and Zelda early on that he has had a vision of a bridge that will lead them to Palestine (8–9). When Tevya asks King Saul to point the way to "Eretz Yisrael," he says, "There is a bridge to cross" (17). ("Again a bridge," Tevya mutters in a moment of *Yiddishkeit*.) The anticipation builds to the play's climax, when the suicidal David is saved by the deus ex machina of a descending bridge from the flies (in a "brightening glare") from which the three soldiers emerge (45). Tevya turns out to have been looking in the wrong places for the bridge, which is not on land but in Jews' souls.

The play itself enacts a bridging of old and new Jewish identities in this liminal postwar cultural moment. The dual heroes of *A Flag Is Born*—situated at opposite ends of that bridge—embody dueling archetypes that were to figure prominently in postwar American Jewish popular culture. In *Fiddler on the Roof* (1964), Sholem-Aleichem's Tevye would become "the personification of the Jewish immigrant and the universal grandfather."[79] In 1958, Leon Uris's bestselling novel *Exodus*—and its subsequent 1960 Hollywood film adaptation—lionized the figure of the Zionist warrior in the character of Ari Ben Canaan, a fighter for the *Haganah* army, rival to the *Irgun*.[80] In *Flag* we see these competing Jewish masculinities already facing off onstage more than a decade earlier, playing out the postwar, post-Holocaust Jewish identity crisis.[81]

When David crosses the long-awaited bridge in the play's finale, his destination is not just the geographic land of Palestine but a place where Jews can finally live freely and have agency *as* Jews. For many, that bridge would lead not just to Palestine but to postwar America. *A Flag Is Born*'s genesis is so enmeshed in the international Zionist politics of its moment that it is easy to forget it was a play created by American theatrical artists for American audiences. Writing *A Flag Is Born* in 1946—and producing it on Broadway—was, thus, not only an intervention into a far-off international dispute but an act of representation at home. Beyond the surface details of its European and biblical settings, the play's more lasting significance is in its dramatic attempt to rewrite the persona of the Jewish American in popular representation at this transitional historical moment.

# 5
# Passion Play for a Jewish "Terrorist"

IN THE SUMMER OF 1947, Hecht received a very unusual commission for a new play. A short, typewritten note was secretly delivered to him from Palestine asking him to memorialize on the stage a recently executed Jewish militant. The note was signed, "Ben-David," which Hecht knew was a code name for the real correspondent: Menachem Begin, commander of the *Irgun Zvai Leumi*. As part of his work with Bergson, the *Irgun*'s chief representative in the United States, Hecht was accustomed at this time, he later recalled, to receiving "secret communiqués, some of them hidden in cigarette packages." (The original missive, preserved in Hecht's archive, is an irregularly shaped paper bearing several folds and creases.)[1] Such security precautions were taken because Begin was deemed by British authorities one of the most wanted criminals in Mandatory Palestine, with a bounty of five thousand pounds promised for his capture.[2] That he took the time to write to Hecht in this moment indicated how the war of propaganda mattered to the *Irgun* almost as much as its military campaign.

The subject of Begin's appeal was Dov Gruner, a thirty-five-year-old *Irgun* fighter who was the first Jewish prisoner put to death by the British in nearly a decade. Although he had been under a death sentence since January, the execution had been postponed while international Jewish leaders appealed the decision and pled for his life to be spared. But British authorities, frustrated by their losing battle against Jewish paramilitary forces, were eager to reinstate the capital punishment for "terrorist" offences and hanged Gruner on April 16 without advance notice. The event shocked observers on all sides, especially since

Gruner—a European-born son of Holocaust victims who enlisted in the British army during the war—struck many as a sympathetic figure. As Bruce Hoffman writes, "However much the British saw him as epitomizing the cold-blooded Jewish terrorist, to other eyes Gruner's life story evoked simultaneously the suffering of European Jewry, the courage and tenacity of a new generation of Palestinian Jews willing to take control of their own destiny, and an ethos of self-sacrifice and personal integrity that reflected positively on the Irgun."[3] Gruner thus became an ideal martyr figure and Begin seized the opportunity to spread his story to generate new support for the *Irgun* at a crucial moment when the tide was finally turning against the British in what turned out to be the final months of their rule in Palestine.

"My dear friend," Begin wrote to Hecht, "I want to suggest that you devote some of your time and ability to a work whose educational value may be decisive: the writing of a play on Dov."[4] The letter reveals Begin's belief in the unique power of theatre to politically engage the public, telling Hecht, "such a work, coming from your brilliant pen, could be a powerful spectacle capable of influencing masses of people more than hundreds of articles and thousands of leaflets."[5] Expressing gratitude for all Hecht has done already for the *Irgun*, Begin flatteringly compares him to Henrik Ibsen, saying that his "readiness to take the stones hurled at you from all sides" on behalf of their mutual cause recalls "the greatness of Dr. Stockman"—the vilified righteous protagonist of *An Enemy of the People*. "There are still Dr. Stockmans in the world," Begin concludes his letter, "and you are one of them."

Hecht's response to this was a one-act play, *The Terrorist*, performed for two evenings in September 1947 at a fundraiser for Bergson's American League for a Free Palestine. It was one of his last contributions to Bergson's cause during a period when his rhetoric was growing increasingly bellicose and confrontational and he had become more personally drawn into the fray of political controversy than ever before. After having devoted the previous six years of activism to appeals to Americans to rescue Jewish victims, he now gave himself over to the cause of championing radical Jewish resistance in Palestine to the point of embracing the label "terrorist" that mainstream political discourse (and even most Jewish leaders) used to denounce such tactics.

## A "ONE-MAN CAMPAIGN AGAINST THE ENGLISH EMPIRE"

As was evident with *A Flag Is Born*, Hecht's Jewish activism hardly subsided after the defeat of Germany and the liberation of the concentration camps. At first a reluctant Zionist, he had been persuaded by Bergson in 1944 (with *A Jewish Fairy Tale*) to start directing his propaganda attacks against British imperialism in Palestine as much as German Nazism. By 1947, Hecht was engaged in what Kurt Weill jokingly referred to as a "silly one-man campaign against the English empire," one that had put him on a rhetorical collision course with the United States' popular wartime ally.[6] The *London Evening Standard* declared *A Flag Is Born* to be "the most virulently anti-British play ever staged in the United States," and copies of the script (which Bergson had published in a limited edition) were banned in all U.K. territories, including Canada, where shipments were seized at the border.[7] In March 1947, the SS *Ben Hecht*—the ship purchased by the *Irgun* with *Flag* funds and named after the playwright—was seized by British guards before it could reach Palestine, putting its hundreds of Holocaust survivors in a refugee camp and its crew in prison.[8] The playwright and his play had found themselves at the center of, literally, an international incident. Hecht remained undeterred by the confrontation; "Britain may be able to patrol the Mediterranean," he quipped, "but she cannot patrol Broadway."[9]

In May, Hecht escalated tensions even further with a widely published newspaper advertisement entitled, "Letter to the Terrorists of Palestine." After a major attack the *Irgun* carried out in Palestine on May 4 to avenge Gruner's execution (they raided the prison where he had been hanged), Bergson capitalized on the news by making a major fundraising push in America and bought advertising space in newspapers nationwide for a rousing statement from Hecht.[10] It was his most hostile anti-British polemic to date in its express endorsement of—even jubilation in—the *Irgun*'s violent methods: "Every time you blow up a British arsenal, or wreck a British jail, or send a British railroad train sky high, or rob a British bank or let go with your guns and bombs at the British betrayers and invaders of your homeland, the Jews of America make a little holiday in their hearts."[11] The advertisement had "an especially chilling effect on Anglo-American relations."[12] So incensed was His Majesty's Government by this "incitement to murder British officials and soldiers" that it lodged a formal complaint with the U.S. State Department challenging the validity of the American League for a Free Palestine's tax-free status, which, they argued, implied Washington's approval of the charitable donations (such as those collected from *A Flag Is Born* audiences) that they suspected were funding *Irgun* attacks.[13] The incident got the attention of President Harry Truman, who was so concerned about not damaging U.S.-British relations that he publicly called upon all Americans to stay neutral and avoid "inflam[ing] the passions" of the Palestinian resistance fighters with any support.[14] "Although he named no individuals," wrote the Broadway columnist Leonard Lyons, "the President's target is Ben Hecht."[15]

By the time Hecht received Begin's letter that summer, he was already receiving a stream of intelligence ("secret communiques") from the *Irgun* front lines bearing "news of every gun it fired, every barrel of dynamite it exploded, of every arsenal it looted and railroad train it tipped over."[16] In his letter to Hecht, Begin offered to send him "as much factual material as we can lay our hands on" about Gruner's case to supply him with research for the play. In addition to his dedication to the cause of Jews in Palestine, this was also an irresistible opportunity for Hecht as journalist to dramatize what at the time was a major international news story, one for which he had the most "inside" sources.

## *THE TERRORIST* (1947)

While Begin had proposed "a play on Dov" that would include "the story of his life, his struggle, his captivity, and his death," Hecht chose to focus his script on the high drama of just the execution itself. And rather than tell only Gruner's story, he again felt compelled to put Jewish terrorism in the context of greater Jewish history—which again meant bringing a ghostly "Tevya" onstage to comment on the action and, ultimately, give his blessing to the bearers of the Jewish future. In *The Terrorist*, Hecht dramatizes even more explicitly than in his other Tevya plays the rise of the new warriors of Palestine out of the ashes of Jewish history.

The Tevya of *The Terrorist* differs from his predecessors in some key aspects. He once again appears to us as the ghost of a murdered Jew in the afterlife. But this Tevya has perished long before World War II, in the Russian pogroms four decades earlier (which actually makes him historically contemporaneous with Sholem-Aleichem's original Tevye). Hecht identifies him as a victim of the Kishinev pogrom of 1903 in particular—an atrocity that attracted worldwide attention for its viciousness, making the very name of the town "synonymous with the worst horrors of Diaspora persecution."[17] Tevya is only the first of many such victims we hear of in *The Terrorist*, which climaxes in a recitation of historical antisemitic attacks going back nearly two millennia.

Another new element is that Hecht gives Tevya another ghost as a partner, a quite different figure from Jewish literary history: the eleventh-century Hebrew poet and philosopher Judah Halevi (whom Hecht renders as "Jehuda Halevy"). As a man of letters, Hecht's choice of a poet to serve as a guide to Tevya in the afterlife (as Virgil does for Dante) makes sense. He had included Halevi in the "Roll Call" of *We Will Never Die* as one of the "many poets of exile," and Halevi held special significance to Zionists. Born a Sephardic Jew in Spain, he made the idea of a return to Jerusalem a centerpiece of his work and—according to legend—made a medieval version of *aliyah* himself and died there. (In 1947, the *Haganah* army named one of their refugee ships the *Yehuda Halevi* in his honor.) Hecht's pairing of Halevi (henceforth "Halevy") and Tevya (and, by extension, Sholem-Aleichem) also brings together onstage the early and late diaspora, the complete span of which serves as an important backdrop to the contemporary story of Gruner's hanging.

These spirits serve as Hecht's framing device for the play, so that the audience watches the Gruner story through their eyes (i.e., in the context of the long history of the diaspora). In an opening image of symbolist mise-en-scène, they appear as just faces suspended in the dark. To the accompaniment of "an eerie Hebraic strain of music," Halevy's "dignified and archaic face" is seen alongside the "small, bearded, almost humorous face" of Tevya (1).[18] "The first Jew has the sound of poetry in his voice," writes Hecht; "The second Jew has the sound of banter and sarcasm." They make an amusing odd couple at first. "It seems I don't know you," starts Halevy, to which Tevya retorts ("a bit truculently"), "Who knows *you*?" (In a nod to Tevya's literary origins, he even offers Halevy a Hebrew greeting of "Sholem Aleichem.") As Halevy explains to Tevya the reason for their presence here—to support "a hero of Israel" in his last moments on earth—the stage reveals Gruner's prison cell; he is asleep and unaware of what awaits him this day. Tevya continues to provide some comic relief as Halevy attempts to awaken Gruner:

HALEVY: Dov, can you hear us?

TEVYA (*nervously*): That good if he hears us? A fine blessing we bring him.

HALEVY: Dov, we have come to be with you in your last hour. Dream of us and we will talk to you.

TEVYA (*sighing*): My advice is—don't dream of us. Better you don't hear what we have to tell. (3)

But that is the extent of Sholem-Aleichem-esque comedy in this, Hecht's most somber Jewish play. Once Tevya comprehends who Dov is and what is happening to him, he expresses an outrage that Hecht's previous Tevyas seemed incapable of: "To hang a soldier—this is against the law! And the English—they are in Palestine against the law. The whole thing is against the law, Reb Halevy!" (3). Hecht wants Tevya's distinctive everyman voice in *The Terrorist*, but the character here is not as central as in *A Jewish Fairy Tale* and *A Flag Is Born*. As a mere observer of the main action, his function is to provide the 1947 audience a perspective through which to watch the Gruner story, a perspective that American Jews in the audience might have recognized as that of their own parents or grandparents.

As the action shifts to the cell itself, the play's dramaturgy changes from symbolist dreamscape to gritty realism. The scene between Gruner and his British guards plays out like a prison drama Hecht might have written for Hollywood, but with a heavy dose of political debate. A succession of four soldiers, each of a higher rank, enters the cell to prepare Dov for execution, climaxing in a violent beating of him when he refuses to stand for the reading of his death warrant (a true story reported at the time). At first, some engage in dialogue with him, enabling the character to give eloquent denunciations of British rule and defend the violent methods of the *Irgun* to drive them out. Just as the real Gruner made waves by giving a defiant speech at his trial refusing to recognize the legitimacy of the British court, Hecht's Dov mocks the legal process and imperial hypocrisy that has brought him to this moment: "A robber comes into your home and steals everything you own. And you cry for the police. The robber grins at you and says, 'I'm the police, old boy, come along.' And he takes you to court. You look up and there sits the robber on the bench as your judge. . . . And the robber then denounces you and sentences you to be hanged for objecting to his thievery. . . . It's the trick by which England has looted and brutalized half the world and still kept its good name for" (8). When he rejects the accusation of treason against him and is challenged, "Do you deny you shed English blood?" he counters, "What was English blood doing on Hebrew soil?" When he objects to being executed in prison garb instead of his *Irgun* uniform because "I was captured fighting for my country" (i.e., as a prisoner of war), he is told "you have no country" and that "gangsters and hoodlums are not entitled to military dress"—proving the Zionist point that without a recognized nation, Jews will continue to be treated as brigands when defending themselves.

Dov's only sympathetic interlocutor is a "Scotch Sergeant," whose own outsider identity within English society makes him more inclined to give the prisoner a fair hearing, comparing "a soldier who's dyin' fer the Jews" to "many a brave laddie [who] once died fer the Scotch" (6). The two men also bond over their shared military service during the war. (The real Gruner fought in the British army for five years.) They learn that they both fought against the Germans in adjacent regiments during the same operation, the pivotal battle in El Alamein during the North African campaign of 1942. Asked why he would now "change sides," Dov reminds the sergeant that for the Jews, the struggle has been the same both during and after the war, only the enemy has changed:

GRUNER: I didn't change sides.
SERGEANT (*angrily*): Ye fought for England once, didn't ye?
GRUNER: I fought for a cause.
SERGEANT (*angrily*): And who didn't man? The overthrow of tyranny in the world.
GRUNER (*quietly*): I'm still fighting for it. (6)

The sergeant further questions Dov's credibility by citing the lack of support for his "Irgoon" even among many of his fellow Zionists. As always, Hecht is eager to accuse more moderate Jews (especially the leaders of Palestine's Jewish Agency establishment) of a lack of solidarity: "It's no fun fighting for a people who cheer when the enemy hangs you and who break out in condolences when you hang one of the enemy," says Dov ("sighing"). The sergeant grows increasingly sympathetic, but when he reassures his prisoner that "lots of folks like Jews right enough and feel sorry for them," Dov fires back: "Yes, if they stay on their knees begging for favors.... But Jews fighting for their rights—that's another story" (7).

The Scottish soldier provides the play with a needed "conversion" narrative—an essential feature of much political propaganda drama. The already committed *Irgun* partisans in the audience can cheer Dov's speeches, but the sergeant stands in for those still ambivalent about lending their full support. (The play was performed at a fundraising event, after all.) The character finally gives himself over to the prisoner's side when he witnesses the cruelty with which his English supporters treat him. The most obvious villain of the scene is a sadistic "English Sergeant" who immediately upon entering calls Dov a "kike" and a "little Jew bastard," telling him with relish that "we're 'angin' ye today—with a nice, thick British rope" and that "ye'll know who owns Palestine when yer 'angin' by yer Jew neck." When a "Captain" and "Major" come to take Dov to the gallows, Dov refuses to stand for the formal reading of his death warrant (as had been reported about the real Gruner), prompting the commanding officer to order that the prisoner be beaten into submission until he is so weak he must be held up by others to obey the order. Hecht calls for a "methodical beating of Gruner" onstage as the English sergeant hits him with the butt of his rifle and "kicks violently at his body" (9–10). Witnessing such violent antisemitism drives the Scottish sergeant to intervene, crying "Stop it! He fought with me at Allemain [*sic*]" and professing, "I'm a Scotchman, not an Englishman!" He too is punished, his sergeant stripes ripped from his uniform. "I'll let the world know!" he warns as he's ordered to detention. "Ye hear me, Dov? I'll tell the world about it, laddie" (10). The play itself, of course, is "telling the world," and the moment reveals another dramatic function of the "convert" figure: to spread the hero's story to new potential followers.

After Dov's sentencing, Hecht resumes the framing device of the ghostly spirits of Tevya and Halevy, who are soon joined by an invisible chorus of other spectral Jewish dead of times past. When they first speak to Dov, he tells them that he wants to "hear the voices of my people" on the gallows: "If I hear them I shall die with pride—because I fought for them" (5). Now, as the audience watches the soldiers march Dov to his death, six offstage voices stand in for what is described as an "endless" procession of "Jews from all the corners of time"—all of them victims of antisemitism (11). Just as in *We Will Never Die*, the dead proceed to tell the stories of their suffering, but now Hecht stages a "Remember Us" for the entire Jewish diaspora. The more recent Holocaust, in fact, is barely referenced in the play, remaining mostly a subtextual current through which to comprehend what Hecht (and many Zionists) considered to be the tragic inevitability of two thousand years of exile.

"Hear our story Dov," says one of the voices at the outset of their litany. "We are the Jews who began the wandering long ago" (12). And so begins a five-page recitation (in Hecht's typescript) of over a thousand years of atrocities against Jewish communities—starting in Alexandria in 400 C.E. and proceeding through the sixteenth century and the extension of the Spanish Inquisition to the New World, detailing over twenty-five examples of distinct violent events or periods of persecution. For example:

FIRST: We were in Spain. We lived in a Golden Age under the Moors.
SECOND: The Moors turned on us. All the Jews of Granada were slaughtered in a single day. This was in the year 1066.
THIRD: We were in Germany when the first storm broke. We were slaughtered by the Emperor Henry in Mayence.
FIFTH: We were in Egypt when the Caliph Hakim declared himself a god and ordered all the Jews of Egypt slain.
SIXTH: Hear our story, Dov. We were slaughtered in the great Christian Crusades—a million of us were slain—and hundreds of thousands of us slew ourselves. (14)

The voices produce not only a generally choral effect but evoke the Greek chorus in particular in their beseeching of the protagonist and their witnessing of his tragedy.

Hecht's source for this exhaustive catalogue appears to have been Heinrich Graetz's multivolume *History of the Jews*, "the classic work of Jewish historiography of the nineteenth century."[19] Hecht cites Graetz frequently in his 1944 book on antisemitism, *A Guide for the Bedeviled*, and says of it, "a gorier tale has never been put to paper."[20] Indeed, as Michael Brenner notes, the work has "constitute[d] the basis for the 'lachrymose' version of Jewish history that Graetz is often accused of."[21] In contrast, the pre-Zionist Hecht drew on the more affirming work of the later historian Cecil Roth for the historical "Roll Call" of *We Will Never Die*.[22] By 1947, we can see how Hecht had grown ever more pessimistic since 1943. Instead of a "roll call" of all the Jewish accomplishments and contributions to civilization, he is now compelled to dramatize that same period of diaspora history as—in the words he gives Halevy—"a long murder, a never finished crime" (11).

This oratorio of oppression, however, does build to a moment of uplift. As the voices in the dark recall the suffering of the past, the stage image before the audience is one of a heroic Dov, willfully ascending the gallows to sacrifice himself for the Zionist cause. A constant refrain is heard from the voices: "We are here beside you, Dov. For we dreamed of you when we were alive" (13). Hecht's stage directions call for Dov to be bathed in light as the soldiers fade away and he emerges alone at the scaffold. At the culmination of the recitations, "the death march music changes to the Hatikva theme," and he suddenly calls out, "I hear you, Jews!," "I hear the voices of my people!," "I promise you justice" (16). The voices quiet, their spirits implicitly watching along with Halevy and Tevya, periodically chanting, "Hallelujah," as Dov utters his last words to the Jews of the future, not the past:

GRUNER: . . . I offer up a prayer of thanks and victory—I see no hangman here. I see no noose. I see a flag over my head that my brothers will raise. . . . I thank you, oh Lord, that it is morning—a bright morning—in my homeland. Hear me, comrades! I will be with you in your battles. In the darkness where I go I will dream of you. I and my slaughtered people from the ends of time will dream of you. Goodbye—my land of Israel. (18)

After a sudden blackout at this climax and a pause "of several moments," Hecht then calls for the spotlight to show the hangman's noose, now empty, but with "the flag of Palestine" flying from the rope above it. This final image perfectly encapsulates the Zionist thesis that only a Jewish state will finally—to paraphrase Hamlet speaking of his murdered father's ghost—give rest to the "perturbed spirits" of the diaspora.

In representing Gruner as a redeemer, Hecht has written a Passion Play for a terrorist. In *A Jewish Fairy Tale*, he playfully presented Tevya as a mock messiah, sent by an imperialistic ruler to punish the Jews. But here he more reverently channels the Christ story in Dov's own version of the stations of the cross—the rejection by his own people, the physical abuse of the guards, and (in the person of the Scotch Sergeant) even a penitent centurion who sees the light. Halevy, during the final scene, makes the comparison explicit: "Another Jew walks up a hill in Palestine to die" (12). The offstage voices even call Dov a messiah—a word Hecht renders in the script as "Mossiah," evoking the original Judaic tradition of an avenging warrior: "He is there in battle," "He stands on his battlefield as we dreamed," "The strong one—the Mossiah who wears Bar Kochba's armor" (17).

As he does with the Ancient Greek chorus, Hecht employs the dramaturgy of the medieval Passion Play to give the death of a martyr theatrical form befitting a stage tragedy. Hecht was a latecomer to Judaism but a lifelong consumer of classic Western literature and well understood the theatrical potency of the Passion Play. (He and Charles MacArthur even mocked the 1920s Broadway penchant for Christian spectacles in their comedy *Twentieth Century*.) Even in the earliest days of his playwriting career—long before his midlife Jewish awakening—he wrote a one-act play called *The Red Door*, the plot of which he later dismissively described as "the 'crucifying' of a Jew, who was a brilliant Zionist, by other Jews who were stupidly averse to Zionism."[23] Even as his message became increasingly anti-diasporic, Hecht still utilized Christian themes and imagery (such as the "heaven" of *A Jewish Fairy Tale*) to communicate to an American audience that he hoped would be broader than just fellow Jews.

The American Jews of the diaspora, though, clearly remained the primary "implied reader" for the play. *The Terrorist* was not a play written for terrorists. Hecht begins and ends the action with the chorus of diasporic onlookers, with Halevy playing the role of Chorus Leader. The real-life audience watches along with them, and in Tevya they could identify an "old country" figure from their own ancestry just two generations back. Hecht knew the Jewish audience in New York would be descended from the Tevyas of the past, not the Gruners of contemporary Palestine. To elicit their support for the latter, his play provides the endorsement of the former.

## PRODUCTION HISTORY

The production of *The Terrorist* appears to have received the least public notice of any of Hecht's propaganda plays. It was presented at Carnegie Hall on two consecutive evenings—September 20 and September 21, 1947—as part of a fundraising event for Bergson's American League for a Free Palestine.[24] (An *Irgun*-sponsored documentary film short, *Last Night We Attacked*, served as a curtain-raiser for the program.) As with *A Jewish Fairy Tale*, also performed exclusively at Bergson rallies, it was not reviewed by theatre critics and no contemporary news reports survive either. The only extant mentions in the press are advertisements Bergson placed in local newspapers during the week leading up to the event, promoting the play as "a dramatic presentation based on the last hours of the Hebrew patriot, Dov Gruner" and "an impassioned dramatic presentation of Hebrew valor."[25] A lack of celebrity performers might have limited the play's appeal to general audiences, as the cast was a largely unknown company of young actors. Instead of Paul Muni or Luther Adler, Tevya was played by the thirty-two-year-old Jonathan Harris (born Jonathan Charasuchin in the Bronx), who had acted in *A Flag Is Born* and later went on to television fame in *Lost in Space*. The role of Dov was played by Simon "Si" Oakland (born Simon Weiss), who became a familiar name on several 1960s and '70s television shows as well. Possibly to provide some star attraction, Hecht added a last-minute prologue speech for Ruth Chatterton, the semiretired 1930s Hollywood star, in this otherwise all-male play.[26] Advertisements could now boast "Ruth Chatterton and a distinguished cast."[27]

Hecht also seems to have had less artistic control over *The Terrorist* than previous Bergson productions. Correspondence from the day after the premiere indicates he was not present for the performance, possibly due to Hollywood commitments.[28] In the letter, he complains to Bergson's associate Samuel Merlin that "no one called or wired me about *The Terrorist*. I waited up most of the night."[29] It was the beginning of the end of Hecht's involvement with Bergson, for whom he continued to write occasional speeches and newspaper ads but no further plays. It was also the beginning of the end of the British Mandate. Behind the scenes, as early as February 1947, "Britain's will-to-rule had reached its end."[30] In the summer, it agreed to cooperate with a United Nations commission devising a blueprint for a future independent Palestine, which resulted in a "partition plan" between Jewish and Arab populations unveiled just three weeks before the performance of *The Terrorist*. The plan was not ultimately implemented, but as civil war broke out between Jews and Arabs, Britain began gradually withdrawing its forces and by early 1948 announced its intentions to officially end their old League of Nations "Mandate" responsibilities that May. On May 15, David Ben-Gurion, the leader of the Palestine Jewish Agency, declared the new independent state of Israel.

By 1948, Hecht was clearly done with his "one-man campaign against the English empire." But Britain was not yet done with him. In October 1948, the Cinematograph Exhibitors' Association of Great Britain barred the release of any films bearing his name on the screenplay. While the rule could only be enforced in the United Kingdom, American studios still became wary of hiring Hecht due to the importance of the overseas English-speaking market. As a result, "during the entire period from late 1947 until well after 1952, because of the threat of the boycott, Hecht found it difficult to obtain work and then only at drastically reduced wages and often with no credit."[31] Only after continued appeals from loyal producers like Twentieth Century Fox's Darryl Zanuck and Spyros Skouras, as well as from Billy Rose, Bernard Baruch, and U.S. politicians who supported the Bergson committees, was the boycott lifted in 1952. In his memoir, Hecht concedes the hardship of those years, but also recalls that when he saw the first report of the boycott, "I beamed on it as the best press notice I had ever received—a solid acknowledgement of the work I had been doing with all my might."[32]

# Conclusion

BY THE LATE 1940S, after more than a decade of activism devoted to Jewish and antifascist causes, Hecht had effectively retired from the propaganda business. The Nazi regime he inveighed against was finally vanquished. The establishment of the State of Israel in May 1948 brought the Zionist campaign to a victorious conclusion. There were also practical reasons to move on. His political writing on behalf of Bergson and others had been largely pro bono or for minimal scale fees. When his rhetorical warfare against the British government resulted in a five-year boycott against exhibiting any Hecht-authored films in U.K. markets, the need for replenishing his finances in Hollywood only intensified.

He did periodically return to the topics of Jews and Nazis in the sixteen years between the birth of Israel and his death in 1964. In a striking coincidence, the film *Notorious*—an antifascist thriller he wrote for Alfred Hitchcock—was released on the very next day (September 6, 1946) after the Broadway opening of *A Flag Is Born*. The postwar plot concerns elite German fugitives in South America whom Hecht's original shooting script explicitly identified as former executives of IG Farben—the pharmaceutical company that supplied poison gas for concentration camps and whose directors were subsequently tried for war crimes. (That specific reference was edited out of the final print by its producers at RKO Pictures.)[1] Much later, when looking for a theatrical vehicle for his young daughter Jenny Hecht, a budding actress, he reached back to the work of émigré authors Lion Feuchtwanger and Bertolt Brecht and their 1942 collaboration *The Visions of Simone Machard*—a retelling of the Joan of Arc story set amid the

French Resistance. Hecht adapted the script himself, but after its premiere at the Cleveland Playhouse in 1962, it had no further productions, despite Hecht's hope of a New York transfer that would mark "the first time Brecht's world famous name will appear as a dramatist on a Broadway Marquee."[2]

As for Israel, Hecht showed little interest other than occasional criticisms of Prime Minister David Ben-Gurion, whose Labor Party was the political rival of Menachem Begin's *Herut*, the party formed by Hecht's Revisionist Zionist colleagues after independence. His only major writing on Israel, tellingly, was his 1961 book *Perfidy*, a denunciation of the Labor government's handling of the controversial 1954 Kastner trial in Jerusalem which concerned accusations of Nazi collaboration during the war. Hecht's motivation in writing this book, aside from revisiting the crimes of the Holocaust, appears to have stemmed more from his continued allegiance to Begin (who used the trial to attack Ben-Gurion's leadership) than an interest in engaging in Israeli current events. Never traveling to Israel for the rest of his life, Hecht mostly retreated from Zionism and, in the words of an old short story title of his, remained a "Champion from Far Away."

Hecht's disengagement from Jewish politics post-1948 only reinforces the import of his political theatre work in the context of domestic American Jewish culture. The postwar moment saw an immediate shift in both public opinion about Jews and in Jewish representation in the arts. "After more than a century of increasing animosity toward the Jews, antisemitism in the United States suddenly began to decline," writes Leonard Dinnerstein, "with the most significant change occurring from 1946 to 1951."[3] A series of landmark Jewish-themed films and plays both reflected and further encouraged such social change, some of which can be linked back to Hecht's work through the involvement of his old collaborators. The Oscar-winning antisemitism exposé *Gentleman's Agreement* (1947) was written by Moss Hart, who directed *We Will Never Die*, and featured an important supporting performance by John Garfield (a *We Will Never Die* performer) as a Jewish army officer.[4] Frank Sinatra's short film about religious tolerance, *The House I Live In* (1945), opened with a dramatic prologue about a Jewish boy being bullied by schoolmates, which Sinatra diffuses by telling the story of the deceased war hero Meyer Levin, a name also invoked in *We Will Never Die*.

Beyond preaching tolerance at home, other works went further in exposing and educating Americans about the Holocaust. *We Will Never Die*'s Edward G. Robinson starred in Orson Welles's antifascist thriller *The Stranger* (1946) as an investigator for the United Nations War Crimes Commission tracking down a Nazi fugitive in small-town America. In a bracing scene, especially for 1946, Robinson's character forces the villain's wife (and the cinema audience) to

## CONCLUSION

watch newsreel footage of the concentration camp liberation. Frances Goodrich and Albert Hackett's 1955 stage adaptation of *The Diary of Anne Frank* ran over 700 performances on Broadway and served as the source of a widely seen 1959 film. And Sidney Lumet, who, as a young actor, replaced Marlon Brando in *A Flag Is Born*, directed his own groundbreaking Holocaust film in 1964, *The Pawnbroker*, considered the first American-made movie to attempt a graphic portrayal of Nazi atrocities.[5]

But even as acceptance of Jews and curiosity about the Holocaust grew more prevalent in the arts and popular culture, Hecht's Jewish political theatre appears to have quickly faded from memory, with no stage revivals and no reprintings of the scripts. When *Fiddler on the Roof* opened on Broadway in the fall of 1964—just a few months after Hecht's death—the musical's nostalgic resurrection of a world that Hecht had declared dead and "disappeared" signaled that postwar Jewish American culture (at least in popular culture) would remain basically optimistic in charting a future beyond the Holocaust. (Luther Adler, who had played Hecht's Tevya in *A Jewish Fairy Tale* and *A Flag Is Born*, actually replaced Zero Mostel's Tevye at one point in the musical's long run.) Hecht's incessantly tragic drama of redemption through combat, sacrifice, and vengeance—especially when combined with his controversial offstage political ties to "Jewish Terrorism"—found few takers. In the heat of the historical moment, Hecht's theatricality thrived as a voice of protest and resistance, but it did not have much to say about healing in the years after.

Some colleagues in Hecht's endeavors even publicly broke with him after the war over the extreme tone his pro-Irgun writings eventually took. The younger Jewish American writer Meyer Levin (not to be confused with the soldier) was once a protégé of Hecht's in Chicago and spent the postwar years developing his own stage adaptation of *The Diary of Anne Frank* that was ultimately considered too uncommercial for Broadway.[6] Writing in 1950, he called *We Will Never Die* "an exciting example of mass-agitation craftsmanship," but faulted Hecht's approach to Jewish advocacy as "parlor terrorism" and "a return to the sometimes primitive morality of our forefathers, whose bloodthirsty battle-cries belonged to . . . the early days of our people."[7] Even Robinson, who had acted in several of Hecht's films and "worked with him in innumerable meetings, rallies and dinners" through the years on behalf of Jewish and antifascist causes, later said he "fell out with him over his support of the Irgun," claiming that "his comments about his delight at the death of every English soldier sickened me" and that "I never acknowledged him again."[8]

Objections to the blunt harshness and bellicosity of Hecht's political rhetoric has surely been one reason behind the general lack of critical attention to—or at least enthusiasm for—his Jewish theatre oeuvre. A more mundane factor has been the extremely limited availability of the texts themselves. Bergson published limited editions of *We Will Never Die* and *A Flag Is Born* as fundraising promotions, and only some of those have ended up in libraries and archival collections. *The Terrorist* appeared in a printing of Bergson's low-circulation newspaper *The Answer*. A typescript of *A Jewish Fairy Tale* survives only in a Palestine Statehood Committee Papers file, along with several miscellaneous records from the work of Bergson's various 1940s committees.[9] They have been more likely to be found by researchers of Zionist history and politics than by American theatre scholars and practitioners.

As a result, they have received little detailed critical analysis in the field of twentieth-century Jewish American drama—usually defined as nonmusical plays, in English, by American writers of Jewish descent about Jewish characters and topics. Ellen Schiff and Julius Novick have written the two most circulated modern studies in this area and neither of them mention Hecht at all.[10] Hecht was certainly a Jewish writer writing about Jews, but Schiff and Novick circumscribe their field within the limits of plays written both by and about Jews in America.[11] In the pre-1945 period, those criteria favor a set of familiar classics about the immigrant experience, especially domestic conflict between first- or second-generation American Jews and their children over the retention of Jewish spiritual values in the face of social and economic pressure to assimilate and prosper—such as Samson Raphaelson's *The Jazz Singer* (1925), Elmer Rice's *Counselor-at-Law* (1931), and Clifford Odets's *Awake and Sing!* (1935). Hecht, in contrast, chose to write about Jews abroad and even—in his encompassing of Jewish history—across geography and time. His engagement with the global experience over the domestic put the political ahead of the personal, offering an implicit rebuttal to the relative insularity imposed by the preference for domestic realism on Broadway.

Hecht's defiance of conventional midcentury Broadway dramaturgy itself makes him an outlier as well, since his Jewish theatre pieces have often been designated as pageants, not plays, and perhaps the extensive musical scoring of some of them excludes them from a narrow definition of spoken drama. Even if one concedes *We Will Never Die* as a musical-spectacle pageant, all three of Hecht's Palestine scripts are dramatic plays in every formal sense, containing individually defined characters in dialogue with each other as well as narratives with beginnings, middles, and ends. Their use of spoken narration, symbolic framing devices, and dreamlike interludes identify them as nonrealist, but not beyond the techniques used by popular modernist American playwrights of the period like Eugene O'Neill and Thornton Wilder. That Hecht was the only Jew-

## CONCLUSION

ish American playwright writing this way about Jewish subjects points to the possibilities of an alternate formal approach to the project of midcentury American Jewish drama.

As far as the presence of Jewish American characters is concerned, these works must also be considered alongside Hecht's own very high Jewish visibility personally. He himself was the offstage Jewish American protagonist of his own propaganda plays. After two decades in the spotlight of Broadway and Hollywood, his name was as recognizable as that of any behind-the-scenes artist could be. Advertisements for these performances gave his name top billing akin to a star actor—and in *A Jewish Fairy Tale*, he even *did* perform on stage as the Narrator. ("Ben Hecht in person will answer Prime Minister Churchill's Threat.") In fact, all the "narrators" and "speakers" in these texts speak in Hecht's unmistakable polemical voice. By making such extensive use of spoken narration, he always made himself a character. Likewise, his frequent use of direct address from the stage by non-narrator characters situated these plays in an American setting (i.e., the theatre or performance space itself, regardless of the far-off geographical places named in the script). When Marlon Brando stared down a 1946 Broadway audience asking, "Where were you, Jews?" specifically calling out "You Jews of America," the spectators momentarily became interlocutors (especially when some shouted back at him, as has been described) (20). In the special monologue Hecht prepared for Paul Muni to read to government dignitaries in the Washington, D.C., performance of *We Will Never Die*, he makes this rhetorical-theatrical device explicit: "There is another cast of actors in this tale whose performance is not done. This cast is our audience. Our audience tonight is a notable cast playing vital roles on the stage of history" (37). Such moments clarify how much Hecht intended these plays for an American audience, not a European or Jewish Palestinian one (let alone post-1948 Israeli). In the largest sense, more than the individual stories of the foreign Jewish individuals depicted, they are all ultimately about the responsibilities that Americans faced at the time, both Jews and non-Jews, to prevent the extermination of a people.

The problematic aesthetic standing of "propaganda" in the mainstream of dramatic studies has also colored Hecht's legacy as a political playwright. Ever since the advent of "Modern Drama," Lara Shalson writes, "overtly activist theatre and performance have often been dismissed as 'bad art,' from which 'good theatre' needs to distinguish itself."[12] Many of the contemporary reviews of *A Flag Is Born* echoed this criticism. "A curiously uneven combination of drama, pageant, and oratory," wrote one critic, as if those elements must always remain separate.[13] The only way to appreciate such a performance is to embrace the possibility that "theatre may in fact become 'good art'—which is to say, formally innovative and exciting art—precisely at the point it intersects with protest."[14] That point may be a uniquely historical one, when the work at hand meets a specific moment in time and place, and those circumstantial factors contribute to the weight of the "art" itself. Regardless of the aesthetic merits of these works of Hecht's, reading them today could never substitute for witnessing their live performance during or shortly after World War II as the news of the slaughter of European Jewry was raw and still unfathomable to most Americans. And the perspective of a 1940s public, when U.S. society was still negotiating its acceptance of Jewish identity, would be different from that of an audience who no longer remembers when Jews, even American Jews, were routinely referred to as an alien race.

The full context of their original historical moment has inevitably impacted the performance viability of these works over time. Aside from the fluctuation of pro- or anti-Zionist (or at least anti-Israel) public sentiment that can amplify some aspects of Hecht's politics and project later meanings onto others, the sheer absence of the full spectrum of his plays' performative elements robs them of their full import. A rare example of an attempted revival of *A Flag Is Born* reveals this problem. When the American Century Theatre company produced the play in 2004, a *Washington Post* critic dutifully observed that it should be "taken in the context as the propaganda piece it was intended to be," but felt compelled to concede that "its post-Holocaust power has largely dissipated"—an unsurprising appraisal of a highly topical work several decades old.[15] But their critique of the "Council of the Mighty" scene revealed an inevitable limitation of resurrecting that particular moment of theatricality: "In Tevye's testimony before an international tribunal consisting of representatives of the United States, France, Russia and Britain. . . . The effect would be powerful if not for all the similar-sounding rhetoric that came before it, most of which is unsuccessfully delivered by [the actor] in a tone that's more kvetching than mournful."[16] By contrast, the critic Elliot Norton, reviewing the original production on tour in Boston, called the scene "electrifying."[17] And Brooks Atkinson, despite his own carping about the play's "turgid stage polemic," still perceived something transcendently immediate and socially significant in Tevya's speech as embodied by the star power and personal biography of Paul Muni in that unique historical moment of September 1946:

> Paul Muni is giving a masterly performance as a vagrant Jew trudging hopefully toward Palestine. Toward the end of the pageant he serves as a spokesman for his race before the world. Anyone who loves great acting should take advantage of the limited engagement of "A Flag Is Born." For

# CONCLUSION

it is obvious that Mr. Muni, who is one of the most accomplished actors of our time, has been stirred by the significance of the part he is playing. . . . His passion as an artist and as a Jew has been aroused by 'A Flag Is Born' and his acting as the composite Tevya is inspired beyond the normal range of the theatre.[18]

Perhaps *A Flag Is Born* could never be fulfilled onstage without the presence of Muni embodying Hecht's theatrical gambit of mid-twentieth-century Jewish American theatre artists overcoming decades of industry-policed silencing of their identity. But that extratextual performative element is what took the play beyond "the normal range of the theatre" into a theatrically compelling, if not always entertaining, realm of public advocacy.

# Appendix 1

## *We Will Never Die (1943)*

[Editor's note: This text mostly adheres to the version published by Peter Bergson's Committee for a Jewish Army shortly after *We Will Never Die*'s final performance in Los Angeles on July 21, 1943. Because that edition contains the late addition of the "Battle of the Warsaw Ghetto" scene, it can be considered an authoritative record of Hecht's final version of a script that had undergone many revisions after its New York premiere in March. I have corrected some apparent misprints and I provide in the editor's notes some notable additional material from the Los Angeles recording. I have also included titles for each scene according to Hecht's list of "episodes" in the official program. Cast and production information for all six productions come from the front matter of the published script, as well as programs and contemporary newspaper articles. Hecht's three extant typescript drafts have also been consulted.]

## PRODUCTION INFORMATION
### WRITTEN BY BEN HECHT
### MUSIC BY KURT WEILL

Source: Ben Hecht, *We Will Never Die: A Memorial Dedicated to the 2,000,000 Jewish Dead of Europe*, New York: Committee for a Jewish Army of Stateless and Palestinian Jews, 1943.

## APPENDIX 1

### DIRECTED BY MOSS HART
### ASSISTANT DIRECTOR AND TOUR DIRECTOR: HERMAN ROTSTEN
### PRODUCED BY BILLY ROSE
### SETTINGS BY S. SYRJALA AND LEMUEL AYERS
### LIGHTING BY MOE HACK

**First performance:** March 9, 1943, at Madison Square Garden, New York

New York Cast:

RABBI: Jacob Ben-Ami
NARRATORS: Paul Muni, Edward G. Robinson
"JEWS IN THE WAR": Herbert Rudley, Luther Adler
"REMEMBER US": Paul Lindenberg, Solvie Wiberg, William Malten, David Leonard, Margaret Waller, Edward Franz, Walter Kohler, Mark Shweid, Eleanora Mendelsohn, Sylvia Sidney, and children of the Israel Orphan Asylum
VOCAL SOLOIST: Kurt Baum
Music performed by the NBC Symphony Orchestra, conducted by Isaac Van Grove

**Second performance:** April 12, 1943, at Constitution Hall, Washington, D.C.

The cast in Washington, D.C. was the same as in New York.

**Third performance:** April 22, 1943, at Convention Hall, Philadelphia

Philadelphia Cast:

RABBI: Jacob Ben-Ami
NARRATORS: Claude Rains, Edward Arnold
"JEWS IN THE WAR": Martin Gabel, Berry Kroeger
"REMEMBER US": Eleanora Mendelsohn, Beaumont Bruestle, Robert Morton, Stewart Wayne, Ben Low, Louis Cordano, Doris Jacobson, Elliot Gordon, Evelyn Creig
VOCAL SOLOISTS: Morris Abrams, Augustin Garcia, Helen Gaber

**Fourth performance:** May 19, 1943, at Chicago Stadium, Chicago

Chicago Cast:

RABBI: Jacob Ben-Ami
NARRATORS: John Garfield, Burgess Meredith
"JEWS IN THE WAR": Harry Drew, E. L. Kiddie
"REMEMBER US": Irving Brown, George Chain, Nina Clowden, Albert Gamze, Sidney Glatcow, Jeanne Juvelier, Maurice Mason, Virginia Paine, Klock Ryder
VOCAL SOLOISTS: Avrum Matthews, Ruth Slater, Edward Stack

**Fifth performance: June 6, 1943, at Boston Garden, Boston**

Boston Cast:

RABBI: Jacob Ben-Ami
NARRATORS AND "JEWS IN THE WAR": Ralph Bellamy, Howard DaSilva, Berry Kroeger
"REMEMBER US": Ludwig Roth, William Malten, David Leonard, Margaret Waller, Mark Schweid, Eleanora Mendelsohn, Walter Kohler, Eleanor Lynn

**Sixth performance: July 21, 1943, at Hollywood Bowl, Los Angeles**

Los Angeles Cast:

RABBI: Jacob Ben-Ami
NARRATORS: Edward G. Robinson, Edward Arnold
"JEWS IN THE WAR": John Garfield, Sam Levene
"BATTLE OF THE WARSAW GHETTO": Paul Henreid, Katina Paxinou, Paul Stewart, and members of the Actors Laboratory Theatre
"REMEMBER US": Edward J. Bromberg, Roman Bohnen, Shimen Ruskin, Art Smith, Akim Tamiroff, Leo Bulgakov, Helene Thimig, Blanche Yurka, Joan Leslie, Alexander Granach
VOCAL SOLOIST: Kurt Baum

# WE WILL NEVER DIE

(*The lights of the meeting hall are dim.*
*Two towering tablets containing the Ten Commandments loom at the back of the stage. A flight of stairs leads down from them to the stage level.*
*There is a space of four feet between the two Tablets.*
*When the Tablets are lighted the music begins. It is the Yom Kippur music. A cantor appears in the orchestra and sings Kol Nidre.*

# APPENDIX 1

*At the end of the singing of Kol Nidre, a bearded figure in white emerges from between the two Tablets. He stands on the steps and blows the shofar. This wild and ancient blast of the Jewish faith ends the Yom Kippur music. The Shofar blower exits through the Tablet space.*

The music resumes. From between the Tablets appears the figure of a RABBI in a satin robe and a white satin hat. The RABBI walks down the steps and takes his place at the central altar near the front of the stage.

The RABBI speaks.)

THE RABBI: Almighty God, Father of the poor and the weak, Strength of the Righteous and Hope of all who dream of goodness and justice; Almighty God who favored the children of Israel with his light—we are here to affirm that this light still shines in us.

We are here to say our prayers for the two million who have been killed in Europe, because they bear the name of your first children—the Jews.

Before our eyes has appeared the strange and awesome picture of a folk being put to death, of a great and ancient people in whose veins has lingered for so long the earliest words and image of God, dying like a single child on a single bayonet.

We are not here to weep for them although our eyes are stricken with this picture and our hearts burdened with their fate.

We are here to honor them and to proclaim the victory of their dying.

For in our Testament are written the words of Habakkuk, prophet of Israel, "They shall never die."

They shall never die though they were slaughtered with no weapon in their hands.

Though they still fill the dark land of Europe with the smoke of their massacre, they shall never die.

For they are part of something greater, higher and stronger than the dreams of their executioners.

Dishonored and removed from the face of the earth, their cry of Shema Israel remains in the world.

We are here to strengthen our hearts, to take into our veins the pride and courage of the millions of innocent people who have fallen and are still to fall before the German massacre.

They were unarmed. But not we!

We live in a land whose arm is stronger than the arm of the German Goliath. This land is our David.

Almighty God, we are here to affirm that our hearts will be a monument worthy of our dead.

## WE WILL NEVER DIE

We are here to affirm that the innocence of their lives and the dream of goodness in their souls are witnesses that will never be silent. They shall never die.

We are here to affirm that we shall stand beside David and in the name of the innocent dead and of human honor battle forever and without end.

Such is the meaning of our Memorial tonight.

Our service will begin with the prayer, Shema Israel, the prayer that holds the last words of the millions who have died in the massacres by the Germans.

This prayer proclaims the soul's allegiance to God. It is out of the pages of Deuteronomy and it has risen from the stricken and the dying in all the lands of the earth—for many centuries.

"Hear, O Israel, the Lord is Our God, the Lord is One. And thou shalt love the Lord, thy God, with all thy heart and with all thy soul and with all thy might."

(*Twenty* RABBIS *in the various costumes of their sects and countries come upon the stage.*

*They take their places in a row in front of the chief* RABBI *who has been speaking.*)

RABBI: The prayer, Shema Israel will be led by our rabbis who have come from the dead ghettos of Europe. They are among the few who have survived. They were witnesses of the killing of our folk in Germany, Poland, Holland, France, Czecho-Slovakia, Roumania, Russia and all the places overrun by the Germans.

(*Four men in white robes holding four Torahs emerge from between the Tablets and take a position behind the twenty* RABBIS. *They hold the Torahs aloft.*

*A light appears, illuminating the choir loft in which sits the choir of cantors. The* RABBIS *begin the prayer of Shema Israel. They recite its first line. The choir of cantors sings its response. The* RABBIS *finish the prayer and the choir again sings its response.*

*The* RABBIS *and the Torah bearers exit. The stage is empty.*)

---

[Episode One—"The Roll Call"][1]

(*From between the Tablets appear two figures. They are not in costume.*

*They are the two* NARRATORS. *They walk down the steps, one going to an altar at the left of the stage, the other to an altar at the right of the stage.*

*The* FIRST NARRATOR *begins to speak.*)

---

[1] In the official programs for each performance, Hecht named the different "episodes" of *We Will Never Die*, which I am interpolating into this text.

# APPENDIX 1

**FIRST NARRATOR:** Long ago there was a tribe that tended sheep and tilled the ground in the half barren places beyond the River Jordan.

There were many civilizations already in the world. Many heroes and philosophers had already entered history.

But in the record of man's rise out of the fogs of savagery there was still one page empty.

It was on this page that the little tribe of shepherds and farmers beyond the Jordan wrote their creed—the creed that was destined to change the soul of man.

They wrote that the soul of man had not come from the beasts but been given him by God.

They wrote that above all the greeds and lusts in the human soul stood goodness, righteousness and justice.

They wrote that the destiny of man called him to serve this mighty creed, to serve it above all the other powers on earth.

Writing thus on the empty page, this little tribe put down the words of a battle cry that has never ended and of a dream that has alone survived all the debacles of history. The first tribesman who wrote on this empty page was named Abraham.

And the handful of farmers who crossed the Jordan with Abraham—were the first Jews.

**SECOND NARRATOR:** Today in the dark lands of Europe the Germans are seeking to destroy the creed written by Abraham and that now belongs to the whole world.

Statisticians have estimated that it costs $50,000 for the Germans to kill a single allied soldier. This is an expensive gesture.

The killing of a Jew is less expensive. It costs nothing.

The Jew of Europe is the step son in the house. The laws of nations do not include his safety, his honor or his inheritance.

**FIRST NARRATOR:** However bravely he dies as a soldier in defense of American fox holes, of British cruisers, of French outposts, however wildly he fights as a soldier under the twenty flags of civilization—as a Jew he is the most inexpensive corpse in history. The killing of two million Jews has cost the Germans less than the killing of a single American soldier.

**SECOND NARRATOR:** It is the cheapness of his death that gives the Jew in military lands a bad name. Against this bad name earned by his helpless death he has only one defense—the value of his living.

**FIRST NARRATOR:** This is his shield.

SECOND NARRATOR: This is his sword.

FIRST NARRATOR: This is his indestructibility.

SECOND NARRATOR: This is his valor and his victory.

FIRST NARRATOR: Here is his roll call.

SECOND NARRATOR: No scroll is large enough to hold all his names.

FIRST NARRATOR: We summon this fame, not to boast, but to give strength to hearts that have forgotten in their sorrow, the shield, the sword, the valor and the indestructibility of their people.

> (*The music is played quietly during the narration. The stage now grows dark.*
>
> *The music swells up. The* NARRATORS *begin the roll call of the Great Jews. During their talk, black robed figures come out of the space between the Tablets and out of doors in the Tablets. Each of the figures carries a lighted candle. The 150 black robed figures in the dark hold aloft the lighted candles, form themselves in patterns on the stairs, and on the stage, as the* NARRATORS *continue. The candle bearers appear in groups of two, three five and ten. They do not follow the name cues called by the* NARRATORS *but offer themselves to the audience as symbols of the light the Jews have brought into the world.*)

SECOND NARRATOR: There was Moses, the lawgiver to the Jews and through them, to the world. Moses who brought down from Mount Sinai the Ten Commandments which are the moral laws of today and which will be the moral laws of a tomorrow—rid of Nazis.

FIRST NARRATOR: There was David, founder of the Jewish kingdom whose voice, lifted in song twenty-eight hundred years ago, still sounds to comfort the heavy laden of the earth.

SECOND NARRATOR: There was Solomon whose wisdom still remains as the homeland of Truth.

FIRST NARRATOR: And around these three, there stands a host of heroes, prophets and poets. Isaiah, Joshua, Saul, Samuel, Jeremiah, Elijah, Amos, Judah of the Maccabees, Mordecai and Hosiah.[2] Thunderers all, whose dreams and phrases molded the soul of man and illumined forever his tomorrow.

SECOND NARRATOR: And if you would know whence the Jewish soldiers in the fox holes, tanks and bombers of today derive their fierceness, look on Bar Kochba. Bar Kochba, the mighty warrior, who marched forth against the Roman legions and scattered and terrified them for three years . . . And who

---

[2] As heard on the Los Angeles recording, Hecht added to this line, ". . . and Jesus Christ of Nazareth, apostle of God and King of the Jews."

# APPENDIX 1

for a year stood with his small army against the entire might of the Roman world . . . and died with all his soldiers on the ramparts of the ancient city of Bethar.

FIRST NARRATOR: Scattered like quicksilver under the hammers of persecution, the Jews raised their voices in the many houses of the world. Theirs was the voice that ushered in the Renaissance and the new light for the world.

SECOND NARRATOR: There were the great rabbis, Hillel and Akiba and Rashi, the commentator. Solomon Ben Gabirol and Abraham Bar Hanasi, philosophers in the Spain of the 12th century, rekindled the torches of learning and beauty that ended the dark ages.

FIRST NARRATOR: With them sang Jehudah Halevi and the many poets of exile.

SECOND NARRATOR: There was Don Isaac Abrabanel, minister of finance to the court of Ferdinand and Isabella who raised money for the venture of Christopher Columbus.

FIRST NARRATOR: There was Baruch Spinoza who in the north erected a tower for soul of man.

SECOND NARRATOR: Far and wide the genius of the Jew—who then as now must die so helplessly—added to the values of life. Amatus Lusitanus, father of European medicine enters the scroll. And Benjamin of Tudela, the first great geographer of Europe. And Dr. Astruc, father of gynecology . . . And Maimonides, the light of reason. The names are many and the scroll is small.

FIRST NARRATOR: There was Montaigne, called the noblest mind of the French.

SECOND NARRATOR: There was Moses Mendelssohn, the little humpbacked Jew of Germany who wrote his people out of the German ghettos. And whose grandson, Felix Mendelssohn made music for the world.

FIRST NARRATOR: Abraham Schreiner of Galicia, discoverer of petroleum.

SECOND NARRATOR: Rachel, the great actress of Europe and Sarah Bernhardt. Pissarro the painter, Ached Hamm, the philosopher.

FIRST NARRATOR: Maurice de Hirsche, genius of industrialism and hero of Jewish philanthropy.

SECOND NARRATOR: Siegfried Marcus, inventor of the benzone propelled engine, forerunner of the automobile.

FIRST NARRATOR: Hyam Solomon who helped finance the armies of the American revolution and Isaac Franks, colonel under Washington and one of the hundreds of Jewish heroes of '76.

SECOND NARRATOR: Sir Moses Montefiore, adviser to Queen Victoria and the great champion of human and political tolerance.

FIRST NARRATOR: Benjamin Disraeli called Lord Beaconsfield, novelist and statesman whose brilliant mind carried England into the East.

SECOND NARRATOR: Zangwill the writer. Shalom-Alechem, Werfel, Feuchtwanger, Sholem Asch, Pinero, Schnitzler, Molnar, Zweig, Wasserman, Halevy, Catulle Mendes, Bret Harte, Olive Schruner—the names of the Jewish writers are many.

FIRST NARRATOR: Marcel Proust . . . Anatole France.

SECOND NARRATOR: Nostradamus, the great astrologer whose prophecies are today coming true.

FIRST NARRATOR: John Howard Payne, American dramatist and author of the song, "Home Sweet Home."

SECOND NARRATOR: And of music makers there is no end. The Jews have sung and played and given songs and symphonies to the world as if Orpheus himself had crossed the Jordan with them. From the great liturgical music echoing through history to the tune makers of the people they have serenaded a hundred lands.

FIRST NARRATOR: Bizet, composer of Carmen.

SECOND NARRATOR: Meyerbeer and Saint Saens.

FIRST NARRATOR: Rubinstein and Oscar Straus, to whose melodies a world still dances.

SECOND NARRATOR: Horowitz, Heifetz, Kreisler, Korngold and Gershwin.

FIRST NARRATOR: Bauer, Offenbach, Berlin, Goldmark.

SECOND NARRATOR: Kern, Schoenberg, Bloch and the last great master of the classics, Gustav Mahler.

FIRST NARRATOR: Luis Ponce de Leon, the greatest lyric poet of Spain.

SECOND NARRATOR: Bialik, the great singer of Palestine.

FIRST NARRATOR: Heinrich Heine, the greatest lyric poet of Germany.

SECOND NARRATOR: And another, Emma Lazarus, whose sonnet stands in bronze on our statue of Liberty—"Send these, the homeless, tempest tossed to me, I lift my lamp beside the golden door."

FIRST NARRATOR: The modern heroes of Palestine—Trumpeldor, Raziel and Jabotinsky.

SECOND NARRATOR: Sir John Hirschel, astronomer and inventor of modern photography.

FIRST NARRATOR: Caesar Lombroso, scientist. Otto Lillienthal of Prussia, inventor of the glider and called the grandfather of the aeroplane.

SECOND NARRATOR: Samuel Gompers, founder of the American Federation of Labor.

FIRST NARRATOR: Louis Brandeis, jurist and philosopher.

SECOND NARRATOR: Ferdinand Lassale and Karl Marx, historians of the future.

FIRST NARRATOR: Cordozo, American jurist and philosopher.

## APPENDIX 1

SECOND NARRATOR: The brothers Zondeck, pioneers in the study of glands.

FIRST NARRATOR: Chaim Weitzman, Jewish patriot and inventor of TNT.

SECOND NARRATOR: Ludwig Traube, founder of the science of pathology whose statue still stands in Paris. Graziadio Ascoli, the foremost Italian philologist.

FIRST NARRATOR: Rosa Bonheur, the painter, Modigliani, Chagall, the painter.

SECOND NARRATOR: Emin Pasha, explorer and statesman, Joseph Israels, painter. Max Nordau, the Voltaire of neurology.

FIRST NARRATOR: Theodore Herzl, founder of Zionism. Max Lieberman, painter, Jacques Loeb, the great biologist.

SECOND NARRATOR: Sigmund Freud, inventor of a new science of thought.

FIRST NARRATOR: The names are too many and the scroll too small but here are our world champions—the Jewish winners of the Nobel Prizes.

SECOND NARRATOR: In 1905, for his work on organic dyes—Adolph von Bayer. In 1907 for his work in meteorology, Albert Abraham Michelson.

FIRST NARRATOR: In 1908 for his invention of color photography, Gabriel Lippman. In 1908 for his work in the cure of syphilis, Paul Ehrlich.

SECOND NARRATOR: In 1908 for his work on bacteria immunity, Ilya Metchnikoff. In 1909 for his invention of the wireless telegraphy with Guglielmo Marconi, Karl Ferdinand Braun.

FIRST NARRATOR: In 1910 for his pioneer work in organic chemistry, Otto Wallach. In 1911 for their literary efforts in behalf of peace, Karl Landsteiner, and Otto Loewi.

SECOND NARRATOR: In 1914 for his work on pathology, Robert Barany. In 1915 for his botanical researches, Richard Willstaetter.

FIRST NARRATOR: In 1919 for his work in chemistry, Fritz Haber. In 1921 for his services in the theory of Physics, Albert Einstein.

SECOND NARRATOR: In 1922 for his work on the atomic theory, Niels Bohr. In 1922 for his work in organic chemistry, Otto Meyerhoff.

FIRST NARRATOR: In 1925 for their work in atomic physics, James Franck and Gustave Hertz. In 1925 for his work in chemistry, Richard Zsigismondo.

SECOND NARRATOR: In 1928 for his work in philosophy, Henri Bergson. In 1931 for his work in chemistry, Otto Heinrich Warburg.

FIRST NARRATOR: The scroll overruns. The halls of fame of a hundred nations hold the names of Jews who have given value to life. The prophet Hosiah spoke of Israel that it was destined to bloom and bud and fill the world with its fruit. Here is that fruit. Here is that Jew who shall never die . . .

(*The music plays and the choir sings as the stage remains filled for several minutes with the black robed figures holding aloft the lighted candles. The candle bearers exit and the* NARRATORS *follow them off. The music ends and the stage is blacked out.)*

---

[Episode Two—"Jews in the War"]

(*A spotlight is thrown on the space between the Tablets. Two American* SOLDIERS *emerge. They stand facing each other and blow Reveille, on their bugles.*

*Three* SOLDIERS, *in torn and soiled uniforms, appear quickly and throw themselves down upon the upper stage. They carry a field telegraph set. When the bugle call ends, we hear the clicking of a telegraph key.*

*Two* NARRATORS, *dressed in soldier uniforms, emerge from between the tablets. Each goes to one of the side altars.*

*The two buglers exit. Red lights play upon the Tablets. The clicking of the telegraph swells for a moment. It subsides and continues under the speech of the two* NARRATORS.)

FIRST SOLDIER: That's a telegraph key clicking. It's a message coming from a faraway place. Listen to it. The date is May 5th. The faraway place is Corregidor. Do you remember Corregidor, the last bastion of American arms in the Philippines? The Japs hit it with a ten to one army and a hundred to nothing air force. It held until this day—May 5th. This is the last hour of its defense. This is the hour of its defeat.

SECOND SOLDIER: A twenty-two year old Jewish boy from Brooklyn, by name Irving Strobing sits at his post and pounds away at his wireless key. He's sending a last message to the world. Corregidor is saying goodbye to the folks back home.

FIRST SOLDIER: Listen to it. This is how an American soldier sounds in defeat. Here's how a Jewish Boy from Brooklyn sends in his last words. We'll translate the morse code for you. Irving is telling the world.

SECOND SOLDIER: "Corregidor calling . . . Corregidor calling . . . They're not here yet. We're waiting for God only knows what. How about a chocolate soda? We've only got about one hour to go. Till noon. They're throwing men and shells at us. They've been shelling us faster than you can count. I am really low down."

(*The telegraph key clicks out in silence again.*)

FIRST SOLDIER: "Enemy heavy cross shelling and bombing. They've got all around us and from the skies. Corregidor used to be a nice place. But it's haunted now . . . I can hardly think. Say, I have sixty pesos you can have for this weekend."

## APPENDIX 1

(*The telegraph key clicks for a moment.*)

"The jig is up. Everyone is bawling like a baby. They are piling dead and wounded in our tunnel. My arms are weak from pounding this key. No rest. Short rations. Tired. Hey, I just got a treat. A can of pineapple."

(*The telegraph key clicks for a moment.*)

"My name is Irving Strobing. Get this to my mother, Mrs. Minnie Strobing, 605 Barbey Street, Brooklyn. They are to get along O.K. My love to Pa, Joe, Sue, Mac, Harry, Jane and Paul. God bless 'em all. Tell Joe wherever he is to give 'em Hell for us. My love to all . . . God bless you and keep you . . . Stand by . . ."

(*The clicking ends. The two buglers blow Taps. When Taps is finished the* SECOND SOLDIER *speaks.*)

SECOND SOLDIER: That was the army's hail and farewell from Corregidor—the salute from the dying delivered by Irving Strobing. It's one of the epics of the war.

FIRST SOLDIER: There are many epics in the war, written, spoken and lived by countless heroes. If we stress for these minutes the deeds of fighting Jews on all the battle fronts, it is not because they are the greatest or the most numerous. It is because they are our own. They are great enough for pride and many enough for history to count. Hundreds of Jewish soldiers, sailors, fliers and marines have been decorated and cited for valor. Thousands of them lie dead and wounded on our battle fields.

SECOND SOLDIER: The Jew, said the Nazis, cannot fight. Wait till Barney Ross gets to Berlin.

FIRST SOLDIER: Wait till the legions of freedom storm across the forests of Bavaria and the fields of Saxony. In the legions under every flag that moves forward will be Jews.

SECOND SOLDIER: They are under the fighting flags now. They have been under them since the first guns sounded in Poland. Bar Kochba's boys are scattered in a hundred armies.

FIRST SOLDIER: They were under the brave flag of the Greeks.

(*An Efzone emerges from between the Tablets. He carries a Greek flag. The music plays a Greek hymn. The Efzone moves down the steps to the front of the stage.*)

SECOND SOLDIER: They were with the Greek heroes who kicked the Hell out of Mussolini's pathetic world conquerors and who stood off the mighty Nazi war machine for the twelve weeks that saved Russia. There were thousands of Jews who died fighting under the Greek flag.

FIRST SOLDIER: They were with the French.

*(The Marseillaise plays and a French* SOLDIER *enters from between the tablets carrying the French flag. He walks to the stage front and stands beside the Greek.)*

They fought in the French retreat defending a flag that was to repudiate them and turn them over to the Germans as Jews fit only for slavery and slaughter. And they clamor still in the concentration camps of France and Africa for a place on the battle field against the Hun.

SECOND SOLDIER: They were under the flag of the Dutch.

*(A Dutch* SOLDIER *carrying the Dutch flag enters as the Organ plays the Dutch anthem. He joins the others.)*

Thousands of them are still fighting in the jungles of Java and Batavia and aboard the ships of the Netherlands.

FIRST SOLDIER: They are under the flag of Russia.

*(A Russian* SOLDIER *enters carrying a Russian flag. The organ plays the Soviet march. The Russian takes his place beside the others.)*

FIRST SOLDIER: Seven hundred thousand of them are on the Soviet fronts from Leningrad to the Don. Their valor is part of the great Russian spirit. Two hundred thousand of them have died standing in the way of the German tanks. These Jews who have shared with the Russians the infernos of the Soviet fronts are the happy Jews of Europe.

SECOND SOLDIER: They have a flag of their own—the Star of David raised above the reclaimed deserts of Palestine.

*(A young man in civilian dress, trousers and a white shirt open at the throat, enters carrying the Palestinian flag.)*

SECOND SOLDIER: There are another hundred thousand sturdy pioneers of Palestine and they cry for the right to fight.

FIRST SOLDIER: We Jews of Europe are being killed as Jews. Give us the right to strike back as Jews. Let the Star of David be one of the flags that enters Berlin.

SECOND SOLDIER: They are under the English Flag.

*(A* SOLDIER *enters carrying the English flag and the organ plays the English anthem or Tipperary.)*

From Burma to Bezerte, in all the Imperial armies, raining death out of the skies over Berlin, Cologne, Frankfort, Milan; in the sieges of Tobruk, in the chase after Rommel, in the headlong drive to throw the Germans into the Mediterranean, Jews march and fly.

*(A procession of* SOLDIERS *carrying the flags mentioned in the next speech emerges from the Tablets space and marches down the steps to stand beside the others . . . The organ swells into a march militaire.)*

## APPENDIX 1

FIRST SOLDIER: Under Mexican, Brazilian and Chinese flags, under the flags of Canada, Australia and South Africa, under the flags of the Serbian guerilla fighters, of the Polish Legions, of the Czech mountain heroes, under the banners of the Turk, the Siberian, and the free Belgian are the Jewish soldiers.[3]

(*When these have all lined up the organ starts playing Over There. And an American* SOLDIER *carrying the American flag emerges.*)

SECOND SOLDIER: And under the flag of the U.S.A., three hundred thousand Jews are marching and sailing and flying forth to battle. And their spirit is the spirit of Washington, Lincoln and Roosevelt—of Yankee Doodle and the Battle Hymn of the Republic—of Bar Kochba and Irving Strobing—

FIRST SOLDIER (*in a ringing voice*): And—Meyer Levin.[4]

(*The* SOLDIERS *dip their flags and all stand silent for a minute.*

*The orchestra starts the Battle Hymn of the Republic—and the choir sings it. During the singing the* SOLDIERS *place their flags in standards at the back. In the dimness the* SOLDIERS *exit down the left and right stairways.*

*The Battle Hymn of the Republic ends. The stage goes completely black.*)

---

[*Episode Three—"Battle of the Warsaw Ghetto"*]

(*The orchestra starts a faint musical overture. The music is woeful. It continues for a time in the darkness. Its sobbing changes gradually into a martial air. Finally the music becomes wild and we hear a battle march filling the darkness. During this overture a wall has been placed on the stage. It is the ghetto wall of Warsaw, 10 feet high and extends across the stage center.*

*The lights go up. We see a street inside the ghetto wall. It is night. The street is empty. The music ends.*

*Two new* NARRATORS *appear at the microphones. One of them is a woman.*)

MAN NARRATOR: This is the ghetto wall of Warsaw. Here no flag flies. Here no bugles sound. This is the wall of doom. Around it stands the might of the Germans. Tank divisions, bomber squadrons, the Elite Guards, and the storm-

---

[3] Added text from the Los Angeles recording: "The Germans murdered two million Jewish civilians without trouble. The Germans are murdering the remaining four million Jewish civilians of Europe without trouble. But those who are marching forward under the flags of freedom, they will not kill so easily. They will have grave trouble killing armed Jews. For every Jew who fights is not only a soldier but an avenger."

[4] Added text from the Los Angeles recording: "We ask of you a minute of silence in honor of our soldiers, all our soldiers, Jew and Gentile, who have died in this war."

trooper regiments surround this wall. It is ringed with death. The eyes of cannon and machine guns watch it day and night.

WOMAN NARRATOR: Inside this wall are the Jews of Warsaw—starving Jews, dying Jews, desperate and doomed Jews, Jews who were once scholars and workers, poets and artisans, soldiers, tradesmen, teachers—Jews who were once busy as human beings wait behind this wall for death. No flag marches to their rescue. No distant bugles sound with hope. Only one activity remains—that of dying.

MAN NARRATOR: They have only one weapon against the might of the Germans that watch the wall. Their weapon is the spirit of man. This remains. Massacre has not blunted it. Doom has not rusted it.

Bright in the history of man are the battles that were fought with this spirit—the unconquerable spirit that shines forever above the victory of its enemies—Thermapoli, the Alamo, Bataan, Stalingrad—here is another battle to place beside them—the battle of the Warsaw ghetto. Here is a battle in which Jews, outnumbered one thousand to one, fought the might of the Germans to a stand-still for three weeks. And though every one of these Jews is dead today, though every man, woman, and child who battled behind the ghetto ramparts has been exterminated, though the ghetto today is empty—empty as a beggar's tin cup in the rain—the spirit of these doomed and half-starved warriors will rise forever among the highest flags of history.

(*During the* NARRATOR'*s talk, groups of men, women and children have been appearing in the street. Old men with prayer books in their hands have appeared and stand facing the wall and praying. Women, holding fast to their children, have appeared and stand in huddles. Younger men have appeared carrying loaves of bread. They cut small slices and give them to the women and children. They seize on the bits of bread and eat like starving people. The bread-bringers offer pieces to the old men praying. The old men refuse the food and continue at their prayers.*

*The woman narrator continues the talk and as she does, the street continues to fill. Ragged, gaunt figures appear. In the corner a woman falls dead. Her children sit crouched around her until she is picked up and carried away. Women sit weeping against the wall. A young man in tatters enters the street. He is playing an accordion. He plays as he walks. The tinny music attracts three little girls. They form a circle, holding hands, and dance around and around as the accordion player pauses to play for them. Then the accordion passes on down the street. The three girls and an old man, who can barely walk, follow after the music. Four men pass through the crowd in the street,*

## APPENDIX 1

*bearing a coffin on their shoulders. They lower the coffin and open it. They remove old rifles and ammunition from it and distribute these to the men and women. A stalwart working man appears carrying a large pot. It is full of soup. He pours a bit into each of the cups that are held up eagerly by the starving crowd.*

*The figures in the street continue to move slowly across the stage. Half of them collapse against the wall. The others continue on.*

*During the foregoing, the* WOMAN NARRATOR *has been talking.*)

WOMAN NARRATOR: In 1941 there were 400,000 Jews in the ghetto of Warsaw. There were another million in the other ghettos of Poland. In 1941 the orders came for their murder. Joseph Paul Goebbels, speaking for the German people, proclaimed over the radio.

GOEBBELS' VOICE (*coming through another microphone*): "The extermination of the Jewish race is of historic importance and there can be no mercy."

WOMAN NARRATOR: That was the order. That was part of the German bid for greatness. Within six months the order was being fulfilled. Within six months the cities of Biolystock, Grodno, Brest, Litovsk, Vilna, Chelm, Crackow were Judenrein—clean of Jews. Every Jew in them had been slaughtered.

MAN NARRATOR: The killing of one million and a half human beings, even though they were helpless and unarmed, required organization and called for ingenuity. And these are talents in which the Germans excel. The Nazi governor of Poland, General Fischer, fell eagerly to work establishing extermination camps.

WOMAN NARRATOR: Remember these names—Trawinke... Oswjecim... Tremblinka. Remember particularly the name of Tremblinka. These were the organized extermination camps. In Tremblinka 7,000 Jews a day were put to death in special steam chambers and the mobile lime pits devised by General Wilhelm Krueger.

MAN NARRATOR: All of the doomed Jews of Poland passed through the ghetto of Warsaw. Warsaw was the embarkation center for death. A million Jews passed through the ghetto of Warsaw on their way to Trawinke, Oswjecim, and Tremblinka—on their way to the steam chambers and the lime pits. The ghetto of Warsaw was ringed with the Nazi divisions, cut off from the world like a section of limbo. But through its walls trickled the cry of the doomed—a faint cry of millions dying that found no echo. No saviors signaled from Heaven or earth.

WOMAN NARRATOR: On the 17th of March, 1943, there were left 35,000 Jews in the ghetto of Warsaw—35,000 Jews and a million ghosts. And on March 17th the Nazi Governor of Poland, General Fischer, issued the order—

"All the remaining Jews of Poland must be killed." This order went to the tank commanders, to the bombing pilots, to the machine gun and artillery officers.

(*The faint distant blare of a German march tune is heard. With it is the rumble of wheels and the sound of footsteps like the wind.*)

MAN NARRATOR: On March 17, 1943, the Germans moved forward on their errand of extermination. The Elite Guards marched into the ghetto of Warsaw at noon. They had come to murder 35,000 helpless people. The Elite Guards arrived at the corner of Dluga and Tonaistra Streets. These are street names to remember—for on the corner of Dluga and Tonaistra Streets a miracle happened. Jews—young, old, weakened with hunger, half-clothed . . . Jews led by an engineer named Michal Klepfis, met the Elite Guard with weapons in their hands—old guns, scant bullets, rusty bayonets—but still weapons; met the Elite Guard and charged them—scattered them and drove them out of the ghetto, killing fifty of their officers.

(*During the foregoing we hear the sounds of distant shooting and the cries of battle. These are not too loud and continue softly under the voice of the* NARRATOR.)

WOMAN NARRATOR: Rally, Jews! Here are old guns from the Polish underground. Here are swords. Here are grenades from the hidden storehouses. And here is battle! Raise your barricades! March—one against a thousand, musket against machine gun, bayonet and club against the finest cannon of Europe.

(*The street inside the ghetto wall becomes a hospital. Here wounded are brought and laid out. The distant cannonading continues. Now fires light up the city beyond the wall. The old men who have been praying turn to take care of the wounded. During the narration, groups of twenty and thirty men and women, carrying various arms, run through the street, shouting and waving their guns.*)

MAN NARRATOR: The Germans brought up their crack divisions. Their famed cannon blasted through the ghetto. Bombers circled overhead dropping shells. Flame and shell filled every alley and highway. But in these streets of a million Jewish ghosts, the Jews held firm. They fought from house to house. They emerged with guns blazing from cellars. They leaped with grenades in their hands from rooftops. They stood firm behind barricades with machine guns captured from the storm-troopers.

WOMAN NARRATOR: Day after day, through light and darkness, the battle rages and there are reinforcements. Five hundred young Jews, on their way to the extermination camp at Tremblinka, turn on their executioners. With the aid of Polish villagers, they overpower their murderers and run all night back to the ghetto of Warsaw to die in battle. Rally, Jews! There is only death at the

## APPENDIX 1

cannon mouth. From the underground radio station SWIT on April 21 comes the single communique of the Battle of the Warsaw ghetto—

RADIO VOICE (*through another microphone*): "Death sentence has been proclaimed on the last 35,000 Jews in Warsaw. Gun salvoes are echoing in the streets. Women and children are defending themselves with their bare hands. Help us!"

MAN NARRATOR: This is the brief cry from the ghetto battle. The only words to come from the ghetto front. They are hurled at the world and the transmitter goes dead. But the battle goes on. The ghetto is in flames. Light, water, oil have been shut off. This is no armed fortress, but naked streets. There are no bomb shelters here. There are no bastions of cannon, yet the ghetto fights on. A thousand Germans are killed the first week, 2,000 the second, 3,000 the third. Coolly, boldly, the men and women of the ghetto stand at their posts, die at their posts, and not all the Elite Guards and the might of the German divisions can overpower them.

WOMAN NARRATOR: And against the ghetto walls the old ones have returned to their praying and the young ones who have no arms, raise their voices and sing as the battle closes on them.

MAN NARRATOR: And now there are flags. Flags go up on the ghetto walls. Flags go up on the rooftops of the warehouses—the flags of far-away countries. The flags of Britain, of Russia, and of Poland rise. No help comes from these lands—but their flags are the faces of freedom, the faces of faraway freedom.

(*The three flags have risen above the wall.*)

MAN NARRATOR: This is the third week of battle and the cry spread through the broken streets of the ghetto, "German tanks are advancing! They are coming down Lange Street."

WOMAN NARRATOR: Rally, Jews! The tanks will roll over the old and the dying, over the weak and the helpless. Rally and meet them!

MAN NARRATOR: This is the last act of the Battle of the Warsaw ghetto. With grenades and pistols, with clubs and swords, all who remained of the fighting Jews storm over the ghetto wall, shouting and singing. They leap from the wall into the street. They rush forward and hurl themselves at the Nazi tanks.

(*During the last of this narration the street has filled with young men and women carrying guns. They bring boxes with them. The boxes are placed like steps against the wall. The fighters climb up on the boxes, one after the other, singing the battle song which was heard at the beginning. They leap from the wall into the street.*

*The* NARRATOR *stops. We hear for several moments the sound of shooting, shouting, wheels, clanking, and above these sounds we hear the singing. The young men and women who leap from the walls continue to sing. The old ones left behind raise their voices and join in the battle song.*[5]

*The stage darkens. In the darkness the singing still continues for a few moments. The boxes and the ghetto wall are removed from the stage during the darkness. The singing ends. The orchestra starts up, continuing faintly the last song of the Jews. All is silent except for the music.)*

MAN NARRATOR: It was a German victory. The German cannon destroyed the last of the Jewish fighters. All of them. Not one with gun or sword in his hands ended the battle until he lay dead. It was a great victory for the Germans. They marched into the ghetto triumphant and slaughtered the 13,000 unarmed old men, women and children who remained. All of them. The extermination of the Jews had been accomplished according to plan. There are only ghosts left in the ghetto of Warsaw today.

WOMAN NARRATOR: Herrenvolk of the Third Reich! Brave, goose-stepping Jew-killers! Swine-hearted knights of massacre and murder—what is it you hear in the ghetto of Warsaw today? Not moans, nor shrieks, nor cannons booming—but a song, faint and endless. The song of the spirit that drifts from every one of the stones you conquered—the song of the brave Jews of Warsaw that will outlive your victories.

*(During the last part of the* NARRATOR's *talk, the voices have resumed singing faintly the battle song that led the fighters over the wall. The* NARRATOR *ends. The stage grows dark and the song continues in the darkness.)*

---

*[Episode Four—"Remember Us"]*

*(The stage is darkened except for the light from the candelabra. The choir balcony is brightly lighted. The choir begins a religious chant. During its singing the red lights and the swirl of cloud and smoke play on the Tablets.*

*These lights end and a large spotlight hits the center of the stage. Into this spotlight come men carrying a long table. Other men bring chairs and place [them] around it. Other men bring the flags of the United Nations and place them in standards on each side of the stage.*

---

[5] As discussed in chapter 2, Franz Waxman and Frank Loesser wrote the "Battle Hymn of the Ghetto" for this scene. Loesser's lyrics are as follows: "We the scum of the human chattel/We of everlasting flight/We will rise in fearless battle/We who cannot live the night./Tears no longer/Tears no longer/Let them taste the death they deal./ And though we die, we die in battle/Not beneath the tyrant heel." The lyrics are not printed in the published script but are featured in the program for the Los Angeles performance. *We Will Never Die* Hollywood Bowl souvenir program, 27.

## APPENDIX 1

*The space between the Tablets lights up. The Two* NARRATORS *appear here and walk down the steps to the microphones.*

*The singing of the choir ends. The organ takes up the music. It plays under the* NARRATOR's *talk.*

*The scene setters have now exited. The long table surrounded by empty chairs and the many flags on each side of the stage remain in the bright spotlight. A separate light shines on the* NARRATOR.)[6]

THE NARRATOR: We come [to] tomorrow. There will be a great meeting hall with tall windows. In this hall will stand a long table. It will be the table of judgment.

(*Three Germans, two in frock coats and one in uniform, with the swastika on their sleeves, enter from the stairs left. They go to the empty table and sit down with their backs to the audience—facing the Tablets.*)

To this table the German peace delegates will come for judgment.

(*Sixteen men follow them to the stage, eight coming from each side stairs. As the* NARRATOR *talks, these men seat themselves.*)

And the men of many countries will sit around this table. The eyes of the German delegates will look into the eyes of American, Russians, Englishmen, Poles, Greeks, Chinese, Belgians, Czechs, Frenchmen, Serbs and Dutchmen. All the victims of the German adventure will be there to pass sentence—all but one. Absent from the table of judgment will be the Jew.

There are two reasons for this. First is the reason that the Jews have only one unity—that of the target. Though they die in many lands, they have no land to represent them at the table of judgment.

The second reason for this is that there will be no Jews left in Europe for representation when the peace comes. They will have been reduced from a minority to a phantom.

Of the six million Jews in German held lands the Germans have said none shall remain. The four million left to kill are being killed—according to plan. When the time comes to make the peace these will have been done to the death.

And these millions who were hanged, burned and shot will have died without the dream of abasements to be avenged or homelands to be restored. For when the Jews die in massacre they look toward no tomorrow to bring their children happiness and their enemies disaster. For no homeland is ever theirs

---

[6] These stage directions clearly introducing "Remember Us" accidentally appear earlier in the published text, after "Jews in the War," an error probably resulting from the late insertion of "Battle of the Warsaw Ghetto" in between the two scenes.

no matter how long they live in it, how well they serve it or how many of its songs they learn to sing.

When the plans for the new world are being thrashed out at the peace table, when the guilts are being fixed and the color and shape of the future determined, there will be nothing for the Jews of Europe to say to the delegates but the sad, faint phrase—"Remember Us."

The dead of many lands will speak for justice through their spokesmen around the table of judgment. The Jew alone will have no one to speak for him. His voice will remain outside the hall of judgment, to be heard only when the window is opened and the sad faint phrase drifts in, "Remember Us."

(*Through the last few moments of the* NARRATOR's *talk the choir has been singing softly. The bright light has illumined the space between the Tablets. The light is removed from the* NARRATOR. *Out of the Tablets come seven Jews, two men, a rabbi, two women and a child. Their faces are grey. They move slowly, and stiffly. The fingers of their hands are curled inward. They advance down two steps and remain motionless facing the peace table. They are the dead and their heads are bowed. One of the dead raises his head. He speaks in emotionless tones.*)

VOICE: Remember us. In the town of Freiburg in the Black Forest two hundred of us were hanged and left dangling out of our kitchen windows. We watched our synagogue burn and our rabbi flogged to death.

(*The voice ends and the group move slowly toward the left of the steps. The choir singing grows louder as they move and as a second group emerges from the Tablets. They are six, two men, a woman and three children. One of the dead raises his face toward the peace table.*)

DEAD MAN: In the town of Szcucin in Poland on the morning of September 3 which is the day set aside for our Atonement we were all in church praying God to forgive us. All our village was there, our bakers and millers and harness makers. All our wives and mothers and sisters were there and every child old enough to pronounce the name of God was there. Above our prayers we heard the sound of motor lorries. They stopped in front of our synagogue. The Germans tumbled out, torches in hand. The Germans set fire to us. When we ran out of the flames they turned machine guns on us. They caught our women and undressed them and made them run naked under whips through the market place. All of us were killed before our Atonement Day was done. Remember us.

(*The group moves to the left. The choir singing swells. Another group appears. These are five bearded old men. One of them raises his head and speaks.*)

## APPENDIX 1

DEAD MAN: Remember us in Wloclowek. The Germans came when we were at prayer. They tore the prayer shawls from our heads. Under whips and bayonets they made us use our prayer shawls as mops to clean out German latrines. We were all dead when the sun set—a hundred of us. Remember us.

*(The five bearded old men move to the left as the choir singing swells. Six women of different ages and four children come out of the Tablets. They stand with their heads bowed. One of them looks up and the quiet voice of a woman is heard.)*

DEAD WOMAN: In Lublin five hundred of our women and children were led to the market place and stood against the vegetable stalls we knew so well. Here the Germans turned machine guns on us and killed us all. Remember us.

*(The women and children move to the right. Out of the Tablets come six workingmen in overalls. They stand bowed as one of them raises his head and the voice speaks.)*

DEAD MAN: In Riga a thousand of us arrived on a transport from Germany as conscripted laborers. We had been traveling in sealed compartments for many days without food. The Germans in Riga unlocked our compartments and looked us over. They decided we were too weak to be of any use in the factories. They put us into sealed wagons and drove us into the fields and dynamited us. Remember us who were workingmen.

*(The six move to the left. Twelve men come out of the Tablets. They stand bowed as one head is raised to speak.)*

DEAD MAN: Remember us who were put in the freight trains that left France and Holland and Belgium and who rode across Europe to the city of Jassy in Rumania—standing up. We died in the freight cars standing up, for there was no food or water or air. Of the 20,000 who made that trip only a few hundreds were taken alive from the box cars. We were too weak for work and the Rumanians killed us. Remember us.

*(The twelve dead move to the right. Fifteen men women and children come out of the tablets. One of their dead speaks.)*

DEAD MAN: Remember us who were in the Ukraine. Here the Germans grew angry because we were costing them too much time and ammunition to kill. They devised a less expensive method. They took our women into the roads and tied them together with our children. Then they drove their heavy motor lorries into us. Thousands of us died this way with the German military cars running back and forth over our broken bodies. Remember Us.

*(These dead move to the left. And now a stream of dead figures comes, one by one, out of the tablets. They do not pause as did the others but continue to move slowly and stiffly toward the dead in the shadows . . . They*

WE WILL NEVER DIE

*form a rough circle around the brightly lighted peace table and the* VOICE OF THE DEAD *continues as they keep entering.*)

DEAD WOMAN: We were in Warsaw. The Germans killed 73,000 Jews in Warsaw in the year 1941. And seventy thousand more in the year 1942. They shot and burned us. . . . In the seven months after June 1941 there were 60,000 of us massacred in Bessarabia and Bukovnia. All of us in Kiev, fifty thousand of us, were killed. There were eighty thousand of us killed in Minsk. We hung from the windows and burned in basements and were beaten to death in the market place. We were used as targets for the German bombing planes to practice on and this was a time of great celebration for the Germans. Remember us.

(*The* VOICE *changes as the Dead keep moving on from between the Tablets.*)

We fill the waters of the Dneiper today with our bodies. There are myriads of us in the waters. And for a long time to come no one will be able to drink from that river or to swim in it for we are still there. And this, too, is held against us by the Germans—that we have poisoned the waters of their rivers with our dead bodies . . .

(*The stage is now filled. The Dead stand in the shadows beyond the brightly lighted peace table. The choir singing swells. There is a pause. Twenty girls in white robes appear out of the Tablets. They remain on the top step as a girl's voice speaks for them.*)

DEAD GIRL: Remember us, too, who were not killed by the Germans but who killed themselves. We were the daughters who lived in Warsaw. We were the daughters of good and pious people. We were young and raised in virtue. The Germans took a hundred and six of us and brought us to a hotel. They gave us perfumes and white robes to put on. They told us that at nightfall they would take us to a brothel and that we were to serve the Germans there. We waited all day. We anointed ourselves with the perfumes and put on the white robes. And when the sun was setting we knelt and prayed and each of us poisoned herself and died. The Germans came but none of us went to the brothel. There were many other thousands like us. Remember us.[7]

---

*[Epilogue]*[8]

(*The* NARRATOR *appears again at his microphone.*)

---

[7] On the Los Angeles recording, one more speech is added to conclude the scene: "We were the Jews who fought the Germans for three weeks in the ghetto of Warsaw. We were outnumbered and alone. The fight seemed hopeless. But we fought until all of us were dead. Remember us."

[8] Hecht does not title the last section, but the break in the action that begins these concluding speeches, leading to the final prayer, signals a dramatic denouement.

## APPENDIX 1

FIRST NARRATOR: These are the two million Jewish dead of Europe today. They will have no one to speak for them at the table of judgment; no voice but ours to echo their cry of "Remember Us."

SECOND NARRATOR: Let us keep their cry alive. Let their dying be not without meaning. Let the manner of their dying be one of the measures of the German soul.

FIRST NARRATOR: Let their myriad corpses piled in the streets, fields and rivers of Europe be as the hound of Heaven on the heels of evil men.

SECOND NARRATOR: Let them who died helplessly make stronger the arm of all those who fight. This is the message from the dead—avenge us.

FIRST NARRATOR: It is not a Jewish message.

SECOND NARRATOR: The massacre of two million Jews is not a Jewish situation.

FIRST NARRATOR: There are four million Jews surviving in Europe. The Germans have promised to deliver to the world by the end of the year a Christmas package of four million dead Jews. And this is not a Jewish problem.

SECOND NARRATOR: It is a problem that belongs to humanity. It is a challenge to the soul of man.

FIRST NARRATOR: In allowing the slaughter of four million helpless people in standing by without utterance, we who are the Four Freedoms of the world, become honorary members of the German Posse. Our silence is part of their massacre.

SECOND NARRATOR: The corpse of a people lies on the steps of civilization. Behold it. Here it is! And no voice is heard to cry halt to the slaughter, no government speaks to bid the murder of human millions to end.[9]

["This text was specially written for the Washington performance."][10]

FIRST NARRATOR: We, the actors who have performed for you tonight are nearly done. But there is another cast of actors involved in this tale whose performance is not done. This cast is our audience. Our audience tonight is a notable cast playing vital roles on the stage of history. It is to this audience more than to any group of human beings in the world that the dead and dying innocents of Europe raise their cry, "Remember Us." And tonight it is not as actors playing parts on a stage soon to be dismantled, but as the spokesmen of a people that

---

[9] At this point, the published version of the epilogue suffers from inconsistencies due to an effort to incorporate the speech Hecht wrote for the Washington, D.C. performance. Guided by the Los Angeles recording and Hecht's typescript drafts, I have slightly rearranged some of the published text here to avoid redundancy and to streamline, for the reader, the flow of the closing speeches and stage action. (The epilogue text on the Los Angeles recording features some further small revisions and additions not reflected here.)

[10] This note appears in the published text.

is being exterminated, that we stand before you—the official, the accredited, the elected makers of history. Two million Jews have been mercilessly destroyed in Europe. Four million surviving Jews are to be destroyed by Christmas according to the pronouncements of the German government. To utter these miserable words anywhere else in the world would be a cry for pity. To speak them here tonight is a summons to action.

SECOND NARRATOR: Better than we, our audience knows the two separate stories of Europe—the story of war and the story of massacre. It knows that as many defenseless men, women and children have been massacred by the Germans as have died on all the battle fronts. The story of the massacre that we have told tonight is incomplete. For we have spoken only of the Jews who lie dead on the steps of civilization. They occupy only part of the massacre ground. Beside them lie millions of Poles, Greeks, Jugoslavs, Czechs, Dutch, French, Norwegians, and others. But we have spoken only of the Jews because the killing of the Jews is a special challenge to history makers. Other peoples have been villainously slain by the Germans in the effort to reform them, subjugate them, silence them or frighten them. The Germans have no such program for the Jews. They desire neither their reform, nor subjugation. They desire only their extermination. Death to all Jews is their cry. And not only death but shame. They must die not as casualties of politics—but as scabrous and undesirable animals unrelated to the human family. The unarmed peoples of Europe have been villainously slain—but only that. The Jews have been not only villainously slain but robbed of their character. Slain and defiled, massacred and robbed of their epitaph as human beings—is the tale of their extermination.

FIRST NARRATOR: Who thus condemned the Jews? Who thus robbed an honorable people not only of life but of their fair name? Was it the Germans alone? It was the German who spoke and killed. But there are other ways of passing sentence than by speech and deed. There is the way of silence. As much by the silence of the world as by the howl of the posse has the Jew been condemned. The silence of our history makers has made them honorary members of the German posse.

SECOND NARRATOR: In this city[11], not far away, are the halls from which Justice has sounded her loudest battle cries, the chambers from which have issued man's noblest promises to tomorrow. Stranger than the mass murder of the civilian millions of Europe, is the silence of these halls today. Stranger than the brutality of the massacre is the quiet of its onlookers in these chambers.

---

[11] i.e., Washington, D.C.

## APPENDIX 1

**FIRST NARRATOR:** For we are more than a nation at war, more than an arsenal, more than a battle line. Above and beyond the valor of our working and fighting millions, America is a dream of justice, a light held aloft to the sacred ways of humanity. We have brave soldiers who are fighting to victory. But the massacre of the unarmed civilians is beyond the reach of their guns. The desert and the Mediterranean are their battle front and they are honorably engaged on it. The massacre of Europe is our battle front—and we are not honorably engaged on it.

**SECOND NARRATOR:** In the historic halls of this city[12] many great deeds and dreams have been forged. We ask that the silence of these halls be broken again. We ask for a second front against the crime of Europe, not a military front of soldiers, tanks and planes. But a second front of the human spirit against massacre. The crime of Europe calls for the mobilization of every shred of righteousness and spiritual power left in the world. On the field of battle soldiers die. On the field of massacre civilization dies. The thunder of civilization against the swamp-like antics of the German government is alone capable of stopping the German crime against life. Such a thunder unleashed by our own representatives and by all the nations that serve the cause of God would be more terrible than an army with banners. Such a moral thunder would strike terror into the souls of the German people.

**FIRST NARRATOR:** For they are people, human creatures, though they serve a vile master blindly. Though they obey his call to the murder of the innocents, they are still people. Steeped in blood, with the mark of Cain blazing from their brows, the obsessed and despairing and murderous Germans still belong to the human family. There are human laws and memories of human brotherhood buried under their blindness. The cry of an outraged humanity can reach them. Moral thunder can shatter the evil beyond the range of shell and flame. The Germans have been told by their masters that the slaughter of Jews is a mystic necessity. And they obey because they are Germans. They obey because the greater master voice of humanity is silent.

**SECOND NARRATOR:** Our valiant soldiers are using to the last ounce of their power the weapons given them. But we who hold the weapons of morality—the cry of wrath and outrage, the words of righteousness which more than armies have made the shape of the world—we do not use our weapons. We betray our victories by not winning them in the name of the decencies for which they are fought. The dead and dying who litter the steps of civilization

---

[12] i.e., Washington, D.C.

## WE WILL NEVER DIE

had only one cry—Remember us. Speak for us, they said, before you become too guilty in your silence even to mourn us. Speak for us and give not only the Jews, but mankind back its fair name.

[RABBI]:[13] The Jews have only one voice left to raise among the governments. It is an ancient voice. It is the voice of prayer, a prayer for their dead. It is the prayer called the Kaddish. It is the prayer spoken by hearts heavy with grief for the dead. But it does not speak of grief. It is the greatest poem of the Jewish soul. For in grief, however great, it affirms the glory of life, and blesses God. Let us sing this prayer for the voiceless and the Jewish dead of Europe.

Perhaps the dead will hear it and find comfort. Perhaps the dying will hear it and find hope. Perhaps the Four Freedoms will hear it and find their tongue.

(*Music starts and the* CANTORS *come upon the stage. Led by their* FIRST CANTOR *they sing the prayer for the dead.*)[14]

(*As the singing of the Kaddish continues, the Dead move slowly back through the lighted space between the Tablets and the stage darkens.*)[15]

---

[13] This text of the closing speech is transcribed from the Los Angeles recording. While the published script assigns it to the First Narrator, it is Jacob Ben-Ami's voice on the recording, indicating that the "Rabbi" from the opening scene reappeared to introduce the Kaddish prayer.

[14] Final stage direction from the published text.

[15] Final stage direction from Hecht's typescript for the New York performance. *We Will Never Die* typescript, Ben Hecht Papers, Newberry Library.

# Appendix 2
# *A Jewish Fairy Tale (1944)*

## PRODUCTION INFORMATION
### WRITTEN BY BEN HECHT
### DIRECTED BY STELLA ADLER
### MUSIC BY SHOLOM SECUNDA

First Performance: December 4, 1944. Carnegie Hall, New York

New York Cast:

NARRATOR: Ben Hecht
TEVYA: Luther Adler
GOD: Ralph Bellamy

**Second performance: February 8, 1945. Academy of Music, Philadelphia**

Philadelphia Cast:

NARRATOR: Ruth Chatterton
TEVYA: Luther Adler
GOD: John [aka Barry] Thompson

Source: Ben Hecht, *A Jewish Fairy Tale* typescript, Palestine Statehood Committee Papers, MS 690, Series III, Manuscripts and Archives, Yale University Library.

APPENDIX 2

# A JEWISH FAIRY TALE

(*Music plays. The* NARRATOR *speaks.*)

NARRATOR: Once upon a time—

This being a fairy tale, we begin with that happy childhood phrase "Once Upon a Time." And we signal by those words that we are going to tell about something that never happened.

Children love to hear stories about things that never happened. And so do Jews. For such stories are usually an improvement on reality. It is for this reason, perhaps, that Jews have been always so eager to listen to fairy tales—beginning with the beaming anecdote about a wondrous God who loved them above all His other children . . . and spent all His Heavenly time watching out for them and hurling thunderbolts at their enemies.

We may be entirely wrong about that anecdote being a fairy tale. It may well be a true story—that story about the wondrous God adored by the Jews. It may well be true that He adores them back and is full of a special interest in all their doings and sayings. If so, there is no great harm done in our calling it a fairy tale, for God has survived many misconceptions of who and what He is and How and Why He works. And if He is really full of devotion for the well being of His special children, the Jews, we ask Him humbly to overlook this little fairy tale—in which He, the Almighty, is also one of the principal characters. And we ask Him please to pay no attention to what we few Jews are saying here tonight—but to listen to the many Jews elsewhere. . . . in their synagogues and kitchens and concentration camps—all singing His praises nobly and a little patiently. And despite all their woes and bewilderment, all adoring Him as their merciful Father. Yes, let Him listen to these and not to us. Although it would be a typical turn in Jewish diplomacy if on this night, God heard not a single Jewish voice rising from the dark and smoking earth, but ours.

Nevertheless, despite such an unfortunate prospect, we will continue with our fairy tale, trusting in the wisdom of God to ignore us. And if He hears us, to chuckle a little over the childlike ignorance which animates all critics of Higher Things.

So we say—once upon a time—once upon a time there was a dead Jew by the name of Tevya who sat on a cloud and hummed to himself as he drifted slowly on his last journey toward the gates of Heaven and the Almighty God waiting to receive him.

We will take you now to this dead Jew afloat on his cloud and talking a little wistfully to himself as he travels upward among the stars. Come in, Tevya from Lublin.

## A JEWISH FAIRY TALE

(*The music softens and changes to a folk song and* TEVYA *speaks.*)

TEVYA: Ah, it's nice air. A pleasure to breathe. No dust, no smoke. Nothing but fine air. A man could be happy all his life just breathing this kind of air. What more does he need? Clean air to breathe and nobody to bother him. So why do I keep worrying about something? What is there to worry about? I feel good. Nothing hurts me. I am riding on a fine cloud. And, everything considered, it's altogether a fine thing to be going at last to Heaven. And to see God and find out what is the meaning of everything. Why He made Jews and Gentiles. Why he sends a wind to blow down houses. Why there are so many people who have to go without shoes. And if it is true that a piece of bread brought into a room by a mouse on the Passover makes the whole house trafe and we must clean everything from top to bottom again. I will find everything out and become wiser than the biggest and holiest rabbi. So what is there to worry about? That I was once alive? But when a thing is over, it is foolish to keep worrying about it. It stands in the Holy Book, a man is only for tomorrow. All right, so I was once alive! Do I have to keep remembering it? No? It is ungrateful to God to remember the little time I was separated from him. After all, how long was it? A few hours. Maybe, as they count time in Heaven, only a few seconds.

NARRATOR: Tevya, the dead Jew, closed his eyes, took a few happy breaths and murmured Shmai Israel and fell asleep, for he was very tired. And while he slept, the cloud on which he lay stood still and advanced not an inch toward the Gates of Heaven. Tevya was unaware of this curious traffic law for travelers between earth and the Pearly Gates—or he would never have taken a nap. For Tevya had always been a very fine character who obeyed all the laws he ever heard of, the laws of God, the laws of men, the laws of friends, the laws of foes. Obeying laws, in fact, had taken up so much of Tevya's time and energies while he was alive, that there had been little left in him for other accomplishments. Which might explain why Tevya had finally died naked, without a rag on his back—and standing up in a lime pit full of burning lime—with ten thousand Jews standing crowded in the same lime pit and all burning with him.

But now Tevya is awake on his cloud again. Awake and talking softly to himself. We take you once more to the interstellar spaces. Come in Tevya, from Lublin.

TEVYA: Why do I keep worrying about something—when I don't even know what it is. Who knows, maybe I am worried because the trip is taking so long. Tevya, you are a king of fools, to even think about such a thing. All right, when you died you didn't jump right away into Heaven like an acrobat. After all it is not the same as catching a train from Warsaw to Lublin. It stands in the Holy Book that the soul of man ascends to God when he dies. But there is no time table that says how fast it goes or how slow.

NARRATOR: And Tevya looked out on the starry wastes about him and fell to repeating softly the prayers he knew so well. There is nothing like a good familiar prayer to make a journey seem shorter—even a journey into heaven. But even while he prayed, the mind of Tevya remained full of thoughts that had nothing to do with praying. We will take you to some of them. Come in, Tevya from Lublin.

TEVYA: I am sure the trip is taking a little extra time because God has figured out that I have a lot of things to forget. The Almighty doesn't want somebody to come hollering into Heaven with all his troubles hot on his tongue. How they killed us. How they burned us. How they butchered the little ones, the old ones. What kind of talk is that to bring into Heaven? So God has figured out, we will give Tevya a little more time, to cool off in the nice air outside of Heaven. And I don't blame Him. It's much better for everybody, if I arrive relaxed, rested, and remembering nothing of what happened down below. A black plague on the world—who wants to remember it? But how I am going to forget—this is something which God will have to arrange. All I can do is tell Him I am willing to forget—and I will be just as satisfied to arrive in Heaven without knowing even that my name was Tevya, or where I came from or why I came from there.

Yes, Almighty God, I am willing to forget and come into Heaven like a happy guest, singing, and with a smile on my face like a little boy. Only You must help me a little. That is, of course, if You want to.

NARRATOR: And now the air around Tevya grew brighter and the odors of bliss began to come into his nose. And Tevya stopped thinking altogether, for it is a waste of time for a man to think when he can see and smell the presence of God.

A great happiness filled Tevya—a happiness that reminded him of a day long ago when he was young and had walked with beating heart to his marriage hour.

And it seemed to Tevya that there were fiddles playing and voices singing again, as on that other happy day. But he couldn't make out whether he was dreaming these things or actually hearing them—so lifted was his heart and so eager did his soul strain to place itself in the palm of God.

And now there is no mistake about it. Whatever doubts Tevya may have had about this journey on the cloud—here was Heaven! Actually Heaven! Radiant as all the pages of the Torah and abloom like all the dreams of Abraham. And there was music and there were voices singing hallelujahs and the stars themselves were playing as if they were guitars.

Tevya sat up on his cloud and looked and despite all he could do he began to cry like a child—tears of gladness that ran down his beard—where other tears had once been. And then, above the beautiful music, a Voice called. And Tevya heard his name and knew Who it was that spoke it.

The Almighty God was summoning little Tevya from Lublin. Come in, God.

GOD: Tevya! Tevya. Step from your cloud, Tevya, and come forward to Me. I am waiting for you, Tevya.

NARRATOR: And Tevya stepped from his cloud, his mouth open wide enough with joy to swallow all of Heaven. And with his head thrown back and words of adoration and thanksgiving pouring from his throat, Tevya moved toward the presence of God. Come in, Tevya.

TEVYA: Oh Lord, our God—Ruler of the Universe . . . Blessed art Thou. Forgive me for worrying. Blessed art Thou who raisest up those who are bowed down. There was nothing to worry about. I can see now! Blessed art Thou, oh Holy Lord, who clothest the naked. Oh Ruler of the Universe who guidest the steps of man. Such clean air. Such beautiful music. Blessed art Thou, oh Almighty God who crownest Israel with glory. Oh, Lord, my soul is filled with love for your goodness and I am prostrate before your sweetness and mercy and all my days are like unto dust blown away by the radiance of your smile. I don't see a gentile anywhere, O Ruler of the Universe, the song of your spirit is like a thunder in my ears. Revered and loved is thy name, hallowed by thy Goodness and Mercy forever.

NARRATOR: And as Tevya continued his rejoicing before the Almighty, a silence fell around him. The angel voices stopped their singing and the guitars of Heaven ceased their celestial strumming. And Tevya in the midst of his transports and exultations became aware of something a little worrisome. He looked nervously around him. Why should the singing stop? Why should everybody be frowning? But despite his new worries, prayers and jubilations fit for the occasion continued to pour from Tevya—until Gud spoke. Come in, O Ruler of the Universe.

GOD: That's enough, Tevya. I have something to say to you.

NARRATOR: The ominous note in the Almighty's voice froze Tevya's soul into silence and he stood gaping—with the holy words of thanksgiving still crowding his tongue. But a command from God is not a thing to be disobeyed—particularly in Heaven. And Tevya closes his mouth as one might dam up a river in flood. Whereupon God speaks.

## APPENDIX 2

GOD: You stand before the Bar of Judgment, Tevya!

TEVYA (*Exultantly*): Glory Be to Israel!

GOD (*Sternly*): Tevya, you have displeased me. You have angered me. You have made My face dark against you!

TEVYA: Forgive me, blessed Ruler of the Universe. Forgive my sins which are many as the trees in the wilderness. Shed thy mercy on me, oh Father—

NARRATOR: Tevya has a solution for all crises. You pray to God. And God hears—and answers.

GOD: Shame on you, Tevya, to come here singing and chanting My name—with a crime on your hands.

(*The Music swells—Pause.*)

NARRATOR: Pardon us. . . . for the delay. We cannot pick up Tevya's answer . . . unless Tevya has been stricken dumb—which is possible. Louder, Tevya! Ah—there is a faint sound—such as the ghost of Tevya might make if it sighed loud enough to be heard from beyond the clouds. Say something we can hear, Tevya! Come in, Tevya from Lublin. Come in! Come in!

(*Music swells—a Pause.*)

We are sure Tevya will speak up in a moment. For a Jew has always his voice . . . It can't be possible that he would lose it in Heaven—that voice of lamentation and laughter . . . Ah—God has the podium . . .

GOD: . . . crime on your hands. . . . great crime. . . . bloody crime on your hands . . . Tevya—Tevya from Lublin—somebody has been killed.

TEVYA (*Faintly*): Ai-ai, somebody has been killed . . .

NARRATOR: Oho—that was Tevya finding his voice. And now Tevya 's heart is heavy with this last disaster—God's anger. His soul is in the dust. His entrails—his ghostly entrails—are burning again as they burned in the cremation furnace.

Opening one eye, Tevya looks for the first time at God and is surprised to see that God is smoking a big cigar and wears a yachting cap. But Tevya puts this down to the confusion of his senses at the moment. He remembers it is written no man can see God plainly, but only through the many veils of ignorance. And Tevya closes his eye again as God speaks.

GOD: Tevya, an Englishman has been killed.

TEVYA (*Softly*): An Englishman . . .

GOD (*Sternly*): An Englishman has been killed—and I don't like it.

TEVYA (*A little more voice*): An Englishman? I don't remember, O Blessed Ruler of the Universe. Did he live in Pogulanki Street, maybe? Was his name Itzikle? Lezerel? Jozefle? There were lots of fine people killed—all from different lands. Cremated. Three million of them. All good Jews . . .

GOD: Not Itzikle or Lezerel or Jozefle. The name of the Englishman who was foully done to death—was a finer name.

TEVYA: Forgive me, O Blessed Lord, there are good names and bad names—I know. Haman as a bad name and Nebuchadnezzar, also. Because they did evil to the Jews. One was hanged and the other went crazy. But that was long ago, of course. Things change. Everything changes. Everything—but Jews . . .

GOD: Quiet, Tevya. You are not here to chatter. The name of the Englishman who was foully done to death was—Lord Moyne.

TEVYA (*Interested*): Lord Moisha.

GOD: Not Lord Moisha. Lord Moyne.

TEVYA (*Sad and very weary*): He was killed someplace?

GOD: Lord Moyne was foully done to death—by assassins.

TEVYA: Excuse me, O Light of the Universe, I am an ignorant man. When I was on earth I knew nothing. In Heaven I know less. But I am very willing to learn. I am sorry to say I don't know who is this specialist—this Englishman? I am a Jew from the cremation furnace—if you will forgive me mentioning it again—from Lublin.

GOD: Lord Moyne was His Britannic Majesty's Secretary of State for the Colonies in the years 1941 and 1942 . . .

TEVYA (*Sadly*): Ah yes—yes. Those years are very familiar to me, O God who raiseth the weak. Only I didn't know you would care to have me talk about them. On the cloud coming here I was trying my best to forget. The years when the massacres began. Black years! Poisonous years! May they rot in a special Hell forever—pooh! Amen!

GOD: I am waiting for an entirely different attitude from you. I am waiting for repentance for your shameful deed—your crime in Palestine.

TEVYA (*Confused*): Crime in Palestine? You mean when Solomon married the Egyptian Queen? No . . . Then it must be when David betrayed Uriah, the Hittite. No—wait a minute. My crime! Egyptian queens I never saw. Or even a Hittite. Something else. Oh! Oh forgive me, Glory of Israel, for not understanding. Now I see. I see you are angry with me because I didn't go to Palestine before I died. But how could I? Please—I am not arguing. Who argues with God? Not Tevya. It stands in the Talmudic writings that every honorable Jew must go finally to Palestine and sing Your praises before he dies. And I did not go. Nobody went. Forgive us all, O Merciful Almighty—we sang them in the furnace.

GOD: Tevya, your furnace arias are beside the point. Jewish immigration into Palestine was pronounced by Lord Moyne in 1942 to be a disastrous mistake. The gates of Palestine were closed against all Jews—by British policy. Is that clear, Tevya?

## APPENDIX 2

TEVYA: Clear, clear. Plain as day, O Light of Israel. You don't have to explain more, I know it is no excuse that our enemies prevented us from going to Palestine. Oh God of Goodness, believe me, we wanted to go. Itzikle, Lezerel, Shmarya, Avrom . . . But what am I talking about! Everybody wanted to go to the Promised Land.

GOD: Tevya—you are before the Bar of Judgment. This is no place to talk politics.

TEVYA: Forgive me, O blessed Father, I am not intending to talk politics. Who cares about politics? They wanted to go to the Promised Land for practical reasons. They wanted to go better than to stay at home and be massacred. O glory of Israel. There were many of us. I am not an engineer but I should say two million. Two million Jews who wanted with all of their hearts to go to Jerusalem. We did everything. We gave bribes. We hid in the forests. We sent letters. We hollered on the radio. We prayed—all the time. Very loud. But nothing came of it—if you don't mind my saying so. O Blessed Lord of Israel—our enemies locked the doors of Palestine. Not the Germans or the Hungarians. But other enemies.

GOD (*Loudly*): Quiet, Tevya!

TEVYA (*Eagerly*): Who can keep quiet about such a thing, O Blessed Lord. I am telling You, O Light of Israel, our enemies locked the doors of Palestine. And the Jews who got as far as the Holy shores were sent back to drown in the sea and to burn in the furnaces . . . hundreds of thousands of them.

NARRATOR: God has been paying no attention to these distracted utterances from Tevya. The Almighty stands frowning into space and chewing on his cigar, a sign that His anger is rising. And he gestures to the Heavenly scribes to strike Tevya's remarks out of the Book of Fate, which bears the curious title 10 Downing Street. And now a stern light fills the eyes of the Almighty and His righteous voice thunders in the Heavens.

GOD: Your wily answers to my charge displease me, Tevya. As you know, I have always been a great friend of all the Jews.

TEVYA (*Happily*): Hallowed be thy name!

GOD: Do I need to remind you how I have labored for the Jews and always planned to make them happy—at the proper time . . . when other business was not occupying my attention too much?

TEVYA: O Blessed Father, we have sung Your praises—while we waited.

GOD: Do not stand now before the Bar of Judgment and try to confuse the issue. The issue is—how have you rewarded my tireless friendship—my dream of Zionism? By producing a new set of gangsters worthy of Nazi Germany . . . By killing an Englishman. By foully doing to death my friend—Lord Moyne.

TEVYA: Me!

GOD: You!

TEVYA: I killed him!

GOD: You, Tevya—the Jew.

TEVYA: Blessed God of Justice, forgive me for even speaking like this—in Heaven where everything is known—even when a sparrow is missing . . . but some kind of a mistake is going on. I swear on the head of my Channah—wherever it is—I killed no one.

GOD: You refuse, Tevya, to accept the responsibility?

TEVYA: What responsibility? O Father in Heaven.

GOD: You refuse to confess your guilt, Tevya!

TEVYA: My guilt! What kind of guilt? If I am guilty, I am guilty. Only what about, O King of the Heavens.

GOD: Lord Moyne was foully done to death by a Jew—two Jews. Maybe three. I find it necessary to the architecture of the Jewish future that all Jews should feel guilty. I find it necessary to the architecture of the Jewish future that all Jews must be punished for what these three Jews have done. Maybe four. Do you understand, Tevya?

TEVYA: Yes—yes—the Jews must stick together . . . O Light of Israel, I understand we are all guilty together—When a Jew does good he does good by himself. But when he does something wrong—we all join him.

GOD: Here is my pronouncement, Tevya . . . All Jews, dead or alive must beat their bosoms and cry shame on themselves.

TEVYA: Shame on me, O Father of Justice, shame on me!

GOD: Lord Moyne was my dear friend.

TEVYA: A black year on me, O Glory of Israel.

GOD: He was a noble and fine gentleman who presided over Zone A of Palestine—the two percent of the Holy Land which I graciously allotted to the Jews.

TEVYA (*chanting*): Ungrateful Jews! Hallowed be thy two per cent, O God.

GOD: It was Lord Moyne who upheld my Word in Palestine . . . who saw to it that hordes of Jews did not pour into Zone A and offend my Colonial Office.

TEVYA: Forgive them, O merciful God. They were dreaming of a place beyond the cremation furnaces. I know. I sinned, too. I also dreamed of Palestine. Forgive me . . .

GOD: You are acquainted with My infinite wisdom and compassion, Tevya.

TEVYA (*Eagerly*): Yes, yes. The three million who were massacred died chanting Your glorious name. You must have heard them.

GOD: Yes, I heard them. And for that reason I am not ready to cast you out of heaven for your unholy crime of killing an Englishman. My mind has been darkened against you but I retain a lingering sentiment in your behalf.

## APPENDIX 2

TEVYA: O light of Israel!

GOD: I am going to give you a chance to win back My love.

TEVYA (*Sadly*): Ai-ai. My heart is filled with gratefulness . . . What do I have to do?

GOD: I am sending you back to earth as My messenger . . . as a Savior for the Jews.

TEVYA: Another one!

GOD: Are you prepared to carry My message to the Jews, Tevya?

TEVYA: If there are any left alive when I get back, O Glorious Father, I will give them Your message.

GOD: Here are My words. The Jews must enter their synagogues and pray to Me to forgive them.

TEVYA: They have no synagogues left, O Glory of Israel. They have been destroyed.

GOD: This must not stop them. Then they must pray in the streets, in the fields. On the beaches. They must pray that My heart will be softened toward them once more.

TEVYA: O Blessed Almighty I will tell them.

GOD: You will tell them that the cause of Israel has been set back another hundred years by this sin against an Englishman . . . That the foul assassination of Lord Moyne makes it impossible for me to love them—for another hundred years.

TEVYA: What are a hundred years? They have passed before. The Jews will rejoice to hear your Holy words . . .

GOD: Return to earth, then, and be My messenger . . .

NARRATOR: And Tevya stepped back on his cloud again, his face pale and his heart stricken. For the way of a Savior is never an easy one. And the cloud drifted back toward the earth, a little faster than it had left it. The sound of singing and the stars strumming faded out of Tevya's ears. And the air around him grew darker and the smell of dust, smoke and blood came into his nose again. And as he sped from Paradise burdened with the Message of the Almighty in the Yachting Cap, Tevya spoke softly to himself. Come in, Tevya—messenger from Heaven.

TEVYA: So what am I worrying about now? It's better to be a Messiah on earth than a Tevya in Heaven. Who can deny this?

NARRATOR: And Tevya sighs and starts praying—and talking to himself—both in one breath. Come in, Messiah Tevya . . .

TEVYA: Oh Glory of Israel who guides the steps of the Jews to their homeland, blessed be Thy name. Of course, I would have liked to bring back from the

## A JEWISH FAIRY TALE

Almighty a different kind of message to the Jews . . . maybe that He was a little sorry they had all been killed and that he was going to bring a black year on their enemies. Hallowed be His name, but why is He so excited about something else always? An Englishman—Lord Shmoyne—gets killed. And everybody has to put on a tallis and pray for a hundred years . . . O merciful light of the Universe, praised be Thy infinite Justice. So much excitement over one Englishman in Heaven, I didn't expect to find . . . More than over Channah and Lezerel and Itzikle and . . . but if I start worrying how will I be a good Messiah?

NARRATOR: The cloud on which Tevya was riding came close to the earth. And Tevya looked down on the land of Europe and saw the broken, empty shoes of his people. And he beheld Palestine for a moment and read the large sign that rises from its soil: "Jews Keep Out—by Order of Their Tireless Friend Winston Churchill." And his voice sounded again. Come in Tevya, Messenger from God.

TEVYA: God forgive me for this, but I keep worrying all the time. In the first place how can I be a good Messiah like God wants me to be when I feel so mixed up. I don't even know if I should cry or sing—with all the honor I got. Better if I stop thinking and start praying. Blessed be thou, O Merciful Almighty who loves an Englishman more than everybody put together—hallowed be thy name . . . On the other hand, how do I know it was God who spoke to me. A beard, he didn't have. And does it say anything in the Holy Books that God wears a cap? No, not one word. What if it wasn't God—but just somebody with a big cigar. Who maybe thinks he's god. Ai-ai. How can I ask such a question. If He isn't God, then who is God? And if I wasn't in Heaven, then where is Heaven? What is there to worry about? He talked in a fine, loud voice and He is mad at the Jews. Not a few Jews here, a few Jews there. But all the Jews. They must suffer together. Put on a tallis and apologize because somebody else got killed—for a change. Tevya, you mustn't argue. This was God. And you must do what he says. God gave you a message to deliver to the Jews. Deliver it . . . no matter what's bothering you.

NARRATOR: Tevya leans over his cloud and looks down on the earth—and a wild light is in his eyes—as he calls out. Come in, Tevya, formerly of Lublin—and now messenger from Heaven.

TEVYA: Ai-ai, Jews. I am coming down now. Watch out for me. I am a savior—a messiah sent by the Almighty with a message for you—what you should do ai-ai—watch out for me, little Jews.

NARRATOR: We hope, good listeners, that our fairy tale has not carried too depressing a moral—and that it will not dissuade Jews from dying and going to

## APPENDIX 2

Heaven, which is their most cherished pastime. And, lest we have been misunderstood and offended the piety of honest folk, we humbly assure them that any resemblance between the character in our story called God and the true God who presides over the heavens, is purely coincidental. And we promise, too, that some day we will write another fairy tale that will end as such tales should—and so they were married and lived happily ever afterward. We will write this more pleasing fairy tale some day—when the flag of Zion is nailed high to some flagpole and the bedevilled soul of the Jew has been given back its good name.

# Appendix 3
# *A Flag Is Born (1946)*

[Editor's Note: As with *We Will Never Die*, Peter Bergson published the text of *A Flag Is Born* privately, in a limited edition. This text is taken directly from that version.]

PRODUCTION INFORMATION
WRITTEN BY BEN HECHT
DIRECTED BY LUTHER ADLER
MUSIC BY KURT WEILL
MUSICAL DIRECTION BY ISAAC VAN GROVE
SCENERY BY ROBERT DAVISON
COSTUMES BY JOHN BOYT
CHOREOGRAPHY BY ZAMIRA GON
IN CHARGE OF PRODUCTION    JULES J. LEVENTHAL

Source: Ben Hecht, *A Flag Is Born*. New York: American League for a Free Palestine, 1946.

## APPENDIX 3

Opening Night Cast:

SPEAKER: Quentin Reynolds
TEVYA: Paul Muni
ZELDA: Celia Adler
DAVID: Marlon Brando
THE SINGER: Mario Berini
SAUL: George: David Baxter
OLD ONE: Morris Samuylow
MIDDLE AGED ONE: David Manning
YOUNG ONE: John Baragrey
DAVID THE KING: William Allyn
SOLOMON: Gregory Morton
AMERICAN STATESMAN: Jonathan Harris
RUSSIAN STATESMAN: Yasha Rosenthal
1ST ENGLISH STATESMAN: Tom Emlyn Williams
2ND ENGLISH STATESMAN: Jefferson Coates
FRENCH STATESMAN: Frederick Rudin
1ST SOLDIER: Steven Hill
2ND SOLDIER: Jonathan Harris
3RD SOLDIER: Harold Gary
SUPERNUMERARIES: William Berg, Randolph Jones, Nick Ferber, Jack Wesley, Allen Lindstrom, Vincent Beck, Jo Davidson, Charles Feurman, George Anderson, Martin Leavitt, Solomon Goldstein, Jack Sloane, Harry Moses, Gilbert Leigh, Jack Buxbaum, Jim Flynn, Norman Kilroy, Jules Preuss, Thomas Arena, Rudolph McKool, Joe Bernard, Daniel Moskowitz, Carl Shelton, Robert Weston, Bill Reid, Ray Johnson, Jim Davidson, Pearl Sugerman, Natalie Norwick, Rona Christie, Selma Stern, Michael Kazaras, Terry Becker, Paul Firestone. Peggy Strange, Steve Gravers, Don Sacks, Eileen Ayres
DANCERS: Evangeline Collis, Anne Wayne, Lilian Ekman, Evelyn Leeds, Anne Widman, Ruth Harris, Audrey Eden, Pearl Borchard, Lee Morrison, Lilian Fisher. Maybelle Lama, Sophia Babert, Virginia Gilchrist, Shirley King, Rosalind Posnick, Jeanne Belkin, Miriam Levy
CHOIR: Paul Mario, Elton Plowman, Joseph Hill, William Durkin, Carl Manning, Allen Lowell, Nicholas Torza, Richard Monte
PERFORMANCE HISTORY
NEW YORK:
Alvin Theatre (September 5, 1946–October 5, 1946)
Adelphi Theatre (October 7, 1946–October 19, 1946)

Music Box Theatre (October 21, 1946–November 16, 1946)
Broadway Theatre (November 18, 1946–December 14, 1946)
NATIONAL TOUR:
CHICAGO: Studebaker Theater (December 26, 1946–January 18, 1947)
DETROIT: Shubert-Lafayette Theater (January 20, 1947–January 25, 1947)
PHILADELPHIA: Erlanger Theatre (January 28, 1947–February 8, 1947)
BALTIMORE: Maryland Theater (February 10, 1947–February 16, 1947)
BOSTON: Center Theatre (February 18, 1947–February 23, 1947)

# A FLAG IS BORN

(*At the stage right, in front of the closed curtain is a* SPEAKER's *stand.*
*The orchestra is in the pit.*
*The overture plays as the lights come up dimly on the closed curtain. The music is wild, bold.*
*It cries out as if a world of torment and exultation were waiting behind the closed curtain. The music grows softer and continues to sound softly behind the words of the* SPEAKER.
*The* SPEAKER *appears and the stand is illumined. The curtain remains closed as he speaks.*)
SPEAKER: This is a tale of a world that has disappeared. It was a little world full of poverty and prayer, full of rueful gaiety and an innocent goodness. It was a world of ghettos and synagogues, of little schools and old leather books, of remembered glories and unpainted villages. On the Sabbath Eve, this little world lit its candles across the land of Europe. In the light of its countless candles, old legends breathed again and old hopes decked themselves out in the white shawls of prayer. This world of Jews—so old, so wise, so harmless—was famed for a single export—greatness. Out of its crooked little streets came scholars and heroes. Poets and philosophers and scientists and great nabobs of industry came without end from its unknown and shambling highways. But none of the greatness it exported ever built fine towers for the little world out of which it came. None of the riches it put forth ever enriched its own little battered streets. It was a magic world—this world that bore the name Jew—flooding the earth forever with greatness and riches and remaining itself forever poor and little and without power.

And remaining forever without friends.

This world of the Jew that had poured its genius and greatness into all cups but its own was, in the hour of its doom, without friends. No friends

## APPENDIX 3

spoke out when its death notice was posted. When its death was decreed, the death of all its streets and houses and people—there were no friends on earth or miracles in heaven to stay destruction. Furtively the governments of the earth kept their silence as a merry and pious little world of Jews was removed from history. Out of his burning houses, out of his crematoriums and lime pits, the Jew of Europe looked on a murderer called the German. But beyond this murder face of the German were other nation-faces to be seen—dim and watchful faces whose silence was a brother of murder. And when the Jew of Europe died, when the six millions were murdered in the furnaces and gas chambers of the German, these cries were in their throats—"Where is Humanity? Where is the goodness of man that we helped create? Where are my friends?"

Nowhere, little vanished Jew. Nowhere, little murdered world—they were nowhere . . . They were busy with other things, little psalm-singer—they were busy with other things.

But all this is known. There is no need to dwell on the whys and wherefores of it. History will sum up the tale someday. And people will read it plainly. History will say, "of all the things that happened in that time—our time—the slaughter of the Jews of Europe was the only thing that counted forever in the annals of man. The proud orations of heroes and conquerors will be a footnote in history beside the great silence that watched this slaughter."

Yes, in the history books it will not be victories—it will be this silence that identifies and condemns our era.

And so it came to pass—we can say in the interests of brevity—and so it came to pass that a world was killed and all its faces and altars, all its kitchens and shops and songs and memories—removed from the earth. The Jew of Europe was hunted into every corner of that land and killed. That is the prologue of our tale. And thus ends the prologue.

(*The* SPEAKER *is silent. The curtain rises. The scene is a graveyard at night. A dark and clouded sky hangs eerily over it. It is a battered graveyard. Only three dead trees stand upright in it. The crumbled wall of the graveyard is visible, most of its stones strewn on the ground.*

*Beyond it can be seen the dirt road that skirts the graveyard.*

*To the stage left is an iron gate twisted and rusted—One of its doors is missing.*

*In the graveyard there are three tombstones. Two of them are tumbled. The third is still erect, although it seems to be tottering. It is a stone five feet high, in front of it is a raised grave covered with a slab of stone.*

*The music swells as the wind whistles through the graveyard. The moon comes out of a cloud and slowly its light illumines the standing tombstone. The music dims and the* SPEAKER *resumes.*)

SPEAKER: This is the scene of our tale. It is a graveyard, a woebegone graveyard that has seen better days. Where is this graveyard—in what land does it greet the pale moon? In a faraway land—in a part of the earth where Jews once lived and live no more.

(*Beyond the broken graveyard wall a man and woman appear. As the* SPEAKER *continues the figures move slowly across the back of the graveyard. They are visible through the broken wall.*

*The man carries a small pack slung over one shoulder. The two figures arrive at the twisted iron gate. Here the light is stronger and we see the faces of* TEVYA *and his wife* ZELDA. TEVYA—*bearded gaunt, fevered, and with more death in him than life;* ZELDA *whose fifty-five years have the look of fifty-five centuries. They enter the graveyard,* ZELDA *leading the way. They move with the quiet rhythm of exhaustion. When they come to the tombstone,* TEVYA *removes his pack and puts it on the slab.* ZELDA *sits down in weariness.* TEVYA, *whose weariness is as great, remains standing. The music continues—softly as the* SPEAKER *talks—through their entrance.*)

SPEAKER: Beyond this shambles of a graveyard two figures are moving down a dark road. Two Jews, two remnant Jews of Europe plod slowly the dark night. Their feet drag, for they carry a heavy burden. Their hearts are like stones that read, "a dead world lies here."

They move in a world without streets or faces. They are moving toward a land of love, of milk and honey, of holy songs—called Palestine. Where is Palestine? Which way does it lie? God only knows. To the south—to the south—the fair land where the lemon trees bloom lies to the south . . . the bright land where God sits in a tabernacle calling his children back.

Eretz Yisrael—Yirushalayim—these are the two words left in the dark night. All the other words are dead. The two Jews on the dark road beyond the graveyard move wearily in the night—toward the two words.

The great world is busy with many projects. The continent of Europe echoes with the tumult and wail of a rebirth. New businesses are being launched, new dreams are hatching in the debris of cities. But these are not for the two Jews wandering the dark night with the spark of Eretz Yisrael in their lame bodies.

Does one open a shop under the gallows where one's father was hanged? Does one return to picnic near the lime pit where one's children were slain?

## APPENDIX 3

Europe is a gallows and a lime pit to these two who wander southward in the dark. There is no doorstep in Europe on which to sit. Out of every window of Europe looks a murderer. There are dead people under every road of Europe—dead Jews—moaning to Jewish feet, "Fly, fly." There are Jewish infants and grandmothers wailing out of all the brooks and rivers of Europe, "Fly. Fly." The word Europe falls like a whip on the shoulders of the two who move in the night—and a voice still echoes out of the seven years of dying—"begone—begone . . ."

(*The* SPEAKER *finishes and the music changes. A Jewish folk melody plays faintly and sadly.* TEVYA *sits down.* ZELDA *talks.*)

ZELDA: Nu, Columbus—you're satisfied? Eretz Yisrael he's going to find! This Sampson without eyes, this little piece of a Jew is going to lead us to the Holy Land of Palestine.

(*She sighs and life seems to ebb out of her.* TEVYA *stands staring and silent.* ZELDA *resumes.*)

Do you know where we are, Tevya? Do you know even in which world we sit—in this world or the other world? Nu, which way do we go now, Tevya? Choochem point me out again—where are the Cedars of Lebanon and the fountains with honey.

(*She coughs and her body writhes with pain.* TEVYA *watches her.*)

TEVYA (*when the coughing is done*): Shh . . . Zelda—you get tired from talking.

ZELDA (*wearily*): From living, Tevya, I am tired. Tired of the day and the night. Ai, my sons and daughters—what is left without them? Two old worms that turn round and round in the night—looking for the Holy Land.

(*She wails at him.*)

Tevya, where are we?

TEVYA: We are in some kind of a park. Sit still and enjoy yourself.

ZELDA (*looking around—and seeing the tombstone behind her*): A park? I can see what kind of a park, a Tevya park—where everybody comes to have a fine time—six feet underground. A graveyard, he calls a park.

TEVYA: A graveyard is the same on top—as a park.

ZELDA: Why don't you ask them—the right road to Palestine?

TEVYA (*looking around*): Who should I ask, Zelda?

ZELDA: The people in the park, Tevya. Lie down on the earth and call down to them—how to go—which way to turn?

TEVYA (*looking at the tombstone, as he half chants*): We will come to Yerushalayim. The Red Sea will open and Tevya and Zelda will walk into the Holy Land and Bevin and Churchill and all the ballabatim will be drowned in the water.

ZELDA (*TEVYA is now peering at the tombstone*): If somebody is going to be drowned, Tevya, I know who it is.

TEVYA: Maybe a Jew lies here.

ZELDA: If it's a grave—a Jew lies there—you don't have to worry.

TEVYA: I remember the grave of Reb Zundel. On his grave it was written what a fine man he was and how he dreamed to go to Palestine before he died.

ZELDA: Ai, a good thing he didn't get started like us.

(*She sighs heavily.*)

Tevya, I don't like it here.

TEVYA: It's not so bad, Zelda. In a graveyard, a good Jew is among friends.

ZELDA (*looking up at him*): Come sit by me, I don't feel so good.

TEVYA: Ai, look—what I found here. The Star of David—here on the stone. It's a Jewish stone. Now I can feel proud to sit here. Some people have government buildings, the Jews have stones in a graveyard—with fine writing on them.

(*He sits beside her.*)

Wait, Zelda, wait till you see in Palestine the writing on the stones. Here lies Abraham—and Saul, too—and David, the King. Abraham—there was a fine man for you—who never did wrong—who brought his whole family with all his cows and sheep to Eretz Yisrael—walking in a warm cloak under the stars—because God told him which way to go, which way to turn, which was the right river to cross, which was the wrong river—

(*His voice becomes a chant.*)

If God will tell me, I will go the right way. I will go like Abraham into Eretz Yisrael, only without my cows or sheep, without my sons and daughters. (*His voice breaks and the rest of the speech is spoken.*) You know where they are, God—close to you in Heaven by your right hand. Only Tevya is left. Tevya and Zelda. I am not asking for many things—like we used to ask in the old days—give us health, give us our daughters should marry good, give us three days of rain for the pasture. Who has daughters now—and pastures? No, nothing I ask now—except, where is it? Which way? Right? Left? Backwards? Forwards? It's easy for You to see from up there. Just point with something—a star—the way to Palestine—Yerushalayim—the land of milk and honey.

ZELDA (*staring in the shadows*): Tevya! Somebody is here!

TEVYA (*turning to her, his voice perplexed*): It can't be an answer. God don't answer so quick, as a rule. It must be somebody else.

(*They look together into the darkness of the graveyard.* ZELDA *holds weakly to his arm. A youth of eighteen has risen from the ground. He comes slowly*

# APPENDIX 3

*toward them. He wears dungarees, a black turtle-necked sweater, a torn cap and shoes. He is gaunt and grim looking. He has the cold look of a lord high executioner. His eighteen years wear a face that has sat in judgment on life and condemned it.)*

TEVYA (*nervously*): You are a Jew?

ZELDA (*clinging to him and whispering*): Ask him first if he is alive or dead.

TEVYA: I know what to ask. If he's a Jew—then dead or alive he is our friend.

YOUTH (*his voice is flat and cold*): I'm your friend.

TEVYA: I am Tevya from Dubinky and this is my wife, Zelda.

*(He pauses and continues nervously.)*

We are resting here—a few hours only—

*(He pauses, then asks shyly)*

Do you belong in this place?

YOUTH: I was sleeping here.

TEVYA (*nervously*): On top—or underneath?

YOUTH: I'm alive—I can still smell the night and see the stars shining. My bones can still move from place to place. I am a very rare type—a young Jew still alive in Europe.

*(The youth scowls.)*

I heard you praying before. I don't like to hear a man praying. I heard prayers in Treblinka.

ZELDA (*wailing*): Treblinka! Treblinka . . . Ai—my sons and daughters—

YOUTH (*coldly*): Did they die in Treblinka, mama?

*(TEVYA and ZELDA cover their faces with their hands.)*

Maybe I saw them. I saw a million Jews die. I used to hide in a tree at night and count them—when they were walking naked—two by two—to the furnaces. And praying.

*(His voice grows mocking as he chants the prayer.)*

Shmai Yisrael, Adonai Elahanu—

*(TEVYA picks up the prayer and continues it, mumbling the words. ZELDA holds her hands over her face. The youth listens to TEVYA for a moment and then continues coldly.)*

My father's God suffered a great misfortune. The earth was His face—but vermin overran it and ate out its eyes, so He couldn't see. One doesn't pray to such a God. One pities Him. And tries to forget Him—like a poor relation. My name is David. I came to the graveyard this afternoon to rest because I have a long way to go.

TEVYA: A long way? Where do you go, David?

DAVID: To Palestine.

TEVYA (*eagerly*): You are going there—to Eretz Yisrael?
DAVID: Yes. The English have forbidden it. The English have put a fence round Palestine. But there are three things that the English fence can't keep out of Palestine—rain, the wind, and a Jew . . .
TEVYA: Zelda, we are saved! I asked God to point and he sends somebody to point for Him.

(*He beams at the youth.*)

Nu—Duvidel—which way. Point the way for us. Talk, Duvidel, which way is it to Eretz Yisrael?

(*A change comes over the youth,* DAVID. *His eyes turn to the shadows in the graveyard. He stares and his voice grows dreamy as he answers.*)

DAVID: Over the bridge.
TEVYA: What bridge! Where's there a bridge?
DAVID (*staring and dreamily*): The bridge is there.
TEVYA (*looking*): Where do you see a bridge, Duvidel?
DAVID (*dreamily*): There—
TEVYA: Don't make fun of us. We are old and sick. Since yesterday my head turning around and around.

(*He moves appealingly to the youth.*)

Duvidel, there's no bridge here. If there was a bridge there would be a river. And if there was a river there wouldn't be a graveyard. So how can there be a bridge?

DAVID (*still staring and dreamy*): It leads to Palestine—the bridge. I saw it when I was sleeping.
TEVYA (*sighs heavily with crushed hopes*): Ai, I thought maybe God had heard me. But why should He hear me, all of a sudden. In Treblinka I talked louder—and who heard?
DAVID (*his voice flat and cold again*): Jewish prayers can't get to God, Teyya, without an English visa. This is the new law. Yesterday our prayers needed a German visa. And the day before yesterday they required a Spanish visa. You see, our trouble is, Teyya, we have been praying in the wrong countries. When I was a boy in Hebrew school I didn't know this. My father taught me that I belonged in the land where I was born; Then, one day, all the Jews in that land were gathered together like a pile of garbage and burned up. From this I learned that the teachings of my father were wrong. Now the English say to me, "Come, go back to your father's village—and start over again and breed another garbage pile for Europe." And I answered them, "A curse on all the lands and villages of Europe. I go to find a corner of the earth where Jews do not turn into garbage—where Jews can die on a battlefield—instead of in a

## APPENDIX 3

crematorium. On their own battlefield, for a change. I go to Palestine—over the bridge.

(*He stops and stands looking tensely again into the shadows. The Marching Theme that played under his talk changes to a folk song accompaniment.* TEVYA *sits, head bowed on the gravestone. There is silence as the folk music swells—and then dims as* ZELDA *suddenly talks.*)

ZELDA: Tevya—I remembered something!

TEVYA (*wearily*): What—what is there to remember?

ZELDA: Tevya, do you know what yesterday was?

TEVYA (*wearily*): Yesterday was nothing. Today is even less. And tomorrow I can give the Malachamuvis[1] for a present.

ZELDA: Tevya—yesterday was Thursday!

TEVYA (*wearily*): A black day in a black year is not something to be noticed.

ZELDA: Tevya—today is Friday!

TEVYA (*looking up at her, excitement coming slowly into him*): Friday? When is Friday?

ZELDA: Tonight!

TEVYA (*bewilderedly*): Tonight is Friday?

(*He rises.*)

It's Friday night, and we sit here—like on a black Thursday! The Sabbath Eve—and I was asking God for travelling advice! When it is forbidden to move, I was praying to Him—how to go! No wonder He didn't answer me. Ai, ai, what a bad Jew He must have thought Tevya was—a Jew who had forgotten His holy Sabbath—

(ZELDA *has been opening* TEVYA's *pack. She takes three candles out of it, a black shawl for herself, and* TEVYA's *tattered white talis and prayerbook.*)

ZELDA: Here's the sider and the talis.

(*Handing them to* TEVYA. *The talis of course is wrapped and only* TEVYA *touches it.*)

TEVYA: On Friday night only a Baal-Tfila wears a talis.

ZELDA: All right—so you are the Baal-Tfila. Who else is there?

(*She lights the candles and puts them in place on top of the tombstone. She covers her head in the shawl.* TEVYA *first washes his hands with earth since there is no water, then puts on his talis and opens his prayer book. The music grows louder during these activities—* DAVID *remains with his back turned*

---

[1] Tevya is referring to the "Angel of Death" of Jewish legend, commonly transliterated from Hebrew as *malakh ha-mavet* or from Yiddish as *malekh-hamoves*.

*to them staring stiffly into the shadows. The music grows fainter as* TEVYA's *voice is raised in prayer.*)

TEVYA (*praying*): Oh Lord, my heart gives thanks—Blessed is the Sabbath rest—Blessed is the Holy One. Exalted and hallowed be God's name in the world. Blessed be his loving kindness in the morning and His faithfulness at night. For Thou, oh Lord, hast made me rejoice through Thy words. I sing Thy praises—

(TEVYA's *voice becomes a mumble of prayer—He continues the mumble, bowed over the prayer book—and* ZELDA *prays, standing beside him. The light appears on the* SPEAKER's *stand. The music is as faint as the mumbled sing-song of the praying. Over these the* SPEAKER *is heard.*)

SPEAKER: Here in the graveyard, a sick and dying Tevya and his Zelda, keep alive the ancient kingdom of the Jew—the little kingdom of Friday Night. Dynasties have come and gone in Europe, but this kingdom of the Jew has remained unaltered by a phrase. In this never-never land of God's word, the Jew of Europe dressed himself up every Friday night in the royal garb of talis and candle light. However lowly his lot or grim his days, on the Sabbath Eve he stepped like a monarch into the realm that waited for him.

It is no less with Tevya on this night. Tevya, broken, half mad, lost and bewildered, looks on the candles of the Sabbath Eve and beholds in their nimbus his Promised Land. It is a mirage of a kingdom but Tevya's soul enters it easily and happily—like an old traveler. There are no voices to sing for him, no Sabbath feast, no synagogue to rejoice in—but Tevya—mighty and ancient dreamer, needs none of these. Heaven is above him full of music, furniture and love. Who can want more? And who can ask for more than to be a king, with the smile of God for a Sabbath crown? So in this graveyard tonight, his soul battered by horrors, his bones stripped almost of life, the incorrigible Tevya, last of a wondrous tribe of Tevyas, raises aloft to God the word spat on by the world—the word Jew—and gives thanks for its presence on his brow.

(*The* SPEAKER *pauses and* TEVYA's *voice rises in prayer again.*)

TEVYA: With everlasting love hast Thou loved the house of Israel—Thy People. Thou hast taught us Thy Torah with its commandments, laws and judgments. The dullard sees not nor does the wicked man understand. When evil men spring up, when those flourish who do only evil, that evil will destroy them. Hear, O Lord, Thy Servant rejoice . . . Hear . . . hear . . .

(TEVYA's *voice again becomes a singsong mumble. To the left of the stage, a part of the dark sky grows luminous and the altar of a synagogue shines dimly. It is* TEVYA's *dream—and it floats like a toy in the sky. The Torah is visible, the robed rabbi walks to it and lifts it down. Around them stands a robed choir of eight men. They sing religious music.*

## APPENDIX 3

*The* SPEAKER *talks as their singing fades for a few moments.)*
SPEAKER: There are dreams in Tevya's head. The memories in Tevya's head make a mist in front of his eyes. And out of this mist come the happy days he knew, come holy people singing in the synagogue of Dubinky, come yesterday and the day before yesterday, come Tevya's friends and Tevya's world—that began long before Dubinky—that began when Abraham and his flock crossed the Jordan.

*(The singing of the Vision choir swells out. Robed figures circle the altar holding the Torah aloft. The singing reaches a climax as the Vision is dimming. Above the climax of the singing are heard suddenly from the right of the stage trumpets blowing. Their notes are wild and shrill. The Choir Vision darkens out as a light comes up in the other side of the sky. Figures appear in this light. Their feet remain in the dark—as they seem to march on the air, out of the sky into the graveyard.*

*They are the figures of* SAUL, *the King, a towering man with a great sword at his side—and of his Captains—all looming and stalwart in their battle dress. The choir singing has ended and the peal and blast of the trumpets fill the stage.*

*The body of warriors stand in the pool of light. There are a dozen of them.* SAUL *stands facing them.)*
TEVYA *(staring rapturously at the lighted figure of* SAUL): Saul, King of Israel! Saul and his mighty captains—Saul!—Saul!

*(Three men enter in the sky just below* SAUL. *The* OLD ONE *is dressed in tattered robes, The* MIDDLE AGED ONE *is richly dressed and The* YOUNG ONE *is in armor and carries a shield. They are frightened and weeping. The* OLD ONE *takes up Tevya's cry.)*
OLD ONE: Saul! Saul!
SAUL *(looking down from his pool of light, his Captains frowning behind him)*: Who are you?
YOUNG ONE: We are men of Jabesh-Gilead.
SAUL: Why are you weeping?
OLD ONE: We are doomed to die.
SAUL *(quietly)*: Who has doomed you?
MIDDLE AGED ONE: Nahash, King of the Amonites.
OLD ONE: His armies overrun Israel.
YOUNG ONE: They stand now before Gilead and order us into slavery.
MIDDLE AGED ONE *(his voice unctuous and appeasing)*: Perhaps not slavery. Who knows? Perhaps we can make friends with the Amonite . . . do nothing to anger him . . . show him how learned and law abiding we are . . . woo him by turning a kindly face to him.

YOUNG ONE (*bitterly*): A kindly face, with one eye in it? Saul! Nahash has ordered the right eye of every Israelite to be plucked out—so that when my left eye is hidden behind my shield I will have no eye to see with. I will no longer be a warrior.

OLD ONE (*wailing*): He will leave our youth enough vision to be slaves!

YOUNG ONE: He has given us seven days to surrender. His soldiers laugh outside our city. And behind our walls men talk like this one—with fear, without hope. Men are ready to yield Gilead, to be blinded, gelded, defiled—men are ready to yield all Israel.

MIDDLE AGED ONE: No, speak truth! Not all Israel! That is stupid talk! Let me put the matter for both sides, King Saul. Nahash the Amonite will take what he wants. But he is only a man. He cannot devour us. The quicker we surrender the less he will take away from us. And what can he carry away from Israel? Houses and land? No! He will leave us our houses and land, and we will raise new flocks, and I say this! a portion of life is better than none at all.

SAUL (*softly*): Is it?

MIDDLE AGED ONE: We are powerless against the enemy, Saul. We have no armies, no armor, no spears.

SAUL: We have hearts!

OLD ONE (*rising*): Hi-koh Sha-ul Ba-a-lu-fov!

(*The rest of the soldiers pick up his cry, in English—"SAUL shall slay his thousands." They shout raising their shields. Saul smiles at them then turns to the OLD ONE.*)

SAUL: End your weeping.

OLD ONE: You will save us?

SAUL: Yes, we go to battle.

MIDDLE AGED ONE: It is you, Saul, who will destroy Israel, not Nahash the Amonite. For we will be removed from the earth. Our houses, our flocks, every stone in Gilead will be dismembered, and every man and child.

SAUL (*quietly*): All this is possible.

MIDDLE AGED ONE (*wildly*): Saul, speak carefully! Words can lead to destruction. Nahash the Amonite is a great and powerful king!

SAUL: A king who comes to a land not his is only as great as its people are little. My kingdom is not a matter of flocks and houses and the earnings of careful men. It is a matter of the spirit. Kingdoms are no more than that—a dream, a love, a symbol of mankind. So I say, men of Jabesh-Gilead, go back to your city and tell your people my words. I go to raise an army from among the shepherds and workers of the tribes of Israel. And if there are any who refuse to join me I will cut the sinews of their oxen so that they will be idle and

## APPENDIX 3

without profit. And if still they refuse to join me and defend their homeland, I will order the sinews of the owners cut along with their oxen. For of what use is a man who is willing for his soul to die that his legs may live—

(*The Captains raise their shields behind him and shout again in unison "SAUL shall slay his thousands." During his talk men and women come onto the field below him—and join the Captains in their shouts. SAUL steps lower out of the sky. The men come straggling on. They are the beginnings of SAUL's army.*)

You, Old Man of brave heart—tell the people of Jabesh-Gilead this for me, for I shall be too busy for speaking. Tell them we have made land for Israel—built it, sweetened it with our dead and living. Its skies are full of our prayers. Its hills are covered with our cattle and our memories. Out of the whole world we have married only this land—and it is our bride. We whisper our love to it at night—Tell your people, Old Man, that a stranger has come for our bride—the fair Hebrew bride of Israel . . . a mighty stranger with robber banners, who wishes to despoil her and use her basely. So be it, if it is to be! Let the stranger take our bride from us—but only after we are stretched bloodless under the sky. Let him have the bride of Israel to sport with—but only after the bridegroom is dead.

(*The Captains raise their arms and shout, and the shout is increased by the stragglers who are still entering.*)

Tell them, Old Man, that however powerfully armed the conqueror is outside, within he is armed only with greed. And that we of Israel are armed within with love, love for every stone, hill, tree, and brook of our homeland; for the sound of its tongue, for the look of its face. Who is there who can conquer the unconquerable—the violence of love? On this the world and its heavens are built—that man loves what belongs to him and that it can only be taken from his dead hands.

(*The Captains and the soldiers shout.*)

Go tell all Israel, that Saul their King, bids them rise from their terrors and come to his side—to battle! And tell them we will win! Go tell them—and give them my promise that no thief from Amon shall take the bride of Israel from our arms!

(*The trumpets peal and the captains shout. The citizens leave the stage to bear the word through Israel. SAUL and his Captains are left alone in a dreamlike silence with TEVYA, hanging over him in the black sky.*)

TEVYA: And they fell on the Amonites and smote them and they won for the Israelites the land of Eretz Yisrael. And Saul, the King went down into the city of Amalek—as God had commanded—and smote the people of Amalek, and Won for the Israelites the land of Eretz Yisrael.

SAUL: Is that Tevya from Dubinky who speaks?

TEVYA (*startled, his voice awed*): You can hear me? You can see me?

SAUL: Why not, Tevya? Have we not always walked hand in hand with you—since you were a child? Did we not follow you down the streets of Dubinky—all our warriors and prophets—since the days of your youth?

TEVYA (*still awed*): You know me!

SAUL: Yes, Tevya, we are alive together in the dream of Israel. And whenever a Jew dies—we all die with him—all the glories and the wisdom of Israel. And whenever a Jew is born—we are all born with him.

TEVYA (*fervently*): God be praised. Hallowed be His name! Whoever thought He would give Tevya these wonders to see. Saul, great King of Israel, if you can hear me and speak to me, then what am I worried about? What troubles have I got? You will tell me—who knows better than you do—you will tell me—where is this holy land? Point out to me which way to go. Help me find your Eretz Yisrael—

SAUL: There is a bridge to cross.

TEVYA: Again a bridge. Where is the bridge? Tell me. Let me see it. I'll cross it.

(SAUL *turns his head to point the way to the bridge. All at once there is a sound of harps and sweet music. The light brightens in the sky and* DAVID, *the sweet singer appears in the clouds. He stands above the warriors, a young and shining figure, holding a lyre. The music continues as he speaks.*)

DAVID THE KING: The Lord is my shepherd; I shall not want.

He maketh me to lie down in green pastures;

He leadeth me beside the still waters.

He restoreth my soul: He leadeth me in the paths of righteousness for His name's sake.

Yea, though I walk through the valley of the shadow of death,

I will fear no evil![2]

TEVYA: David, wonderful king—what a fine face you have! My heart opens up when I look at you. I remember when you danced in the streets of Yerushalayim—before the ark of the covenant. What a fine day that was! Hallelujah! Hallelujah!

(*The vision begins to fade in the sky.* TEVYA *holds out his arms pleadingly.*)

Just one minute—before you go to smite them, David—Saul, I shouldn't ask you—when you are busy—but if you can't point me the way to Eretz Yisrael—talk to me a little. Tell me—is it still there? Such a place? Such a land?

---

[2] This speech quotes the first four verses of Psalm 23.

## APPENDIX 3

*(The music swells as* DAVID *answers.)*

DAVID [THE KING]: The judgments of the Lord are in all the earth. He hath given His covenant forever, the word given to a thousand generations; the covenant made with Abraham and his oath unto Isaac—saying, touch not mine anointed and do my prophets no harm. And the Lord gave the children of Abraham the land of their desire. And He broke the gates of brass and cut the bars of iron asunder. And he turned the wilderness into a standing water and dry ground into water springs. And He gave them the fruits of their labor and the land of Israel in which to keep his laws.[3]

*(The trumpets blow loudly. The warriors move.)*

SAUL *(to his soldiers)*: Now the night is deep and Israel draws its sword.

*(The trumpets peal again and the warriors return into the sky, led by* SAUL. *The light fades as the troop marches into the darkness. When the sky is black again, the sounds of the trumpets and battle cries are still heard echoing as if from far away. The clamor dies out.* TEVYA *is left standing by his tombstone staring into the dark graveyard. The folk music theme starts up softly.* ZELDA *has finished her prayers before the candles. She removes her shawl and busies herself removing a half loaf of bread and a pot from* TEVYA's *pack. During her activities* TEVYA's *eyes remain riveted on the empty darkness. He ignores* ZELDA's *talk.)*

ZELDA *(wearily, her movements slow)*: Git shabis—we have lit candles. We have prayed. Now God should feel happy, if nobody else. Tevya, sit down. We'll eat. Not fish, not meat, not noodle soup—but a piece of old bread—and some bones.

*(She looks up at him.)*

Who are you looking at, Tevya? What is there to see? Do you expect Reb Zundel to come out of his grave with a chicken cooked in each hand? Sit down, Tevya. Here is the full supper—not enough to live on—but enough to keep from dying.

*(She sits munching the bread and looks at the youth* DAVID. *She calls to him.)*

Young boy, David. If you are hungry, come here by our table and sit down.

*(*DAVID *goes to the tombstone.)*

In a minute Tevya will make the prayers and the food will taste better—to the Almighty.

*(She looks up at* TEVYA.*)*

Tevya—come eat.

TEVYA *(sighing)*: I'm not hungry.

---

[3] This speech combines language from Psalms 105 and 107 with Hecht's own paraphrases of scripture pertinent to God's "covenant" with Abraham.

ZELDA: An hour ago you were falling down with hunger. Who has been feeding you, the ravens of Elijah?

TEVYA (*softly*): Maybe I'm hungry, but it seems to me I don't want to eat.

(*A feverish little chuckle has come into* ZELDA'*s talk and her mind has grown vague. She forgets now her worry about* TEVYA *and busies herself handing* DAVID *his portion of the "meal."* TEVYA *remains standing beside the tomb, his eyes still searching the shadows for more wonders.* ZELDA *talks to the preoccupied youth.*)

ZELDA (*glowing with memories*): On Friday night everything in the house was scrubbed clean and lovely to see. The white curtains ironed—hanging on the clean windows. The floor polished. The kitchen smelling with fresh bread.

(*She chuckles as she gnaws at the bread in her hand.*)

And lots of people sitting around our table for supper.

(*She pauses—and then wails softly like a frightened child.*)

Lots of people—in our house . . . oh, so many people . . .

(*She looks feverishly at the shadows around the tomb. The spot in front of her grows brighter as she stares into it.* ZELDA *beams at the growing brightness. She nods at it, her mouth wide with smile. She speaks in a strong voice that belongs to another long ago.*)

Wait—Shmulik, Yussella—your papa has to make a prayer first. Nu, Tevya! God is waiting to hear from His favorite brocha-maker. Amen!

(*Standing in the half dark beside the tombstone,* TEVYA *automatically begins to mumble his "brochas."* ZELDA *sits silent and smiling as she listens to the familiar words. The lighted spot in front of her brightens and she stares at it with deepening delight.*)

ZELDA (*softly*): How nice everybody looks! What are you doing, Rochella? Enough lukshen! Leave some room for the fish. Yussella—Yussella—use a napkin! Don't wipe hands on the table cloth. Estherel—you are not eating. Stop sitting there in a dream—and eat.

(*She chuckles—and then pauses, her head cocked as if she were listening. She then adds softly and gloatingly*)

Ai, ai—excuse me. The Barala is crying again.

(*She starts singing softly the lullaby of "Rozinkas and Mondlen"*[4] *For several moments the stage is motionless as* ZELDA *sits singing and rocking and looking into the lighted place in front of her.*)

---

[4] "Raisins and Almonds." See discussion of this song in chapter 4.

## APPENDIX 3

*The light and music dim and the bright place vanishes.* ZELDA *sits again silent in the night.*)

(DAVID *rises and turns away from them. He raises his face and remains looking wildly into the night that is over the audience. A strong shaft of light comes down, a second shaft of light bisects it, making a cross of light. He stands in front of the crossed beams. Torment is in his face. He is silent. Then he speaks to the darkness beyond him. His voice begins softly and full of pain.*)

DAVID: Where were you—Jews? Where were you when the killing was going on? When the six million were being burned and buried alive in the lime pits, where were you? Where was your voice crying out against the slaughter? We didn't hear any voice. There was no voice; You Jews of America! You Jews of England! Strong Jews, rich Jews, high up Jews; Jews of power and genius! Where was your cry of rage that could have filled the world and stopped the fires? Nowhere! Because you were ashamed to cry out as Jews. You would rather let us die than speak out as Jews! A curse on your silence! That frightened silence of Jews that made the Germans laugh as they slaughtered. You with your Jewish hearts hidden in your American boots! You-with your Jewish hearts hidden behind English accents—you let the six million die—rather than make the faux-pas of seeming a Jew. We heard—your silence—in the gas chambers. And now, now you speak a little. Your hearts squeak—and you have a dollar for the Jews of Europe. Thank you. Thank you!

(*The lighted cross fades out behind him. He covers his head in his arms and stands crouched.*)

TEVYA (*staring at him from the tombstone on which he leans*): Don't, Duvidel!

DAVID (*turning to him, his voice cold and raging*): You are the one who prays, Tevya. Pray to God, then, to save us who are left from that last curse—the charity of frightened Jews. Those Jews who were afraid to cry out—are sending us now bagel and pieces of meat. They are going to feed the beggar with wild eyes—at the backdoor of the world. Feed him for a few days—and then slam the door in his face.

TEVYA (*sighing*): To eat for a few days—is not too bad, Duvidel.

DAVID: I spit on their food.

TEVYA: If we weren't so hungry, maybe we could move a little faster to Eretz Yisrael.

DAVID (*pleadingly*): Tevya—you are a wise man. Then understand! It's not us they are feeding-but their own timid souls. We want freedom from the pogrom, from the hate of Europe that smolders around our feet—we want a land to live in—and they send us instead scraps from their rich tables. And they tell each other, "Look how noble we are, how good we are. We have fed some Jews."

TEVYA (*sighing*): Me, they haven't fed yet. And if they fed me something, I would be wise enough to eat it. A wise man always eats first and figures out what is wrong—afterwards.

DAVID: Afterwards! What afterwards, Tevya? After we eat a few more meals—we go back to being garbage people again. And the noble, money giving Jews can go back to their silence. The silence that will keep the roads to Palestine closed for us—as they kept the gas chambers of the Germans open.

TEVYA: Maybe they are not silent, Duvidel. In a place like this—you don't hear very much.

DAVID (*grimly*): They are silent.

TEVYA (*sighing*): My son, my son, we have worse enemies than Jews with bagel.

DAVID: To die in front of enemies—I dream of that.

(*His voice grows flat and cold again.*)

But to die alone in the night—and not even hear guns—but hear only the voices of Jews arguing. Arguing. Arguing a race out of existence. That's written as our fate. We will die—the rest of us—not on the spears of our enemies, but in the arguments of the Jews outside.

(*His voice grows quieter and colder.*)

I thought I saw a bridge. There is no bridge, Tevya. You were right. We sit in a graveyard—and our homeland—is underneath. Nowhere else—underneath.

ZELDA (*calling—weakly*): Tevya—are you here, Tevya?

TEVYA (*turning to her*): I'm here, Zelda. Where else?

ZELDA: I have to lie down, Tevya. Help me lie down.

(TEVYA *kneels beside her and takes off his talis.*)

TEVYA: It hurts you someplace?

ZELDA: No, Tevya. Nothing hurts.

TEVYA: You are tired—

(*He helps her lie down beside the grave-slab.*)

ZELDA: Yes, tired.

(*She sighs.*)

Tevya, pray for me in the synagogue today.

TEVYA: Around here, Zelda, there's no synagogue.

ZELDA: It must be—someplace—there's always someplace a synagogue.

(*She sighs.*)

A bed, I wouldn't ask for. How would Tevya know where to find a bed and food—how does Tevya know where food grows. But God—my Tevya always knows where to find him. God—and his synagogue. Find one, Tevya and go pray for me.

(*She is silent.*)

## APPENDIX 3

**TEVYA:** Yes, Zelda, I will find.

*(He rises and puts his talis on again and stands against the tombstone staring into the shadowy night. The music swells—and the light on the* SPEAKER's *stand goes on. The* SPEAKER *talks as* TEVYA *remains motionless in his talis staring.)*

**SPEAKER:** And so Tevya goes looking for a synagogue—not with his legs but with his hungry and fevered soul. And Tevya's soul—like a bird fleeing a bitter clime, moves southward, moved southward toward the land of milk and honey. And his inner eyes behold the wonders of which he has read and dreamed since childhood. The inner eyes of the ghetto Jew of Europe were not for seeing God only but for looking on his own manhood. This is Tevya's last secret in the graveyard—that he dreams of the glory of being a man. His soul has not accepted the lower levels designed for it by the hate and villainy of a world. It will not bow to contempt or murder. Condemned to survive as human rubbish, it will lift itself up out of the dust and move bewilderedly toward its destiny—manhood. Such is the reason of Tevya's journey to Palestine. There his manhood lies. There he will go—or die reaching for it. And so Tevya leans against a tombstone—as his soul goes looking for a synagogue—the little Jew in his talis for whom hope will never die.

*(The graveyard beyond* TEVYA *has grown luminous. And out of the eerily lighted sky figures have begun to appear; sandaled women, garlanded and lovely. They are a procession of Jews on its way to the great temple. Robust and hieratic music accompanies them. Grandeur and happiness are in their ranks.*

*This parade of wondrous Jews and all their fineries drifts past. The procession ends and the dim light in which it moved begins to brighten and the music to rise.*

*Out of the stumbling shadows, appear the bronzed pillars of a great structure. We see stretching beyond its magnificent entrance, the interior of Solomon's Temple. It stands, shining and with incense smoke curling out of its depth.*

*A throne has appeared in the Temple on a dais. Seated on this throne is the glittering figure of* KING SOLOMON. *Around the floor of the dais, lovely women are grouped. Robed priests appear and stand like a guard to the side. Glittering warrior captains appear and stand to the other side. The* KING *holds a papyrus in his hand. The music plays—a strumming of lutes, a sweet cry of fifes—and a beating of cymbals at intervals.*

*As* KING SOLOMON *begins his song of songs, the women rise. They dance slowly before him. The warriors and priests remain in their places. Through the music and the dancing comes the lyric voice of the* KING.*)*

SOLOMON: The voice of my beloved! behold he cometh leaping upon the mountains, skipping upon the hills. Rise up, my love, and come away.

For, lo, the winter is past, the rain is over and gone:

The flowers appear on the earth; the time of the singing of birds is come, and the voice of the turtle is heard in our land.

My beloved is mine and I am his; he feedeth among the lilies.

I will rise now, and go about the city in the streets and in the broad ways.

I will seek him whom my soul loveth.

Come with me from Lebanon;

Look from the top of Amana

From the top of Shenir and Harmon

From the lions' dens,

From the mountains of the leopard.

Awake, O North wind and come thou South; blow upon my garden, that the spices thereof may flow out. Let my beloved come into his garden, and eat his pleasant fruits.

I charge you, O daughters of Jerusalem, if ye find my beloved, that ye tell him that I am sick with love. Thou art beautiful, O my love, as Tirzah, comely as Jerusalem; terrible as an army with banners. Set me as a seal upon thy heart; as a seal upon thine arm.

My vineyard is before me. Make haste, my beloved, and be thou like a young hart upon the mountains of spices.

(*The music swells after the* KING *is done reading and the dancers bring their dance to its climax. The music becomes faint and the dancing girls, priests and warriors and* KING SOLOMON *return to their original posture—and stillness.* TEVYA, *who has stood by his tombstone, watching and listening to these wonders, walks slowly toward the couch of* KING SOLOMON *and stops halfway.*)

TEVYA (*awed and exultant*): It is like it is written. Every stone stands like it is written. The Temple of Solomon, ai what a thing to see!

SOLOMON: Come nearer to me, Tevya of Dubinky.

TEVYA: How is this possible? How can King Solomon, in all his glory, know Tevya?

SOLOMON: The pleasant fruits of my garden are yours, Tevya.

TEVYA: It's enough I can see you and talk to you. Who wants more presents? I am in Eretz Yisrael! I stand in the Holy Land—in front of King Solomon.

SOLOMON: Yes, the upright shall dwell in the land and the perfect shall remain in it.

TEVYA (*continuing the proverb*): But the wicked shall be cut off from the earth and the transgressors shall be rooted out of it.

## APPENDIX 3

SOLOMON: You know my sayings, Tevya?

TEVYA: Who doesn't? What other land have we got to dwell in—than your sayings, King Solomon. Where else are the transgressors rooted out—than in your lovely words? So we live in them. And we die in them. They are our Holy Land—where everything goes on fine—better than anyplace else. Blessed be the name of the Lord and the wisdom of Solomon.

SOLOMON: He that despises his neighbor, sinneth; but he that hath mercy on the lowly, happy is he.

TEVYA (*fervently*): Amen! Ai what a pleasure it is to listen to the wisdom of Solomon.

(*He sighs.*)

Even when you are hungry and dying, wisdom is always a pleasure. Ai, food, houses, children, life—everything else they can take from you. Wisdom they have to leave you. It's the only thing a Jew has that they don't want.

SOLOMON: You weep, Tevya.

TEVYA: Who weeps? I should come to King Solomon—and weep in front of all his glories! No, Tevya says only "Hallelujah—hallelujah."

SOLOMON: There are tears in your words. Bitterness laughs in them. I am a Judge in Israel, Tevya. If you have a complaint that calls for a judgment, bring it to me.

TEVYA: A complaint? Yes, maybe I have a complaint.

SOLOMON: Against whom is your complaint, Tevya?

TEVYA (*softly*): Against whom?

SOLOMON: What is the name of your enemy, Tevya?

TEVYA (*sighing*): The name of my enemy?

SOLOMON: Speak, Tevya—his name?

TEVYA: It's a name I don't like to say aloud, King Solomon. Who has a voice to say such a name? Not Tevya.

SOLOMON: Is it the name of a powerful king, Tevya?

TEVYA: A king's name I could speak. Even two kings. But this is a name bigger than kings.

SOLOMON: You are in a court of God's justice. You have nothing to fear, Tevya.

TEVYA: Afraid, I am not, King Solomon. But ashamed. Anyway, I'll give you the name of my enemy. Why not? It's no secret. The name of my enemy is the WORLD.

SOLOMON (*slowly*): The world? You mean the land in which you live?

TEVYA (*sighing*): The land in which I live. The land in. which I don't live. From here to there—and across and around—the whole world up and down—this is what I mean.

SOLOMON: What have you done to make so great an enemy, Tevya?

TEVYA: I'm a Jew.

SOLOMON: The name that brought glory to the world.

TEVYA: Glory it brought, but not for Jews.

SOLOMON: The reason, Tevya?

TEVYA: The reason, I don't know. Who can know the reason for why he is hated? Because we are weak, we arc hated. Because we are strong, we are hated. Because we are rich, because we are poor, because we are wanderers, because we refuse to wander—wherever there's a reason—that fits nothing and nobody—that's the reason why we are hated.

SOLOMON: Speak on.

TEVYA: God scattered us from our house. So we went to new lands and helped build new houses. And when the house was built, the owner said every time, "I have a fine house now. There is only one thing wrong with it. In the basement, under the kitchen, where the coal is kept, lives a Jew. If we throw him out, then we will have a finer house."

SOLOMON: I will give you my judgment, Tevya. My judgment is that you return to your own house.

TEVYA (*exultantly*): Fine! Fine! I am going! I am walking with Zelda at night looking for Eretz Yisrael. But how can I go? They stop us.

SOLOMON: Who stops you, Tevya?

TEVYA: Who? Everybody. The world stops us. In Europe, they burned us—millions and millions. Because they didn't want us in the land of Europe—in the houses we helped build. So when they are finished killing us and we who are left start to run from the ashes—they say, "stop! Jews can't leave the land of Europe." And the doors of the Holy Land are closed against us—who are left.

SOLOMON: Who closes the doors, Tevya?

TEVYA: Who? The same one. The world.

SOLOMON: This is my judgment, Tevya—go to the World, speak to it, be not afraid of its mighty councils. For in you is my own wisdom—and the wisdom of the Books you have treasured, the wisdom of God whose name you have kept bright—Go to them, Tevya, and find their soul that is hidden beneath the vanities of their power and the veils of their hate.

(*The Temple and the* KING *begin to fade into the shadows. The Voice of* SOLOMON *continues out of the vanishing Vision and the falling dark.*)

SOLOMON: In you, Tevya, is the tongue of greatness, the tongue that fashioned the eternal words of justice. Speak with it to the councils of the mighty, Tevya. Speak and be not afraid.

## APPENDIX 3

(*The music has started as* SOLOMON *finishes. The stage has darkened and* TEVYA *is left in his graveyard. The music is that of fanfares, as if a parade were moving somewhere in the distant shadows.*

*The fanfares dissolve into a medley of satyrically patriotic themes—the "Punishment To Fit the Crime," "Give My Regards To Broadway," "The Marseillaise," the "Russian March," etc. The martial music swells, the light fills the graveyard and the Council of the Mighty emerges. On a great dais sit a row of statesmen and behind them stand other rows of statesmen, generals, admirals and factotums from all the nations. And behind and over this concourse of great personages are the flags of all the nations. They sweep up in a cloud into the sky.*

TEVYA *stands beside his tombstone staring at this Vision as it brightens. The Music reaches a climax. It dissolves into mounting trumpet peals and drum rolls. Between these trumpet peals and rolling of drums, the* SPEAKER *continues his words.*)

SPEAKER: Mighty of the earth—frock coats from whom all blessings flow . . .

Festooned and elderly custodians of History . . . Powerful faces carved out of the dreams and confusions of the peoples of the earth . . . High Priests from the bloody altars of Tweedledum and Tweedledee . . . Panoplied Spokesmen for Armadas, Atom bombs and the lusts of trade and politics . . . Wazirs, Satraps, Poohbahs, Princes and Kings of Protocol and Pronouncement . . . Majestic visages whose eyes glitter with the wrath of Governments, whose tongues sound the High Mass of Ownership . . . Mighty of the earth who stand guard before the doors of the future, a delegate comes to address you—a man, a small man with somewhat weary feet.

(TEVYA *has moved slowly forward toward the great vision. He stands looking up at the Spectacle of the Mighty. The* SPEAKER *finishes. The music swells out. The Mighty sit in silence under their heaven of flags.* TEVYA *speaks after a pause.*)

TEVYA: Excuse me, I didn't know I had my talis on.

(*He starts removing his talis and folding it carefully.*)

A talis you don't wear for asking a little favor—on earth . . .

(*He puts it under his arm and raises his face to the Mighty.*)

First I want to thank you for all being here. It is a great honor for Tevya from Dubinky to stand in front of so many fine people—even if he has got nothing to stand on, except a grave. A grave, I say! Who knows where I'm standing? On a grave. On a barrel. On plain air. All I know is—I'm standing! And it seems to me I'm also talking. And it even seems to me—the whole world is listening. More, nobody could ask.

AMERICAN STATESMAN (*sternly*): We are unusually busy today, Tevya.

## A FLAG IS BORN

TEVYA (*happily*): It even speaks to me!

AMERICAN STATESMAN: Be as brief as you can, Tevya. We have a full agenda.

TEVYA: Don't worry, I'm used to fitting into an agenda. Reb Zundel in Dubinky used to say "Tevya, when the world comes to an end—with a Messiah or without a Messiah—there will have to be a second ending to take care of the Jews. Because Jews are not in the world. They are on the agenda."

RUSSIAN STATESMAN: Russia has no time to waste, gentlemen.

AMERICAN STATESMAN: Nor has the United States.

FRENCH STATESMAN: Nor France.

ENGLISH STATESMAN: Nor England.

AMERICAN STATESMAN: Be brief, Tevya.

TEVYA: Brief? Why not? What have I got to say that takes long? I want to go to Palestine.

ENGLISH STATESMAN (*slowly*): Is this a Jew?

TEVYA (*beaming*): Who else wants to go to Palestine?

ENGLISH STATESMAN (*sternly*): You will answer without oriental evasions!

TEVYA (*modestly*): Without oriental evasions, I'm a Jew. And with them, I'm also a Jew. However you twist him and turn him, Tevya is left, a Jew.

ENGLISH STATESMAN: Your presence here is decidedly bad form. Utterly bad form.

SECOND ENGLISH STATESMAN (*beside the first*): More than that. I'd say, his presence here is distinctly a breach of international courtesy. A deplorable breach.

ENGLISH STATESMAN: Why is it that the Jews always push themselves to the head of the line—Tevya.

TEVYA: The Jews are not at the head of a line but at the bottom of misfortune. And they did not push themselves there, they were pushed—by gentlemen maybe like yourself—who think that as long as a Jew is standing, he is in the wrong place.

ENGLISH STATESMAN: I see no reason to listen further to this illegal interloper. No reason at all.

AMERICAN STATESMAN: Speaking for the United States, I think we could stretch a point and permit this delegate to talk.

BOTH ENGLISHMEN: What do you mean?

AMERICAN STATESMAN: Mind you, off the record, gentlemen.

ENGLISH STATESMAN: I object most strenuously, sir, to identifying this fellow as a delegate. A delegate from where? He hasn't a rag or a pot to his name.

RUSSIAN STATESMAN: Objection overruled!

ENGLISH STATESMAN: I take exception to your attitude, Russia. My word, man, we're at war with the Jews.

# APPENDIX 3

RUSSIAN STATESMAN: There are no Jews! Russia does not tolerate either anti-Semitism or Semitism.

ENGLISH STATESMAN: My dear fellow, this is hardly the time or place for such idealistic twaddle. I speak for a nation engaged in the blood and sweat and tears of a great crisis—a nation at war with the Jews.

TEVYA (*angrily*): Excuse me—but I would like to ask what you are doing here, sitting in a front seat! You Germans were already defeated. So what is Germany doing in a front seat again?

ENGLISH STATESMAN: I am not Germany. I am England.

TEVYA: England! England is having a war with the Jews! Who can believe such a thing!

(*He stares intently at the* STATESMAN.)

Excuse me, are you sure you are England!

SECOND ENGLISH STATESMAN: Don't answer the fellow. He was always a wily beggar, with a genius for giving his betters a bad name.

TEVYA: Dead Jews in a gas chamber have this genius. But not Tevya. Not yet.

AMERICAN STATESMAN: I advise you, Tevya, not to exhaust our patience with emotional name calling.

TEVYA: Who is calling names? Not Tevya. He bows to you fine gentlemen. And if there are tears in his eyes, please look somewheres else. Because I am not here to sit shiva. I am here only to speak to somebody about a very small piece of ground, hardly big enough to be noticed. Not even ground! Sand. Sand and flies and no water. A piece of worthless but Holy land called Palestine.

ENGLISH STATESMAN (*sternly*): Search him! See if the rascal is armed!

TEVYA: Who is armed? I have two arms to work with, if there's work. And to eat with, if there's food—sometimes. What other arms has a Jew?

ENGLISH STATESMAN: Your mockery is ill-timed, Tevya. The Jews are attacking the English with weapons of war—guns, bombs, dynamite, mines.

TEVYA: God Almighty, is this true! Twice you have told me! But how can it be? The Jews should attack England, and try to overthrow such a great country! Who wants to live in London? Or even Birmingham?

AMERICAN STATESMAN: Gentlemen, I move that we clarify the situation for Teyya.

FRENCH STATESMAN: France seconds the motion.

RUSSIAN STATESMAN: Gentlemen, Russia considers the clarification unnecessary and imperialistic. There is no Tevya!

FIRST ENGLISH STATESMAN: More Muscovite twaddle! By Jove, I say there is a Tevya.

RUSSIAN STATESMAN: Niet! Niet! Niet!!

FIRST ENGLISH STATESMAN: And I stand ready to implement that fact.

SECOND ENGLISH STATESMAN: There are certain irrefutable facts of which Russia is not aware.

AMERICAN STATESMAN (*cutting through the second* ENGLISH STATESMAN): Gentlemen! Gentlemen! Please! This is no barroom. This is a court of nations. I move we put the issue to a vote.

FRENCH STATESMAN: France seconds the motion.

AMERICAN STATESMAN: All those gathered here under the covenant of the Four Freedoms who believe there is a Tevya, so signify by saying "Aye."

(*There is a thundering chorus of "Ayes"" from the Mighty*)

All those who believe there is no Tevya, so signify by saying "NO."

RUSSIAN STATESMAN (solo): No.

AMERICAN STATESMAN: The "ayes" have it. There is a Tevya.

RUSSIAN STATESMAN: Russia Walks!

AMERICAN STATESMAN (*nervously*): Where were we?

FRENCH STATESMAN: We were going to clarify the situation for Tevya.

AMERICAN STATESMAN: Yes, yes, indeed. Now that we have admitted his existence, I think the next move, in all logic and decency, is to clarify it. I suggest that England be allowed that privilege.

ENGLISH STATESMAN: Thank you very much.

(*to Tevya*)

The situation, Tevya, is very simple The Jews in Palestine have taken up arms against British law and order.

TEVYA: Is it the law and order left over by Buchenwald and Dachau—maybe?

ENGLISH STATESMAN: It is the law and order of the British Empire that prohibits the entrance into Palestine of refugee Jews from Europe. The Jews of Palestine have broken that law.

TEVYA: If somebody makes a law against humanity who is the law breaker?

SECOND ENGLISH STATESMAN: I object to submitting ourselves to this campaign of vilification.

TEVYA: Who is vilifying? If a pig looks into a looking glass, is it a campaign of vilification—who looks out?

ENGLISH STATESMAN: I take it that the pig in question is an Englishman.

TEVYA: Not always.

SECOND ENGLISH STATESMAN: I see nothing to be gained by quibbling with this bold and mocking Semite. It is too late for words. England has declared a state of war against Palestine and—

AMERICAN STATESMAN (*interrupting*): Let me assure you, Tevya, this was done without the knowledge or consent of the United States.

## APPENDIX 3

TEVYA: Thank you, thank you. That's almost as good as making a protest. Not quite, maybe. But it's something. Reb Zundel used to say, "A dead Jew is always grateful that somebody didn't consent to his being killed."

AMERICAN STATESMAN: I must ask you to curb your unhappiness, Tevya, and not to give up hope We have scheduled a number of conferences on the Palestine situation. The subject is not closed.

TEVYA: Fine, fine, fine. This is the usual situation for the Jews. The subject is always open—but everything else is closed. Look, gentlemen, I would like to talk to you. I have come a long way to talk to you about why the Jews belong in Palestine.

ENGLISH STATESMAN: Impossible, my dear fellow! A censorship has been declared against anything you have to say.

TEVYA: How can you make a censorship against people who have nothing left but a little voice?

AMERICAN STATESMAN: I move that Tevya be given the floor.

FRENCH STATESMAN: France seconds the motion.

ENGLISH STATESMAN: The motion is out of order. The Jew is a criminal in Palestine and has forfeited all parliamentarian rights.

TEVYA: How did I forfeit? What did I do wrong? Palestine was given to the Jews, and England was told to take care of it for a while and make it into a Jewish homeland. This I remember from yesterday. And everybody said, "Don't worry about Palestine now. Good England is fixing up the Holy Land for the Jews." So who is the criminal now—the policeman who stole or the beggar who was robbed?

FIRST ENGLISH STATESMAN: I demand the arrest of this traitor!

SECOND ENGLISH STATESMAN: I demand his arrest immediately! Immediately!

AMERICAN STATESMAN (*talking down the two* ENGLISHMEN): Please—Please—We must proceed according to rule. The motion has already been made and seconded that Tevya be given the floor.

SECOND ENGLISH STATESMAN: A bloody outrage! How would you Americans like some stupid red skin to come into this court bellowing for the return of the State of Pennsylvania?

AMERICAN STATESMAN: All those in favor of Tevya having the floor so signify by saying "Aye."

(*The Mighty thunder a chorus of "Ayes."*)

All opposed so signify by saying, "No."

FIRST AND SECOND ENGLISH STATESMEN: No.

AMERICAN STATESMAN: The "ayes" have it.

(*He places his hand on the* ENGLISHMAN's *shoulder.*)
Sorry, pal.

ENGLISH STATESMAN: Quite all right, old boy.

(*The* RUSSIAN STATESMAN *comes walking back, bows to his colleagues, and resumes his seat.*)

AMERICAN STATESMAN: Proceed, Tevya, the floor is yours.

(*Trumpets peal. Drums roll. The theme of the Hatikva is heard, as the clamor climaxes. The music grows softer. Above it are heard faint voices calling in Yiddish. They are from faraway and are wailing.*)

YIDDISH VOICES: Tell them, Tevya. Tell. Tell, speak to them, Tevya. Speak. Speak for all the dead and the living. Tevya speak . . . speak . . . for us . . .

(*The wailing Yiddish voices subside and a folk music theme starts faintly under* TEVYA's *words.*)

TEVYA: I am a single hungry and tired old Jew in front of a great world. But listen to me. Because there are many voices that speak out of Tevya's mouth. Who knows—maybe even God has a few words to say with Tevya's mouth. It stands written that God speaks out of everything . . . stones, clouds, trees— so why shouldn't He speak out of Tevya?

(TEVYA *pauses, his eyes closing wearily. And the Yiddish voices start up again, wailing in the distance and out of the earth.*)

YIDDISH VOICES: Speak, Tevya. Hurry. Hurry. Tell. Tell. Speak for the dead and the children of the dead. Speak for us, Tevya . . . Tevya speak . . . speak . . .

(*The voices waken* TEVYA *and his eyes open. The Hatikva theme grows louder for a few moments. The light on* TEVYA *brightens and his figure casts a towering shadow against the sky. The music dims as* TEVYA *resumes.*)

TEVYA: Oh world—it is like this. In the old days the Jews did not need Palestine because they had many fine homelands in Europe. Wherever you looked were Jews, sometimes rich, sometimes poor. And they worked hard in all the lands. And they made songs and wrote books. And they sat with other people and helped make inventions and operas and armies. And in the old days when somebody said to me, "Tevya, go to Palestine and live in the Holy Land like a good Jew," I answered them back, "Why do I have to go anywhere? I am through going. Name me a place in the world, and I have gone in, gone out. Now I have a home. Europe."

(*The Yiddish voices wail out of the earth.*)

YIDDISH VOICES: Save us, Tevya. Speak and save us . . . Tell . . . tell . . . Tevya. Tell.

(TEVYA *is silent as the voices wail—and the music swells up. Then he resumes, softly.*)

## APPENDIX 3

TEVYA: Then it turned out that this was only a dream about a home. A dream that died in a gas chamber.

(*He pauses.*)

So it died. And all the Jews died with the dream. Forgive me—not all ... almost all. So how can we who didn't die still have such a dream?

(*The Hatikva theme begins to sound again.*)

No, the dream is gone. Now we look for another home—another place where we can dream we are human beings. So where is there such a place? Where else but Palestine? Palestine, where we came from long ago. Palestine, that was given to England to hold for us—because England was an honorable country ... because the Jews fought beside England and drove the Turks from the land. Because the honor and conscience of the world said, "Palestine belongs to the Jews. Guard it, England, for them. Fix it for them. Let them have a home, there, ready."

So—who is the home for now? Jews? No—Englishmen. Why Englishmen? Have the Englishmen no other place to live? Look on the world. On one fourth of it live Englishmen. How rich must a man become before he doesn't steal a last crust from his brother? And when he steals this crust why must he cry robber at the hands he has emptied?

(*The lights on the flags dim—leaving only the English flag in brightness. The music plays an English theme.*)

Listen to me, Englishmen, do you remember how the Jews helped to build Europe? And England, too. Have you forgotten so soon how the Jews fought beside you in the bad battles—Tobruk and Alemein?[5] So I tell you as we built and fought and brought honor to the world—that is how we will build Palestine.

Look Englishmen, look how nice it would have been if you had acted a little different toward America long ago. If you had not hired German Hessians to go to fight the young Americans as you are hiring Arabs to go fight the Jews now. Think how nice it would have been if you had not said to the colonies in America, "No—no! You can't have what you want. You must be punished for daring to be men and defying English law and order."

Ai, if you had not said No! No! to your halutzim in America, then you would have a finer Empire today ... an empire nobody would have to help and save all the time ... yes, a fine empire with a British land called America. Besides, can't you remember, Englishmen, that you have never won a war against a people that wanted to be free? So why make such another war

---

[5] Hecht is referring to El Alamein in Egypt, the site of major battles between British and Axis forces in 1942 during the North African campaign of World War II.

and lose it? And lose your own honor, also. Lose all the fine things that Englishmen fought for—when they were defending themselves and called the world to help them by crying, that everybody should be allowed to live on earth without fear or oppression.

Who wouldn't fight for such a cause? How can it be that when you win such a cause, you start fighting Jews? Why? For a little oil you are ready to put out all the lights of English honor? Why? Because you don't want to do wrong by the Arabs? Since when does England worry about doing wrong to people whose land it steals? And who would treat the Arabs better, Jews who are their brothers, or Englishmen who are their masters? Ai, we know who the Arabs are. They are an English lie with a burnoose on it. They are an English lie so that England will seem like a nation with a cause—and not a robber with a camel for a disguise.

(*The lights dim on the English flag and come up brightly on the American flag,* TEVYA *has paused and the music takes an American theme. The Yiddish voices wail again out of the earth.*)

YIDDISH VOICES: Speak, Tevya . . . More. Tell. Tell. Speak for us. Save us. Speak for the dead and their children. Tell . . . Tell . . .

TEVYA (*his eyes on the* AMERICAN STATESMAN *and the illumined flag over him*): Listen to me, Americans, my people were killed in Europe by the Germans—and Tevya is left with a handful. Let them into Palestine or they die—all that are left. Why did you fight the Germans, so you could take over their work of killing the rest of the Jews? You have conferences. You have more conferences. How many conferences do you need to hold before one of the Freedoms for which your soldiers fought and died—can exist . . . ?

(*The lights illuminate all the flags and statesmen.*)

Look—I see Jewish faces here, standing among the great ones of the world. Let me talk to the great Jewish faces who belong to other lands. Jewish faces—in the old days Palestine was no business of yours. You could look at Europe and say, like Tevya, "Why should the Jews go to Palestine? They're in a fine place now. Living fine. Doing fine." And you could feel proud when you looked at the Jews of Europe. They were covered with honors. They were your relatives. But now—who are your relatives? Broken, wandering Tevyas. Is it nice to be related to such people like Tevya—and nobody else? Will you be able to feel grand and hold up your heads when the word Jew becomes a word like the word beggar, like the word pariah, like the word vermin? And there is no other word for him?

If your relative is a beggar, how rich are you in the eyes of the world? If your relative is a piece of rubbish—a beaten, hunted scarecrow of a Jew—

# APPENDIX 3

how much does your neighbor think of your silk hat? How much better if you have a fine relative in Palestine—a relative who builds a land, a relative who makes inventions and operas and armies again.

So Tevya says to you Jewish faces—Palestine is now the business of every Jew, wherever he is . . . if he wanders the forbidden roads of Europe whipped and dishonored, or if he sits in the finest houses of England or America.

And Tevya says to everybody, to the whole world here, under all its fine flags—the Jews are tired of building a sickness in the souls of others. Be tired with us. You couldn't swallow us. And who wants to swallow you? Let us go and become a nation instead of a sickness in strangers' lands. Let us go and build a little land of our own. Let us go and become part of the world—an arm, a hand, a finger of the world—instead of a fever in alien veins. Tevya says, open one little door for the Jews who have opened so many big doors for everybody else. Open one little door to Palestine, to Eretz Yisrael.

(TEVYA *stops. Trumpets peal out and the drums roll. The* AMERICAN STATESMAN *rises and lifts his arm.*)

AMERICAN STATESMAN: I say yes—absolutely yes! Tevya is right!

FRENCH STATESMAN: Yes, yes . . . Let us give Tevya what he wants!

ENGLISH STATESMAN: Rather well put, Tevya.

SECOND ENGLISH STATESMAN: Not bad at all—that point about the American Colonies. We should never have lost them, you know.

FIRST ENGLISH STATESMAN: By heavens, if we're not careful we'll lose them again! The Jews have a right to live.

RUSSIAN STATESMAN: Russia is in favor of life!

ALL THE STATESMEN: Hear! Hear! He is right! etc.

AMERICAN STATESMAN: Gentlemen, you will please come to order. I move that the doors of Palestine be opened to the Jews of Europe. All those in favor so signify by saying "Aye."

(*There is a mighty chorus of "Ayes."*)

This conference of nations gathered here in solemn conclave has decided again I say, has decided again, that the cause of the Jew is honorable. That the world owes the Jew a birthright. That Tevya and all his sorely aggrieved and much sinned against people are entitled to a haven on earth. You may go, Tevya, the doors of Palestine are open!

TEVYA: Blessed be the Lord and all his wonderful works! Ai, what a thing to hear! We can go! We can live!

FIRST ENGLISH STATESMAN: I move that a commission be appointed to investigate the best ways and means of opening the doors of the Holy Land to the Jews. We can't go about this thing blindly.

TEVYA: I stood and talked and I reached the hearts of the powerful, like Solomon the wise King told me—and they gave us Palestine again!
FIRST ENGLISH STATESMAN: Gentlemen, I move we adjourn, and put the matter of the Jews on tomorrow's agenda.
AMERICAN STATESMAN: The Jews are on the agenda.

(*Each* STATESMAN *in turn repeats "agenda" to the next and begins to chuckle. Through the rising laughter,* TEVYA *is heard pleading.*)

TEVYA: No, no! An agenda again! No, don't go away! If you go away there will be another conference. If you go you will forget again! Great Statesmen, Kings, Presidents, Prime Ministers, Ballabatim—you spoke to me! Don't go away from Tevya now! Don't leave him in the dark, on a wild road with a promise in his ears . . . a promise that every wind blows away . . . a promise that dies . . . dies . . .

(*He holds out his arms pleadingly. The vision is gone.*)

(TEVYA *is left in the dark graveyard beside his tombstone. The music ends. The laughter of the* STATESMEN *and the Mighty continues out of the darkness. It fills the shadowy graveyard with mockery and derision. Another laugh is heard—a quiet bitter laugh that takes up the theme of derision by itself. It comes from the lighted figure of the youth,* DAVID. *He stands looking at the stricken* TEVYA. *His laughter turns* TEVYA's *face to him.*)

DAVID (*mocking*): Look at him! Tevya! Holding out his heart like a beggar's cap! To whom, Tevya? To the hyenas in the night? Listen and you can hear them laughing—laughing at Tevya and his beggar's cap. With whom are you pleading there, Tevya? With the hyenas? Dead ears, Tevya. The dead and the living have the same ears for the Jew—dead ears.

(*The folk music theme plays softly.* TEVYA *is silent. He turns and goes to* ZELDA, *calling to her softly.*)

TEVYA: Zelda. Zelda. Zelda? Zelda!

(*She lies motionless on the ground. He kneels beside her figure and slowly puts on his talis. He stares for moments. The music of the Kaddish plays and* TEVYA *rises and begins his prayer of death. First he rends his garment with his fingers in ancient tokens of his grief.*)

TEVYA: Baruch Dayan Emet.
Yit-ga-dal v-yit-ka-dash shmeh ra-ba
Be-al-ma de-bra hir-u-teh v-yam-li'h mal-hu-teh v-yats-ma'h pur-ka-ne, vi-ka-reb m-shi-heh Amen.
B-'ha-ye'hon ub-yo-me'hon, up-'ha-ye d'-hol bet yis-ra-el, ba-a-ga-la u-biz-man ka-rib ve-im-ru Amen.

(DAVID *stands rigidly listening to the Kaddish.*)

## APPENDIX 3

DAVID (*coldly*): Now there's one less.

(TEVYA *continues his praying softly.*)

I will dig a place for her.

(*He pauses and* TEVYA *prays on*) And we will go without her.

TEVYA: Without her.

DAVID: She will walk with us with the other ghosts.

TEVYA: She will walk beside us.

DAVID: She gave me bread and food.

TEVYA: She gave me sons and daughters.

DAVID: The dead have a home together.

(*A vast shadowy figure appears in the sky. It is the black cowled figure of Death, one arm held across its face, the other reaching out.* TEVYA's *back is to the shadow. He sits beside the dead body.*)

TEVYA (*quietly*): My wife. Sleep. My little bride who loved me, sleep. My little girl. So quiet. Nothing to remember. My tired bones, my broken heart, my friendly face—sleep in peace. Sleep long.

(*He rests his head on the body.*)

DAVID: Stand up, Tevya.

(TEVYA *sits up and looks at the sky. He sees the great figure of the death Angel.*)

We have a long road to go Tevya.

TEVYA (*staring at the Angel*): No, I can't go. Don't you see—there's somebody here for me.

DAVID (*staring around*): Where?

TEVYA: There! Standing! I can see him—the Angel of Death—the Malachamuvis. Look how he stands—with one arm over his face. Why does he hide his face from me? I have seen worse faces than his.

(*He pauses and smiles dimly as he looks at the Angel.*)

Old friends of the Jews—I'm coming. Not to Eretz Yisrael, but to an even older place. Duvidel, go on alone. Leave behind Tevya and his old legs. Tevya and his old words and his burned out houses. Go find new words and new houses.

DAVID (*sharply*): Tevya!

TEVYA (*he pauses and smiles at the great Shadow*): Sh! sh! He comes. Ah, how soft he walks! How friendly he sighs! Ah, what's so wrong with death? Welcome—brother . . .

(*He sinks beside Zelda and is still.* DAVID *remains looking at his body. The Angel vanishes out of the sky. The* TEVYA *death music, all the rollicking folk themes of his past, swells up—and then dims.* DAVID *draws a knife from his belt. He holds it gleaming in the light. He speaks in a low, tense voice.*)

DAVID: Is it better there, Tevya? Is the ground softer, Tevya? Is the darkness sweeter, Tevya?

(*He moves toward the two bodies and spreads* TEVYA's *old tattered talis over him. Then cries out*)

Why not? Better to be dirt than to be a Jew! Dirt, cold dirt, that feels nothing when feet walk on it! Lucky Tevya!

(*He mimics his voice.*)

Go on Duvidel . . .

(*Bitterness flames in him.*)

Where? With what? The world tears my heart out—and you want it to beat with hope! A heart on the end of a stick—beating with hope! The hate of a world chews on my brain—and you want it to dream!

(*He raises his head to the clouded night.*)

Of what use is a man in darkness? Of what use is a Jew in a world of poison and shame? You—World—who made a garbage pile of my people, you didn't kill me. An oversight—to be corrected. You kill me now. You—land and sky forbidden to Jews—I give you my unlived years, my uneaten bread. I give you my unused loins, my brain that never dreamed, my heart that never sang. I go back to the garbage pile you made for me and mine.

(*He places the knife against his heart. A light appears at the right of the stage. It grows brighter. In the brightening glare a bridge stands, reaching out of the shadows. The music starts faintly, martial music, threaded with the Hatikva theme. A voice calls from the hidden end of the bridge.*)

FIRST SOLDIER: David! David!

(DAVID *remains holding the knife against his body. Three figures appear on the other side of the bridge. They move a few steps into the light. They are dressed in the uniforms of Palestinian soldiers. One of the* SOLDIERS *steps forward on the bridge. He speaks in a strong sharp voice.*)

FIRST SOLDIER: We're waiting for you, David.

DAVID (*dully*): Who are you?

SECOND SOLDIER: We are the Hebrew army of Palestine. We are the soldiers of the Haganah and the Irgun.

THIRD SOLDIER: We are the army of the Sternists.

DAVID (*dully*): What do you want of me?

SECOND SOLDIER: You! We fight in Palestine. In the streets of Jerusalem and Tel Aviv. In the hills of Lebanon—in the deserts of Judea. We hold the gates of our land open at night—for the Jews of Europe. We fight to open them in the daylight. We need you.

DAVID (*dully*): You are far away.

## APPENDIX 3

THIRD SOLDIER: No, we are in your heart.

DAVID (*dully*): Far away.

(*The sound of distant guns is heard.*)

SECOND SOLDIER: Don't you hear our guns, David? We battle the English—the sly and powerful English. We speak to them in a new Jewish language, the language of guns. We fling no more prayers or tears at the world. We fling bullets. We fling barrages.

(*Another of the* SOLDIERS *steps forward.*)

THIRD SOLDIER: We die in the streets, fighting. And our enemies die with us.

FIRST SOLDIER: We fight for Palestine.

SECOND SOLDIER: Come, David, no one laughs at Jews in Palestine. Torture, yes; violence and death, yes. But no laughter. It's no laughing matter to kill a Jew in Palestine. It takes tanks and planes and armies.

FIRST SOLDIER: The past is dead, David. We have thrown it into the Red Sea. It lies on the bottom of the sea—the whole black past of the Jews. Today our ancient wisdom speaks out of cannon mouths. The youth of the Jews die singing and chanting tomorrow's victory.

SECOND SOLDIER: Come David, Saul and the Maccabees live again in Palestine. Their strong arms are bared again. We promise you an end of pleading and proverbs. The manhood the world took from us roars again in Palestine.

THIRD SOLDIER: We promise you war—a war against the sly and powerful robbers of England. We promise to wrest our homeland out of British claws—as the Americans once did. And the Dutch of Africa. And the Irish. We promise you barricades and a loud battle cry.

FIRST SOLDIER: We promise you a war that will not be done until the dishonored flag of Israel flies white and spotless over Palestine. We promise you courage that will avenge all the Jews who have died under the grinding heel of the world.

SECOND SOLDIER: We promise you a battle front of Jews that will stand and die and stand again until a Hebrew nation rises out of the Hebrew soul.

DAVID: How do I go to join you?

(*The* THIRD SOLDIER *steps forward.*)

THIRD SOLDIER: There's a bridge to cross—a shining bridge. It's the bridge of cunning and fortitude, of youth and wild courage. That bridge is in your heart. It's the bridge that reaches from the dark in which you stand into the promised battle and the Promised Land. Put your feet on this bridge and walk. You will scurry down dark roads. You will hide under trains and in the dark corners of ships. You will rob, lie, kill, and claw your way forward through many hostile lands. But the bridge will bear you always. It will carry your feet and your soldier's hands—to us and the streets of battle . . . to the land where manhood and a gun wait for you . . . Come David, and fight for Palestine.

FIRST SOLDIER: Come, David, help us give birth to a flag . . .

(DAVID *turns to the dead* TEVYA. *He takes the talis from him. He takes a blue star from his own pocket. He puts the star on the talis, cutting away the talis fringes with his knife. From beyond the lighted bridge comes a chorus of soldiers singing the Hatikva in the distance beyond the bridge . . .* DAVID *tacks his talis-flag to a branch. He pauses and through the singing he hears the sound of guns, distant guns growing louder. He looks at* TEVYA. DAVID *turns toward the shining bridge. Holding his flag high, he walks toward the light, the singing and the sound of guns . . .*)

(*The curtain falls.*)

# Appendix 4
# *The Terrorist (1947)*

[Editor's note: Peter Bergson published the text of *The Terrorist* in his private newsletter *The Answer*. That text is identical to Hecht's typescript except for the late addition of a "Prologue" speech written for the actress Ruth Chatterton.]

## PRODUCTION INFORMATION
WRITTEN BY BEN HECHT
DIRECTED BY MOE HACK
MUSIC BY ISAAC VAN GROVE
SETTINGS AND COSTUMES BY JOHN BOYT

Performed September 20–21, 1947, at Carnegie Hall, New York

Cast:

PROLOGUE: Ruth Chatterton
JEHUDA HALEVY: Joseph Silver
TEVYA: Jonathan Harris

Sources: Ben Hecht, *The Terrorist* (typescript), Erwin Piscator Papers, Special Collections Research Center, Southern Illinois University Carbondale; Ben Hecht, "The Terrorist," *The Answer*, September 19, 1947.

APPENDIX 4

DOV BELA GRUNER: Si Oakland
SCOTCH SERGEANT: Joseph Keen
ENGLISH SERGEANT: Harvey Lembeck
ENGLISH CAPTAIN: Clark Howat
ENGLISH MAJOR: Jabez Gray
VOICES OF THE DEAD: Ruth Hill, Rudy Bond, Bernard Grant, Joseph Keen, Vincent Beck, R. Spelvin

## THE TERRORIST

PROLOGUE: There are those whom death does not remove
　　　Nor silence, whose voices speak
　　　Out of covered graves.
　　　So speaks the soldier, Dov Bela Gruner,
　　　Hebrew fighter for the Land of Israel
　　　Who was hanged by the English in Palestine.
　　　He was one of the heroes who, with the world against them,
　　　Fight on for a better world.
　　　He was of the riders to lost battles
　　　Who die in darkness
　　　Yet so brightly burned their living souls
　　　That, dead, they leave a light behind.
　　　He was of that human handful
　　　Of whom tomorrow says—
　　　So deep their Faith was,
　　　Their dream of justice so profound,
　　　So dedicated were their days—
　　　That death struck vainly at them
　　　And left them glowing in our midst
　　　More precious than ourselves
　　　And more alive than we.
　　　So glows and lives the soldier, Dov Bela Gruner
　　　Hebrew fighter for the land of Palestine.[1]
　　　(*The stage is dark. An eerie Hebraic strain of music begins. A bearded white face appears out of the dark. A spotlight lights it dimly. It is the face of an ancient Jew. A black robe covers the body. The music continues as this*

---

[1] The "Prologue" speech appears in the text published in *The Answer* but not in Hecht's typescript.

*dignified and archaic face hovers motionlessly in the dark. A few moments later another face appears. The second face, although white and ghostly as the first, is of a different quality. It is a small bearded, almost humorous face. The music grows fainter. The two Jews speak. The* FIRST JEW *has the sound of poetry in his voice. The* SECOND JEW *has the sound of banter and sarcasm in his talk. With the music still playing faintly, the* FIRST JEW *speaks.*)

FIRST JEW (*slowly and without looking at the other*): It seems I don't know you.

SECOND JEW (*turning and speaking a bit truculently*): Who knows you?

FIRST JEW: It stands in the Talmud that the dead are not strangers.

SECOND JEW: Your name I don't know. Your face I have never seen. And dead I am—like Yussel's horse that was drowned in the Dnieper. But if it says in the Talmud we are not strangers—good. I believe. Amen.

FIRST JEW (*without turning*): To believe and believe through one darkness into another is the happiness of the Jew.

SECOND JEW (*wryly*): Fine, fine. Nobody can say I'm not a happy Jew. (*He sighs heavily*) Ai, usually I can't remember my name—who I was, where I lived. But tonight I remember, I was Tevye Feifle, a man of many troubles.

FIRST JEW: I was Jehuda Halevy—who wrote many poems.

TEVYA: Sholem Aleichem.

HALEVY (*motionless*): Aleichem Sholem.

TEVYA (*turning to inspect his companion*): You are dead long?

HALEVY: Longer than you.

TEVYA (*sighing*): Yes, you look rested.

HALEVY: It takes a long time to find rest—Even after the One with the iron knuckle knocks on your door.

TEVYA (*he looks around nervously*): I was sent here. But what is there to see? Nothing. The same nothing. Do you think, Reb Halevy, we have come to the right place?

HALEVY: How could God send us to the wrong place?

TEVYA: Forgive me. I didn't know who it was sent us.

HALEVY: There is no power but God and we are the Lord's messengers.

TEVYA (*nervously*): Who wants to argue? (*He sighs*) If God sent me then I'm here—and no place else. Like he wants. (*He prays with sudden piety*) Schmai Israel Adenoi Aluhanu—

HALEVY (*joining the prayer*): Schmai Israel Adenoi Achud—

(*The music grows louder and voices singing a prayer are heard in the dark. The two faces remain motionless and silent until the singing grows softer.*)

TEVYA (*nervously*): Did you hear?

HALEVY: Yes.

## APPENDIX 4

TEVYA: There are others?

HALEVY: This is a place of importance. Many dead have come. They are all around us.

TEVYA (*looking around him*): Fine, fine.

HALEVY (*motionless*): This is a place where a hero of Israel sleeps. A young one whose heart is like a lion on a hilltop.

(*The singing swells out. A light appears. It shines dimly through a barred cell window and falls on a young man on a cell-bench. He is dressed in red trousers and a torn shirt. His right arm is crudely bandaged. He is motionless in sleep.*)

TEVYA (*turning and staring at him*): You know who he is?

HALEVY (*without turning*): His name is Dov.

TEVYA (*still watching the figure*): Ai—he sleeps like a baby.

HALEVY: It is his last sleep.

TEVYA (*sighing*): Ai, I should have known. If Tevya Feifle is there—it's no good. (*A pause*) He dies soon?

HALEVY: When he wakes he will be hanged.

TEVYA (*softly*): He knows?

HALEVY: Not yet.

TEVYA (*sighing*): Why so they hang him, Reb Halevy?

HALEVY: Because it is needful to take away his good name. It is his good name the English hang—so that he shall seem a criminal instead of a Hebrew soldier who fought to free his homeland of an invader.

TEVYA (*excitedly*): To hang a soldier—this is against the law! And the English—they are in Palestine against the law. The whole thing is against the law, Reb Halevy!

HALEVY (*quietly*): Nothing that is done to the Jews is against the law—if it is done by a nation. A nation can only commit a crime against another nation. And the Jew, however numerous he be, is forever outside the law, because he belongs to nowhere.

TEVYA: This I know, Reb Halevy—a Jew breaks the law when he is born. This I found out in Kishinev.

HALEVY: Dov, can you hear us?

TEVYA (*nervously*): That good if he hears us? A fine blessing we bring him.

HALEVY: Dov, we have come to be with you in your last hour. Dream of us and we will talk to you.

TEVYA (*sighing*): My advice is—don't dream of us. Better you don't hear what we have to tell.

HALEVY (*softly*): Many friends are here, Dov—Jews from yesterday and long ago.

## THE TERRORIST

(*A pause.* GRUNER *speaks from his bench. He remains motionless and asleep as he talks. His voice throughout his dream is tranquil and almost childlike.*)

GRUNER: Who are you?

HALEVY: You will know us when you meet us.

GRUNER: Where will I meet you?

HALEVY: In a better world.

TEVYA (*sighing*): Ai, a better world—if you can get used to it.

HALEVY: Tomorrow comes not.

GRUNER: What are you doing here?

HALEVY: We are here in your last sleep.

GRUNER: My last sleep—

TEVYA (*chanting ruefully*): Oh Lord, I would like sometime to bring good news to a Jew. But naturally God is wiser than I am so He sends me here.

GRUNER (*softly in his sleep*): My last sleep—The sun will be rising when I wake up. The hills will be bright with dew. And the cedar trees will look wet and young. I have always liked the morning. (*A pause*) Is the gallows high? What will I see when I stand on it?

HALEVY: You will see the dream in your heart.

GRUNER: My wise brother from long ago, I do not want to look at a dream when I stand there. I have not been a dreamer among Jews.

HALEVY: What do you desire when you stand there, Dov?

GRUNER: I want to hear the voices of my people—the voices that called to me out of the slaughter in which my people died.

HALEVY: You shall hear them, Dov.

GRUNER (*softly*): If I hear them I shall raise my head and feel a gun again in my hands. And though I am beaten and sick and the rope is on my neck—if I hear them I shall die with pride—because I fought for them.

TEVYA (*wailing softly*): You fought for us. You die for us. Tell me where is the hope for my children. Where is a land without death or wickedness for our own?

GRUNER (*softly*): I will answer you on the gallows, Old Jew. Here—·here where the gallows stand is our homeland. Here where the hangman walks is the house of the Jews. Here where the thieves of England come to fatten is Eretz-Israel.

(*The music swells out and voices sing sadly for a moment.*)

TEVYA (*sadly*): Look how he sleeps there with no one but a stranger—a dead one—to weep for him.

(*The singing fades out.*)

GRUNER (*gently*): Don't weep for me, Old Jew. Remember instead my brother who is young and alive and who fights on without me—stronger because I have died for his cause. In my last sleep it is pleasant to dream of them—of all my brothers hidden among the hills and people and in the desert waiting. And when I am dead, I pray that God gives me eyes to see them drive the robbers from our home—the English robber with his whip, his lies and his gallows.

(*The music starts again.*)

HALEVY: The bad hour comes soon. Sleep a while longer. Dream once more of battles won—of happy Jews in the happy land of Palestine. Dream once more—

(HALEVY's *voice trails off . . . The music rises . . . Voices singing triumphantly fill the dark . . . The two apparitions begin to vanish. The light goes from their faces . . . The singing softens. The light on* GRUNER *brightens. A figure appears. It is that of a* SCOT SERGEANT. *The* SERGEANT *stands looking down on the sleeping* GRUNER *. . . The music and singing end.*)

SERGEANT (*with a Scotch accent*): I'm here to wake ye up, Gruner. (*He shakes* GRUNER's *shoulder*) Time to get up.

(GRUNER *wakes. He sits up slowly. He looks beyond the sergeant to where the two ghostly visitors stood. He frowns. Then he looks at the Scot.*)

GRUNER (*softly*): Is it morning?

SERGEANT: It is that.

(GRUNER *raises his eyes to the light in the window.*)

GRUNER: The sun's up eh? What time is it?

SERGEANT: Nearin' five o'clock.

GRUNER (*quietly*): You're an hour early, aren't you?

SERGEANT (*curtly*): I got me orders.

GRUNER: I know.

SERGEANT (*sharply*): Ye know what?

GRUNER (*quietly*): Is the gallows ready?

SERGEANT: I'm givin' no information.

GRUNER (*softly*): Tomorrow comes not.

SERGEANT: Who's been talkin' to ye?

GRUNER: Two old friends.

SERGEANT: Yer lyin'. There's been a double guard on ye since last night with no visitors passin' through.

GRUNER: How soon will the hangmen be here?

SERGEANT: I'm tellin' ye nothin'.

(*He paces in front of the cell, scowling.* GRUNER *sits watching him. The music plays softly a Scotch bag-pipe air. The* SERGEANT *pauses and looks at* GRUNER.)

SERGEANT: The lads were tellin' me you were an English soldier once.

GRUNER: That's right.
SERGEANT: It's a hard thing to believe. (*He paces and then stops again.*) See any action?
GRUNER: Quite a bit.
SERGEANT: Where abouts?
GRUNER: Allemain.[2]
SERGEANT: Is that a fact? I was there. Fifth Highlanders. What outfit were ye?
GRUNER: The Buffs Regiment.
SERGEANT: The Buffs, eh? A very good outfit. They were on our right.
GRUNER: Yes, I remember the bagpipes when the charge started.
SERGEANT: I piped me head off. A fine day that was, when the Krauts started breakin'.
(*He pauses and looks angrily at* GRUNER. *The music ends.*)
And it's a fine mess yer in! A fine mess for any man who was at Allemain. And it's yer own fault. No man has the right to change sides.
GRUNER: I didn't change sides.
SERGEANT (*angrily*): Ye fought for England once, didn't ye?
GRUNER: I fought for a cause.
SERGEANT (*angrily*): And who didn't man? The overthrow of tyranny in the world—
GRUNER (*quietly*): I'm still fighting for it—
SERGEANT (*angrily*): A fine cause it is when your own Jewish people call ye a lawbreaker and a terrorist! And a murderer, too!
GRUNER (*sighing*): It's no fun fighting for a people who cheer when the enemy hangs you and who break out in condolences when you hang one of the enemy.
SERGEANT (*sarcastic*): They're all out of step but yourself, eh?
GRUNER: It's easy to be wrong—when you're frightened.
SERGEANT: So that's your theory, man! The whole world includin' nearly all the Jews is wrong—and only you and your Irgoon is right! It is a fine fancy to have.
GRUNER: That's the fancy—I'm going to die for, Sergeant.
SERGEANT: If it was only the English who were for hangin' ye, I'd say maybe the man is a soldier who's dyin' fer the Jews—as many a brave laddie once died fer the Scotch. But how do ye explain it when the English are again' ye and your own people equally again' ye? Answer me that?
GRUNER (*softly*): My own people—

---

[2] Hecht is referring to El Alamein in Egypt, the site of major battles between British and Axis forces in 1942 during the North African campaign of World War II.

## APPENDIX 4

SERGEANT: Yes—I've yet to hear a good word for your Irgoon from a Jew or Christian—And even the Jews who are dreamin' to live in Palestine callin' ye names for spoilin' their chances—by fightin' and breakin' the law. Answer me that.

GRUNER (*quietly*): My people have lived in disgrace for a long time. They've been like an unwelcome guest in the world. That's why they don't like to see Jews fighting—even for existence. They're more afraid of giving offense than of being slaughtered. I'll tell you something queer, Sergeant—millions of Jews have died without fighting back—for fear of adding to their unpopularity.

SERGEANT: Man, there's lots of folks like Jews right enough—and feel sorry for them—

GRUNER: Yes—if they stay on their knees begging for favors that nobody will give them—people don't mind Jews so much. But Jews fighting for their rights—that's another story. Even the nicest Christians get angry about it. Maybe they wonder if the Jews are going to start killing their enemies—where will they stop? (*A pause*) They coming yet, Sergeant?

SERGEANT (*looking down the corridor*): Yes—

(*A pause. The music plays softly the Hatikva theme.*)

GRUNER (*softly*): Yes—any other people fighting for their homeland would be hailed as patriots. But Jews fighting and dying for their Palestine—are gangsters and murderers.

(*An* ENGLISH SERGEANT *appears. He is tough and snarling.*)

ENGLISH SERGEANT: Wot's he gabblin' about?

SCOT SERGEANT: Oh, just jawin' about his troubles. Where's the brass?

ENGLISH SERGEANT: Comin' along shortly. (*He looks at* GRUNER) Does 'e know about 'is little party?

SCOT SERGEANT: I didn't mention the matter to him.

ENGLISH SERGEANT (*sneering at* GRUNER): 'Ellow, ye little Jew bastard—I've the pleasure of informin' ye that we're 'angin' ye today—with a nice, thick British rope.

GRUNER (*quietly*): Thanks.

ENGLISH SERGEANT: Yer welcome, ye bloody little kike. Ye'll know who owns Palestine when yer 'angin' by yer Jew neck enjoyin' the 'olyland breezes.

(*An* ENGLISH CAPTAIN *enters.*)

CAPTAIN (*curtly*): Shut up, Atkins.

(*The two* SERGEANTS *salute. The* CAPTAIN *returns the salute.*)

ENGLISH SERGEANT: 'E was shootin' off 'is Jew mouth.

CAPTAIN (*ignoring him and turning to* GRUNER): Major Brooks will be here shortly. The sentence imposed on you by His Majesty's Court last January will be carried out immediately.

GRUNER: Am I going to be hanged in this outfit, sir?

CAPTAIN: Yes.

GRUNER: I was captured in uniform.

CAPTAIN: Gangsters and hoodlums are not entitled to military dress, Gruner.

GRUNER: I was captured fighting for my country.

CAPTAIN: You have no country. You might as well face the facts of who and what you are in your last hour—and go out with a bit of sanity in your head. You're a Jew brigand without a leg to stand on. You were tried by a British Court of law and found guilty. And the verdict has been approved by the world.

GRUNER (*quietly*): Yes—I was tried.

(*He stares at the* CAPTAIN *and continues softly.*)

A robber comes into your home and steals everything you own. And you cry for the police. The robber grins at you and says, "I'm the police, old boy, come along." And he takes you to court. You look up and there sits the robber on the bench as your judge. And your own frightened brother appears as a witness against you—testifying you had no right interfering with the robber's work. And the robber then denounces you and sentences you to be hanged for objecting to his thievery. And the world looks at you hanging and says, "He got what he deserved for defying law and order." And the world shakes hands with this English robber for disposing of another Jewish scoundrel. It's the trick by which England has looted and brutalized half the world and still kept its good name for—

ENGLISH SERGEANT (*interrupting angrily*): Are ye goin' to let this Jew bastard insult 'is Majesty, Captain? Wot 'e needs is a rifle butt across 'is stinkin' Jew mouth—and so 'elp me—I'll—

CAPTAIN (*sharply as the* SERGEANT *raises his rifle*): Hold it, Sergeant. He's paying a fair price for his notions in a few minutes—(*To* GRUNER) Are you done calling us names, Jew?

GRUNER: You'll hear them for a long time, Englishman.

ENGLISH SERGEANT (*sneering*): Not from you, sonny boy.

GRUNER: You'll hear them when the world wakes up to your red handed theft of Palestine—and to your crimes against the Jews of Europe. You'll hear them when you hold out your hand begging for help again—and the decent world comes to you with contempt instead of gold.—

(*A British* MAJOR *has appeared during the last part of* GRUNER'S *answer.*)

## APPENDIX 4

MAJOR: What's all this?

(*The* CAPTAIN *and the two* SERGEANTS *salute him.*)

CAPTAIN: The prisoner is airing some final views on the Empire, sir.

MAJOR: You've got to expect it from Jews. They never stop talking. (*He turns to* GRUNER *who is sitting on the cell bench*) Stand up, Gruner. I have something to say to you.

GRUNER: What is it?

MAJOR: A death warrant. You will please stand.

GRUNER: I do not recognize the legality of your warrant, sir, and will not stand up to hear it.

MAJOR: Come now, Gruner, there's no sense in being difficult about it. I shall have to insist that you obey the formalities imposed on His Majesty's criminals.

GRUNER: I am a soldier, sir, and not a criminal.

ENGLISH SERGEANT: You bloody little Jew traitor—stand up!

GRUNER: I'm no traitor—

MAJOR (*to the angry* SERGEANT): No interruptions, Sergeant. (*To* GRUNER) So you're no traitor, eh? Do you deny you shed English blood?

GRUNER: What was English blood doing on Hebrew soil?

CAPTAIN: Aren't we wasting time, Major?

MAJOR: I'll ask you once more Gruner. Stand on your feet to hear His Majesty's warrant.

GRUNER: I have only one weapon left against the English robber of my people—that's the knowledge that you and not I are the criminal. I'll die with that weapon in my heart.

MAJOR: Stand him up, Sergeant.

ENGLISH SERGEANT (*stepping to* GRUNER): On yer feet, ye dirty Jew!

GRUNER (*quietly*): No.

(*The* ENGLISH SERGEANT *swings his rifle and hits* GRUNER's *body with its butt.* GRUNER *sways in his seat.*)

MAJOR: Keep it up—Sergeant—till he stands up.

(*The* SERGEANT *starts a methodical beating of* GRUNER. *The prisoner falls to the floor. The* SERGEANT *kicks violently at his body. In the midst of this kicking the* SCOT SERGEANT *cries out.*)

SCOT SERGEANT: Stop it! Stop it! You can't do this to a man who's goin' to die!

(*He dashes toward the* ENGLISH SERGEANT. *The* CAPTAIN *seizes him.*)

CAPTAIN: Quiet, you fool!

SCOT SERGEANT (*struggling with the* CAPTAIN): Stop it! He fought with me at Allemain.

MAJOR (*stepping up to the* SCOT): How dare you open your stupid mouth—while on duty!

SCOT SERGEANT: I'm a Scotchman, not an Englishman! I'm a man! And as a man I ask ye to stop what you're doin'!

MAJOR: Take his stripes off, Captain.

(*The* CAPTAIN *is holding the* SCOT. *He rips his sleeve stripes off.*)

MAJOR: Go to your barracks, we'll talk to you later.

SCOT SERGEANT (*backing away from the* CAPTAIN *who has drawn his gun*): You'll not be the only ones who talk. I've got a tongue of me own. I'll let the world know! Ye hear me, Dov? I'll tell the world about it, laddie—

CAPTAIN: Get out!

(SCOT SERGEANT *goes away.*)

MAJOR: Will you stand now, Gruner?

GRUNER (*from the floor*): Never.

MAJOR: Pick him up, Sergeant—give him a hand, Captain.

CAPTAIN: Yes sir.

(*The two lift* GRUNER *to his feet end hold his limp form erect.*)

MAJOR (*removing a paper from his uniform and reads*): "In accordance with the sentence imposed by His Majesty's Court, by order of His Majesty's Minister of War, special defense regulations 1470—supplement 2—dated 28 January, 1946, the convicted Dov Bela Gruner has been found guilty of committing an offense in violation of part 3, section 58, paragraph D, and has been condemned to death as a member of a group or body of persons, any one or more of whom has committed an offense against this regulation. Namely the condemned Dov Bela Gruner did contravene His Majesty's regulations and in accordance with the findings of the General Military Court that the convicted, Dov Gruner, be put to death by hanging by the neck until dead—we hereby as officers of His Majesty's service order you to the gallows in fulfillment of the sentence given." Take him out.

GRUNER (*faintly*): I have a request to make, I would like a rabbi of my faith to come with me to the gallows.

MAJOR: Request denied. Take him out.

(*The lights dim out. The music of the death march starts up in the dark.*

*The stage remains in darkness for a few moments as the death march swells and ebbs.*

*A light slowly illumines the faces of the two apparitions—*TEVYA *and* HALEVY. *The faces are close together in the center of the dark stage.* TEVYA *is peering from left to right as if watching some marvel.* HALEVY *remains motionless.*

## APPENDIX 4

*The death march music changes into a Hebrew strain as the two faces become visible. The singing voices are heard again.*

*After a few moments the voices and the music remains faintly under the talk.)*

TEVYA (*a-marvel*): So many are here! Look!

HALEVY (*motionless*): I see them.

TEVYA (*in awe*): Who are they?

HALEVY: Jews from all the corners of time.

TEVYA (*whispering*): So many! So many! Why are they here, Reb Halevy?

HALEVY: He asked to hear the voices of his slaughtered people. And they have been sent to him.

TEVYA (*looking up*): He can hear us when he stands up there—still alive?

HALEVY: He will hear us. We will be like a sound out of a dark meadow. He will stand with his lips silent and his body broken. But his heart will remain like a lion on a hilltop and his spirit will speak bravely to the darkness.

TEVYA (*shrinking as he looks slowly around*): More come! Look—how many! Endless—endless!

HALEVY: The darkness is not vast enough to hold them.

TEVYA (*softly*): Ai—who has killed so many Jews?

HALEVY: Ask who has not.

TEVYA (*awed*): From everywhere—from all the years!

HALEVY: It is a long murder—never a finished crime. The face of the earth changes, but one thing remains the same—the killing of Jews.

TEVYA: Why—why?

HALEVY: Ask that question not of a Jew. For he who is murdered knows only his innocence.

*(The music swells and the singing is heard faintly.)*

TEVYA: The Cossacks came like a black wind riding into our kitchens—killing, killing! And there was no reason. "Die, Jew, die!" they yelled. So we died. Why—why?

*(Voices are heard out of the dark. They come from both sides of the stage. The voices echo* TEVYA's *word.)*

VOICES: Why—why—why?

*(The cries subside and the singing ends ... A light appears at stage left. It reveals* GRUNER ... *The music of the death march plays ... Behind* GRUNER *walk the* BRITISH MAJOR, CAPTAIN *and* SERGEANT. *They are in half shadows ...* GRUNER *moves slowly. He is climbing an incline. His head hangs, his body wavers ...* TEVYA *watches his progress with a pained face ...)*

TEVYA: He is here, Reb Halevy. Look—

HALEVY (*without turning*): Another Jew walks up a hill in Palestine to die.
TEVYA: He is weak—there's nobody to pray for him—(*He starts praying in Hebrew*) Baruch attu Adenoi Elohenu.
HALEVY (*chanting with him*): Baruch attu Adenoi Echod.
  (*The light on* GRUNER *brightens as he moves upward toward the gallows platform . . . The death march continues and swells . . . Voices speak out of the dark. As they fill the stage, the slow moving* GRUNER *raises his head as if he heard them—he pauses, straightens, moves on, his head turning toward the voices coming to him.*)
FIRST VOICE (*calling tenderly*): Dov—Dov.
SECOND VOICE: Dov, we are beside you.
THIRD VOICE: We are the voices you asked to hear.
FOURTH VOICE: The voices of the slaughtered.
FIFTH VOICE: Your slaughtered people.
SIXTH VOICE: The slaughtered—we are beside you, Dov.
  (*The light has remained on the faces of* TEVYA *and* HALEVY. *It brightens now.*)
TEVYA (*shrinking as he looks and listens*): They are like an army, look—look! Like an army!
HALEVY: A pale army without banners.
  (*The light grows dimmer on their faces. The light brightens on* GRUNER. *His shadowy English escort is gone. He stands listening for a moment, moves, pauses, climbs on.*)
FIRST VOICE: Hear our story Dov. We are the Jews who began the wandering long ago.
SECOND VOICE: We were driven naked out of the city of Alexandria—by the Christian Bishop Cyril. And this was in the year 400.
THIRD VOICE: We had lost our nation. No home was ours anymore. We were driven forth and we carried the land of Israel in our hearts—
FOURTH VOICE: The Sabbath was forbidden us. The Persian King slaughtered us. Our bodies were nailed to crosses on the bridge of Marchuza.
FIFTH VOICE: We are here beside you, Dov. For we dreamed of you when we were alive.
  (*The singing is heard. The light brightens on the faces of* TEVYA *and* HALEVY. TEVYA's *eyes are everywhere in wonder.* HALEVY *is without movement. The singing fades. Under its soft hum, the apparitions speak.*)
TEVYA: You know them, Reb Halevy?
HALEVY: Yes, I know them. They were the survivors of the Hebrew nation that was hammered to bits. They were the bits that refused to die—and flourished

# APPENDIX 4

again under the last Hebrew Princes of the Captivity. They were the Mishna and the Talmud writers, the remnant of Israel, that was torn out of its last house and flung across the earth.

(*The light grows dimmer on the two feces. The music rises.*)

FIRST VOICE: Hear our story, Dov. In the year five hundred we were slaughtered in the land of Byzantium.

SECOND VOICE: The Emperor Zeno bewailed the fact that there were not enough Jews left in Byzantium to make another good bonfire.

THIRD VOICE: We died with prayers on our lips and our hearts turned to Palestine.

FOURTH VOICE: We are beside you, Dov. For we dreamed of you when we were alive.

(*The singing fills the dark. The singing ebbs. The two apparitions speak again and the light brightens on them.*)

TEVYA: Explain to me, Reb Halevy, what they mean? How could they dream of him so long ago—

HALEVY: He will tell us—when he speaks.

TEVYA: He knows?

HALEVY: He will know soon—

(*The music increases. The voices resume as the music ebbs.*)

FIRST VOICE: Hear our story, Dov. We are from the slaughter of the years that began in 532. The Emperor Justinian passed a law forbidding Jews to appear in any Christian court as witnesses. We were condemned without voice—we were driven out again—to wander further.

SECOND: We lived in all the lands from the Mediterranean to the North Sea. We were men of learning and we were welcomed. We toiled beside the workers of all the lands. We fought beside the soldiers of all the nations. And out of the battles we shared, many countries were built.

THIRD: But the light was taken from our faces, the slaughter was begun again. We were forbidden to appear in the street on Christian holidays. This was in the year 538.

FOURTH: We were massacred in the town of Clairmont, in France, under the Bishop of Aeverniu.

FIFTH: Laws were passed by all the Bishops of France forbidding us to sit down in the presence of Christians—and we were slain in our synagogues.

SIXTH: The Emperor Dagobert called for the killing of all Jews alive in the Empire of France—and were slaughtered. This was the year 629.

FIRST: We are beside you Dov—for we dreamed of you when we were alive.

SECOND (*exultantly*): Hear us! We battled where you stand, Dov! We were the Jews who lived hidden in the hills and cities of Palestine.

THIRD: The soul of Bar Kochba entered our hunted bodies and we struck against the Romans. We stormed Jerusalem! We drove them out. That was in the year 614.

SECOND (*exultantly*): For fourteen years the land of Israel was ours again.

FOURTH: Persia and Rome—and the might of the world came down upon us. And all our soldiers were slain.

FIFTH: Heraclius entered the Holy City and the law was made that every Jew left alive in Palestine be slain.

SIXTH: Our children, our old and our women fled. We were the last Jews to leave the land of Israel. And in our wandering, we dreamed of you, Dov.

FIRST: We were in Spain. We lived in a Golden Age under the Moors.

SECOND: The Moors turned on us. All the Jews of Granada were slaughtered in a single day. This was in the year 1066.

THIRD: We were in Germany when the first storm broke. We were slaughtered by the Emperor Henry in Mayence.

FIFTH: We were in Egypt when the Caliph Hakim declared himself a god and ordered all the Jews of Egypt slain.

SIXTH: Hear our story, Dov. We were slaughtered in the great Christian Crusades—a million of us were slain—and hundreds of thousands of us slew ourselves.

FIRST: All the towns of the Rhine became Jewish graveyards.

SECOND: We were in the land of Bohemia. The Counts of Bohemia stripped and slaughtered us and we went wandering into Poland. This was in the year 1098.

(*The light brightens on* HALEVY.)

HALEVY: A thousand years of torment—and we were still alive. We were the bits that refused to die. Hear the song that was in us, Dov. We sang of Jerusalem. "Oh City of splendor, oh bright home of the Jews, our spirit flies to thee from the many lands. In the East—in the far land of the cedar and the lemon trees our hearts lie, and our souls swell beside the sun gone down on Israel." This we sang in the years when massacre of Jews became the spiritual life of Europe.

FIRST: Hear our story, Dov, our long story. On the banks of the Seine, the Rhine, the Moselle, the Danube, the Dnieper—and in all the lands of Europe we were hunted and slaughtered. This was after the year 1146.

SECOND: The Second Crusade swept us from the earth.

THIRD: King Louis the VII of France ordered our destruction.

FOURTH: We were slaughtered in the cities of Carenton, Cologne and Wurzburg.

FIFTH: In Morocco the Caliph Abdul Mumon ordered the death of all the Jews alive in Africa. We went wandering. And in our wandering we dreamed of you who stand on the gallows.

# APPENDIX 4

FIRST: Count Theobold burned us in the land of France, after decreeing we were murderers.

SECOND: King Phillip Augustus of France stripped us of all we owned to the clothes on our backs, slaughtered us and drove us out of Paris.

THIRD: We were in England when the bloody cries of Thomas à Becket filled the land.

FOURTH: All the synagogues of London were destroyed. All our homes were pillaged.

FIFTH: The Archbishop of Canterbury cried out for our blood and denounced our protector, King Richard the Lion Hearted. "Hell take our King," he cried, "for his friendship to the Jews."

SIXTH: And when Richard left England on his new Crusade, the English slaughtered us in the cities of Lynn and Stamford, Norwich and London.

FIRST: We fought them in the tower of Dover until our ammunition was gone—then five thousand of us leaped to our death on the rocks below.

SECOND: King John, the new King of England robbed us of our citizenship. Bounties were paid for dead Jews. This was in the year 1220.

THIRD: Pope Innocent ordered the extermination of all the Jews in Europe. We remember his words—"The Jews, like Cain, are doomed to wander the world as fugitives and vagabonds and their faces must be covered with shame."

*(During the last speech GRUNER has stopped moving. His face, lighted vividly, remaining motionless ... A light suddenly picks out a large noose hanging beside his head ... The death march music changes to the Hatikva theme ... GRUNER raises his head and calls softly to the dark.)*

GRUNER: I hear you, Jews!

FIRST: We dreamed of you, Dov, when Philip the Good drove us from France again.

GRUNER *(exultant and soft)*: I hear the voices of my people!

SECOND: When the shepherd gangs on the Garone slaughtered us—and in Toulouse.

THIRD: When the knight Von Doggenburg hunted us out of Bohemia and Austria.

FOURTH: When two thousand of us were burned at the stake in Strasburg. This was in 1348.

GRUNER *(his voice is exultant and soft as if he were speaking in a half dream)*: I promise you justice.

*(The voices come more quickly.)*

FIRST: We dreamed of you, Dov.

SECOND: When they massacred us in Worms, Frankfurt, Nuremburg—in Breslau and Vienna.

HALEVY (*his arms raised to* GRUNER): There is no nation in the world that has not burned the house we built.

THIRD: When Louis, King of Hungary, slaughtered us—

FOURTH: When Henry the Third, King of England, stripped us and slaughtered our thousands in London.

FIFTH: We waited for you—

HALEVY: In whatever land we thrived we have always known that our thriving was short—that tomorrow would bring us exile and slaughter.

TEVYA: Look, Reb Halevy, he is not afraid. His eyes are bright.

FIRST: In Spain—

SECOND: In Spain, red with fires of the inquisition.

THIRD: In Spain—when Pope Gregory the Ninth called on Europe to exterminate us.

FOURTH: When our three thousand children were slaughtered in Bordeaux and Anjou.

FIFTH: When all the Jews of Munich were burned.

SIXTH: When all the Jews of England were given yellow badges—and torn asunder by horses.

FIRST: When Switzerland became the new center of Jew hatred—and we were slaughtered in Zurich and Berne charged with bringing the black plague to Europe.

SECOND: When we were outlawed from Alsace and Basle—and all the Jews of Freiburg were burned.

THIRD: When all Europe became a gallows for the Jews—

FOURTH: We dreamed of you coming, Dov—

FIFTH: When we fled before the slaughter of Pope Clement the Fourth—dressed in yellow hats—

SIXTH: When the 30,000 were massacred in Seville.

FIRST: Massacred on the island of Majorca.

SECOND: And no Jew left alive in Portugal.

THIRD: Hunted down and burned in the new lands of Mexico and Peru and Brazil.

FOURTH: When the man called Capistrano led our slaughter in Silesia.

FIFTH: When he came to Poland—and inflamed our friends to massacre us.

(*The light brightens on* HALEVY.)

HALEVY (*his arms raised to* GRUNER): During all this time of torment and humiliation we dreamed of a Jew who would rise from our ashes and cry, "Hold! Enough!" to the world. We dreamed of a Jew who would stand on Israel's

# APPENDIX 4

soil and say to our enemies, "I am done with being the unwelcome wanderer. I am done with being the guest who must be destroyed. Here in Palestine is my home. Here I will fight and die for my homeland. If you would kill me again, kill me in battle with a gun in my hands."

SIXTH: He is there in battle.

FIRST: He stands on his battlefield as we dreamed.

SECOND: The strong one—the Mossiah who wears Bar Kochba's armor—

THIRD: He battles for our children and our children's children.

FOURTH: For they have no other home than the land of Israel.

(*The light brightens on* HALEVY *and* TEVYA.)

TEVYA: Where else! Where else! Under the hooves of the Cossacks I found no home!

HALEVY: No where else. Destroyed, we rise again to fresh destruction. Such is our history. No generation has passed in 2,000 years without witnessing our slaughter. We waited long for you, soldier on the gallows, and now you are here we sing hallelujah in the darkness.

VOICES (*in chorus*): Hallelujah—Hallelujah!

HALEVY: We have been summoned to watch a Jew die for a new reason—not because lunatics said he drank the blood of children—or because lunatics cried he scattered plague germs, or because he once watched another Jew die on a cross—not even because he bears the curse of being a Jew. Not for any of those ugly reasons, but for a reason that is like a light in the sky—because he fought for his people—a reason that makes all the pale and bannerless dead of Israel rejoice around his gallows.

FIRST: We sing Hallelujah to a hero of Israel!

SECOND: We dreamed of him in the furnaces of the Germans that destroyed six million of us -

THIRD: We dreamed of him in the pogroms of a hundred lands—and he is here!

HALEVY: Speak to us before you die. And we will remember your words in eternity.

VOICES (*in chorus*): Speak—speak to us, Dov.

(*The light brightens vividly on* GRUNER. *The music begins the Hatikva theme.*)

GRUNER (*his voice now full*): I speak to you! The English are hanging me. They have beaten and cursed me—and they stand now sneering at me—waiting for me to moan and cry out for their mercy. But I don't moan or cry out. My heart answers them—"I would rather live a moment on this gallows in my homeland, than survive for years in the little frightened corners of the Earth."

VOICES (*in a soft chorus*): Hallelujah.

GRUNER: I and my comrades are sick of Jewish voices begging Englishmen for what is ours. We are sick of Jewish voices pleading with the contempt of their enemies.

## THE TERRORIST

VOICES (*in Chorus*): Hallelujah! Hallelujah!

GRUNER (*raising his eyes*): Dear Lord, the English refused me a rabbi—so I pray to you myself. I thank you, God, for having sent the voices of my people into my heart. I thank you for having given me the courage to live and die as a friend of my people and an enemy of their enemies. I thank you for my brave comrades who will fight on when I am gone. And here on my gallows I offer up a prayer of thanks and victory—I see no hangman here. I see no noose. I see a flag over my head that my brothers will raise.

VOICES (*in a louder chorus as the music swells*): Hallelujah!

GRUNER: I say goodbye to the morning. And I thank you, oh Lord, that it is morning—a bright morning—in my homeland. (*His eyes lower and his voice rings out.*) Here me, comrades! I will be with you in your battles. In the darkness where I go I will dream of you. I and my slaughtered people from the ends of time will dream of you. Goodbye—my land of Israel.

(*The lights go out. The music swells up in the darkness and voices sing triumphantly.*

*The stage remains black for several moments.*

*The light appears on the noose. It hangs emptily.* GRUNER *is gone. From the rope above the noose, as from a flagpole, the flag of Palestine flies.*)

# Acknowledgments

This project began with my doctoral dissertation in theatre history at the City University of New York (CUNY) Graduate Center and this book would not exist without my advisor David Savran's intellectual inspiration and encouragement. It was also a great honor and gift to have such esteemed scholars as Marvin Carlson and Morris Dickstein on my doctoral committee. It saddens me that Morris did not live to see this book, since his spirit informs so much of it and his expertise in the Jewish American literary tradition was such a priceless resource for me.

Some of the research institutions I relied on for my dissertation continued to be essential during work on this book. None has been more crucial to me than the Newberry Library in Chicago, the repository of Ben Hecht's main archives and (since the death of Hecht's widow, Rose Caylor Hecht, in 1979) the executor of his estate. Beginning with a Summer Research Fellowship in 2009 and continuing with several subsequent visits, I have been indebted to the expertise and generosity of the Newberry staff, particularly the Hecht collection curators, first Martha Briggs and then Alison Hinderliter. I owe very special thanks to Daniel Greene for his continual support of this project over the years at the Newberry, first as a senior director and later as president. The other institution I have benefited most from is the Kurt Weill Foundation for Music, especially their archivist Dave Stein for his assistance and trust in sharing with me invaluable documents and resources related to Weill's collaboration with Hecht. The foundation also provided research grants that supported my travel to other collections.

## ACKNOWLEDGMENTS

Special collections staff at several academic libraries have facilitated digitized copies of key materials: the Manuscripts and Archives division of Yale University Library; Hebrew Union College-Jewish Institute of Religion in Cincinnati (both the Jacob Rader Marcus Center of the American Jewish Archives and the Klau Library); the Special Collections Research Center of Morris Library at Southern Illinois University; the Harry Ransom Center at University of Texas, Austin; the Rubenstein Institute at the United States Holocaust Memorial Museum; and the Library at the University of Hawai'i at Mānoa.

Other supporters of my dissertation research I wish to acknowledge are the YIVO institute for Jewish Research for awarding me a Drench Memorial Fellowship and Temple University's Feinstein Center for American Jewish History for its summer research grant. Yale's Irving S. Gilmore Music Library, the Morgan Library and Museum Reading Room, and the Library of Congress's Recorded Sound Division supplied several valuable archival finds. As always for theatre historians, frequent visits to the Billy Rose Theatre Collection at the New York Public Library for the Performing Arts were essential.

I am grateful to many academic colleagues and mentors for their offers of resources, opportunities, and advice—most especially Alisa Solomon, Edna Nahshon, Jonathan Shandell, Brian Eugenio Herrera, Chrystyna Dail, Annette Levine, Henry Bial, and Avinoam Patt. I must also single out the late Ellen Adler, Stella Adler's daughter, for granting me an extended interview to share her firsthand memories of *A Flag Is Born* and her legendary family's involvement in it. Joshua Rotsten was likewise generous with his time in talking to me about his father Herman, who played a key role in *We Will Never Die* as Moss Hart's assistant director.

I have greatly benefitted from my wife Alissa's encouragement, her expertise in all things editorial, and her willingness to endure several conference talks about a project that has been gestating since before our marriage. I thank my now nine-year-old daughter Ariel for forgiving her father for "typing on the computer so much." My mother, Marilyn Eisler, and my in-laws Anita and Daniel Heyman have provided much-needed support, both material and emotional. My father, Lawrence Eisler, passed away in 2014, but I am grateful he saw the early fruits of this labor, since it was he (under the stage name Eddie Lawrence) who initiated me into the world of theatre and whose perspective and experiences, both as an artist and a Jewish American World War II veteran, inform me still.

Finally, I want to acknowledge the entire staff of Rutgers University Press, especially the acquisition editors who successively shepherded this project at different stages from proposal through production with patience and courtesy: Elisabeth Maselli, Christopher Rios-Sueverkruebbe, and Carah Naseem.

# Notes

## INTRODUCTION

1. I wish to acknowledge a 2007 lecture by the musicologist Tamara Levitz for introducing me to *We Will Never Die*. Tamara Levitz, "Kurt Weill's Kol Nidre and Jewish Memory," Center for Jewish History, May 8, 2007. A scene in Bernard Weinraub's 2007 play *The Accomplices* depicting the first *We Will Never Die* performance was also influential.
2. Harley Erdman, *Staging the Jew: The Performance of an American Ethnicity, 1860–1920* (New Brunswick, NJ: Rutgers, 1997), 8.
3. Quoted in J. Hoberman and Jeffrey Shandler, eds., *Entertaining America: Jews, Movies, and Broadcasting* (Princeton, NJ: Princeton University Press, 2003), 137.
4. "In the late 1920s and early 1930s, American Jews were vibrant presences in Hollywood cinema . . . After 1934, Jews weren't vilified on the American screen; they just vanished from it. . . . The strict enforcement of the Code stemmed the flow of Jewish-American characters and coinages." Thomas Doherty, *Hollywood's Censor: Joseph I. Breen and the Production Code Administration* (New York, Columbia University Press, 2009), 213.
5. Arthur Miller, *Collected Essays* (New York: Penguin, 2016), 382.
6. Edna Nahshon, "Jewish American Drama," in *The Cambridge History of Jewish American Literature*, ed. Hana Wirth-Nesher (New York: Cambridge University Press, 2016), 243.
7. Henry Bial, *Acting Jewish: Negotiating Ethnicity on the American Stage and Screen* (Ann Arbor: University of Michigan, 2005), 26.

8. David S. Wyman, *The Abandonment of the Jews: America and the Holocaust, 1941–1945* (New York: Pantheon, 1984); Rafael Medoff, *Militant Zionism in America: The Rise and Impact of the Jabotinsky Movement in the United States, 1926–1948* (Tuscaloosa: University of Alabama Press, 2002); David S. Wyman and Rafael Medoff, *A Race against Death: Peter Bergson, America and the Holocaust* (New York: New Press, 2002). Other Bergson biographers have spotlighted Hecht's contributions to that movement as well: Louis Rapoport, *Shake Heaven and Earth: Peter Bergson and the Struggle to Rescue the Jews of Europe* (Jerusalem: Gefen Publishing House, 1999); and Judith Tydor Baumel, *The "Bergson Boys" and the Origins of Contemporary Zionist Militancy*, trans. Dena Ordan (Syracuse, NY: Syracuse University Press, 2005).
9. Another field that has produced scholarship on these works is the life and career of Hecht himself, as interpreted by several biographers over the years: Douglas George Fetherling, William MacAdams, Jeffrey Brown Martin, and, more recently, Adina Hoffman and Julien Gorbach. Each places Hecht's Jewish theatre writing in a different context, but never American theatre itself. Hecht's own 1954 memoir, *A Child of the Century*, also remains an invaluable biographical source.
10. Stephen J. Whitfield, "The Politics of Pageantry, 1936–1946," *American Jewish History* 84, no. 3 (1996): 221–251. Erika Fischer-Lichte, "Towards the Rebirth of a Nation—American Zionist Pageants, 1932–1946," in *Theatre, Sacrifice, Ritual: Exploring Forms of Political Theatre* (London: Routledge, 2005), 159–196. A similar framing is adopted by Rachel Merrill Moss and Gary Alan Fine in "Pageants and Patriots: Jewish Spectacles as Performances of Belonging," *The Journal of American Drama and Theatre* (Fall 2018).
11. A 1989 dissertation by Atay Citron combined all three Weisgal titles with Hecht's works. Atay Citron, "Pageantry and Theatre in the Service of Jewish Nationalism in the United States, 1933–1946" (PhD diss., New York University, 1989). Citron's exhaustive account of all these works remains extremely valuable, drawing in part on oral histories collected from surviving members of the Bergson group.
12. The Jewish American writer Ludwig Lewisohn provided the translation. Franz Werfel, *The Eternal Road: A Drama in Four Parts*, trans. Ludwig Lewisohn (New York: Viking, 1936).
13. See Joan FitzPatrick Dean, *Pageant* (London: Bloomsbury, 2021).
14. Brooks Atkinson, "The Play," *New York Times*, September 7, 1946, 10.
15. Ben Hecht, *A Flag Is Born* (New York: American League for a Free Palestine, 1946), 39.
16. Ben Hecht, *A Child of the Century* (1954; repr., New York: Primus, 1985), 528.
17. Aaron Berman, *Nazism, the Jews, and American Zionism, 1933–1988* (Detroit, MI: Wayne State University Press, 1990), 11, 13.
18. Berman, *Nazism, the Jews, and American Zionism*, 17.
19. Hasia Diner, *The Jews of the United States, 1654 to 2000* (Berkeley: University of California Press, 2004), 227.

20. Victor S. Navasky, *A Matter of Opinion* (New York: Farrar, Straus and Giroux, 2005), 280.

## 1 PROTESTING ANTISEMITISM VIA ANTIFASCISM

1. Thomas Doherty, *Hollywood and Hitler, 1933–1939* (New York: Columbia University Press, 2013); Ben Urwand, *The Collaboration* (Cambridge, MA: Harvard University Press, 2015); Steven Alan Carr, *Hollywood and Anti-Semitism* (Cambridge: Cambridge University Press, 2001).
2. Harley Erdman, *Staging the Jew: The Performance of an American Ethnicity, 1860–1920* (New Brunswick, NJ: Rutgers University Press, 1997), 8, 145.
3. Quoted in Bial, *Acting Jewish*, 25.
4. Bial, *Acting Jewish*, 30.
5. Nahshon, "Jewish American Drama," 248.
6. The canonical status of *Awake and Sing!* is evident in the title of Ellen Schiff's anthology *Awake and Singing: 7 Classic Plays from the American Jewish Repertoire* (New York: Penguin, 1995), reissued in 2004. Odets briefly addressed antisemitism in one scene of his *Waiting for Lefty* (1935), but he did not write about Jewish life again until his last play, *The Flowering Peach* (1954), a retelling of the Noah's Ark story in a modern Jewish idiom.
7. "Although the Yiddish and the American Jewish stages have had much in common, particularly in the first decades of the 20th century, they are posed on separate axes and serve different constituencies. The Yiddish theatre faces inward, speaking its own language.... The American Jewish stage has faced in exactly the opposite direction from the Yiddish—outward." Ellen Schiff, *Awake and Singing, New Edition: Six Great American Jewish Plays* (New York: Applause Theatre and Cinema Books, 2004), 20, 22.
8. According to Michael Denning, "The antifascist numbers [in *Pins and Needles*] were probably the best-known of the topical sketches.... They included the early satires of Mussolini, 'Mussolini Handicap' and 'Public Enemy No. 1'; an attack on British appeasement, 'Britannia Waives the Rules'; a sketch on the Nazi suppression of the work of Heinrich Heine, 'Lorelei on the Rocks'; and an allegorical account of the Biblical tyrant Belshazzar, 'Mene, Mene, Tekel.'" Michael Denning, *The Cultural Front: The Laboring of American Culture in the Twentieth Century* (London: Verso, 1998), 298.
9. Another Jewish American playwright notable in this context is S. N. Behrman, whose 1934 drama *Rain from Heaven* contains a startling scene in which an émigré Jewish writer proposes a futuristic novel about "the extermination of the Jews" based on what he has seen in Germany, but the character only figures in an isolated subplot. S. N. Behrman, *Rain from Heaven* (New York: Samuel French, 1936), 28–29.
10. Julius Novick, *Beyond the Golden Door: Jewish American Drama and Jewish American Experience* (New York: Palgrave Macmillan, 2008), 3.

11. Ben Hecht, *A Guide for the Bedevilled* (New York: Charles Scribner's Sons, 1944), 208–209.
12. Hecht, *A Guide for the Bedevilled*, 208.
13. Hecht, *A Guide for the Bedevilled*, 62. Despite numerous sources identifying 1894 as the year of Hecht's birth (including his own tombstone), Adina Hoffman claims official records prove he was born one year earlier. Adina Hoffman, *Ben Hecht: Fighting Words, Moving Pictures* (New Haven, CT: Yale University Press, 2019), 221.
14. Hecht, *A Guide for the Bedevilled*, 62; Hecht, *Child of the Century*, 87.
15. Quoted in William MacAdams, *Ben Hecht: A Biography* (New York: Barricade Books, 1999), 181.
16. "My salary ran from five thousand dollars a week up. Metro Goldwyn-Mayer in 1949 paid me ten thousand a week. David Selznick once paid me thirty-five hundred a day." Hecht, *A Child of the Century*, 467; United States Bureau of the Census, "Income of Families and Persons in the United States: 1948" (Washington, D.C., 1950), via HathiTrust Digital Library, accessed October 13, 2022.
17. In *A Child of the Century*, Hecht claims to have written "the first nine reels" of *Gone with the Wind* (i.e., approximately the first half of the 221-minute film) when the producer David O. Selznick begged for his help at an impasse in the film's development (489). The director John Ford told William MacAdams that Hecht contributed much to the outlining of the *Stagecoach* screenplay. MacAdams, *Ben Hecht*, 197–198.
18. Stuart J. Hecht, "Kenneth Sawyer Goodman: Bridging Chicago's Affluent and Artistic Network," *Theatre History Studies* 13 (1993): 140.
19. Hoffman, *Ben Hecht*, 78–79. Hecht wrote some of the "Alfred Pupick" pieces with his friend Herman Mankiewicz when the two briefly published a humor magazine, *The Low Down*, in 1925.
20. In his 1959 essay "The Jew in the American Novel," Leslie Fiedler critiques *A Jew in Love* at length, calling its protagonist a "caricature of the anti-Semite come to life" and the novel itself "a work of inspired self-hatred; a portrait of the Jewish author as his own worst (Jewish) enemy." Leslie Fiedler, *The Collected Essays of Leslie Fiedler*, vol. 2 (New York: Stein and Day, 1971), 81–82. Hoffman offers a more nuanced reading, speculating: "Are we meant to despise Boshere [the protagonist] or to pity him for having internalized the most grotesque stereotypes ascribed to his people?" Hoffman, *Ben Hecht*, 105.
21. Hoffman, *Ben Hecht*, 107.
22. Hecht, *A Child of the Century*, 517.
23. Hoffman credits Rose Caylor Hecht, "his feisty Vilna-born wife," with prodding Hecht to take on the cause of European Jews as his own. Hoffman, *Ben Hecht*, 118.
24. Ben Hecht, "On Broadway," *New York Daily Mirror*, July 31, 1935.
25. Ben Hecht, *To Quito and Back* (New York: Covici-Friede, 1937), 140, 180.
26. Quoted in Julius Gorbach, *The Notorious Ben Hecht: Iconoclastic Writer and Militant Zionist* (West Lafayette, IN: Purdue University Press, 2019), 109.
27. Mary McCarthy, *Sights and Spectacles* (New York: Farrar, Straus and Cudahy, 1956), 6.

28. Roy S. Waldau, *Vintage Years of the Theatre Guild, 1928–1939* (Cleveland: Case Western Reserve University Press, 1972), 255.
29. Olga J. Martins, *Hollywood's Commandments: A Handbook for Motion Picture Writers and Reviewers* (New York: H. W. Wilson, 1937), 288.
30. *The Life of Emile Zola*, directed by William Dieterle (Warner Home Video, 2005), DVD; *The Mortal Storm*, directed by Frank Borzage (Warner Archive Collection, 2010), DVD; *Dr. Ehrlich's Magic Bullet*, directed by William Dieterle (Warner Archive Collection, 2009), DVD.
31. *Let Freedom Ring*, directed by Jack Conway (MGM/UA Home Video, 1994), VHS. According to the IMDB website, shooting for the film began on November 25, 1938. "Filming and Production," *Let Freedom Ring*, Internet Movie Database, https://www.imdb.com/title/tt0031565/locations?ref_=tt_dt_loc.
32. Ben Hecht to Rose Caylor Hecht, telegram, January 16, 1939, Ben Hecht Papers, Newberry Library, Chicago.
33. Peter Sidney, "'Let Freedom Ring' a Fine Film about U.S.A.," *Daily Worker*, March 11, 1939.
34. MacAdams, *Ben Hecht*, 214.
35. "Screen News Here and in Hollywood," *New York Times*, January 24, 1941.
36. "News of the Screen," *New York Times*, February 24, 1941; "Screen News Here and in Hollywood," *New York Times*, July 12, 1941; "Screen News Here and in Hollywood," *New York Times*, July 29, 1941. Hecht's early involvement with *Journey into Fear* has led some to inaccurately include the title in his filmography as an uncredited work, even though none of his material was ultimately used in the final film. Simon Callow confirms that Hecht's early draft of the screenplay was discarded. Simon Callow, *Orson Welles*, vol. 2, *Hello Americans* (New York: Viking, 2006), 13, 49.
37. *Foreign Correspondent* was intended by the producer Walter Wanger as a dramatization of the memoir *Personal History* by the American reporter Vincent Sheean, who covered the early rise of fascism in Europe. But by the time the film was approved for production, all that remained from the book was the figure of a journalist hero loosely based on Sheean. Hecht's contribution to the screenplay went uncredited but is documented by Matthew Bernstein in *Walter Wanger: Hollywood Independent* (Minneapolis: University of Minnesota Press, 2000).
38. *Foreign Correspondent* (Warner Home Video, 2004), DVD.
39. Denning, *The Cultural Front*, 50.
40. Hecht, *A Child of the Century*, 365.
41. Hecht's name appears many times in the reports of the Un-American Activities Committee as a member and/or signatory affiliated with "Communist Front Organizations," including the League of American Writers, the National Citizens' Political Action Committee, Russian War Relief, Inc., and the American Committee to Save Refugees. See United States. 1938–1944. *Investigation of Un-American Propaganda Activities in the United States. Hearings Before a Special Committee on Un-American Activities, House of Representatives, Seventy-Fifth Congress, Third*

*Session - Seventy-Eighth Congress, Second Session.* Washington, D.C.: U.S. Government Printing Office, 1944.
42. Denning, *The Cultural Front*, 16.
43. Ben Hecht, *1001 Afternoons in New York* (New York: Viking, 1941), 26. Viking published this anthology of Hecht's PM columns in October 1941. The original column about Kennedy ("A Diplomat Spikes a Cannon") appeared in the January 16, 1941 edition of *PM*.
44. Fight for Freedom announced its formation on April 18, 1941. The organization's leaders (including university presidents, Wall Street executives, and newspaper editors) were hardly radicals, but they operated in typical Popular Front fashion by building a broad coalition of antifascist allies, including leaders of organized labor and show business progressives. See Fight for Freedom, Inc. Records, Mudd Manuscript Library, Princeton University, http://findingaids.princeton.edu/collections/MC025.pdf.
45. I discuss both the "Fun to Be Free" rally and Hecht's pageant within it in greater detail in my essay "Ethnic Americanism vs. Isolationism: Pluralistic Antifascism in Fun to Be Free," in *Experiments in Democracy: Interracial & Cross-Cultural Exchange in American Theatre & Performance, 1912–45*, ed. Cheryl Black and Jonathan Shandell (Carbondale: Southern Illinois University Press, 2016), 191–212.
46. "17,000 See 'Fun to Be Free,'" *Variety*, October 8, 1941.
47. Contemporary documents inconsistently refer to both the pageant and the overall event as alternately "Fun to Be Free" or "It's Fun to Be Free." To avoid confusion, I refer to the rally as a whole as "Fun to Be Free" and use the title *It's Fun to Be Free* only for the Hecht-MacArthur pageant within it.
48. Ben Hecht and Charles MacArthur, "It's Fun to Be Free," in *Best One-Act Plays of 1941*, ed. Margaret Mayorga (New York: Dodd Mead, 1942), 240. All further citations from the play are from this publication. The script was also published by Dramatists Play Service for licensed performances. Ben Hecht and Charles MacArthur, *Fun to Be Free: Patriotic Pageant* (New York: Dramatists Play Service, 1941).
49. "Fight for Freedom Fun," *Life*, October 20, 1941, 38.

## 2  BREAKING THE SILENCE

1. "2 Million Jews Slain, Rabbi Wise Asserts," *Washington Post*, November 25, 1942, 6. A similar, slightly longer version of the AP story ran in the *New York Times* as "Wise Gets Confirmations: Checks with State Department on Nazis' 'Extermination Campaign,'" *New York Times*, November 25, 1942, 10.
2. Paul Fussell, *Wartime: Understanding and Behavior in the Second World War* (New York: Oxford, 1989), 137–138.
3. Ben Hecht, *We Will Never Die: A Memorial Dedicated to the 2,000,000 Jewish Dead of Europe* (New York: Committee for a Jewish Army of Stateless and Palestinian Jews, 1943), 11. Hecht's full script for the pageant was published in this limited edition shortly after the final performance in Los Angeles on July 21, 1943. Further citations from this version are given in the text.

4. Hecht, *A Child of the Century*, 520.
5. Hecht, *1001 Afternoons in New York*, 166–167.
6. Hecht, *1001 Afternoons in New York*, 164–165, 167.
7. Hecht, *1001 Afternoons in New York*, 167.
8. Bernard Avishai, *The Tragedy of Zionism: Revolution and Democracy in the Land of Israel* (New York: Farrar, Straus and Giroux, 1985), 120.
9. Rafael Medoff, *Militant Zionism in America: The Rise and Impact of the Jabotinsky Movement in the United States, 1926–1948* (Tuscaloosa: University of Alabama Press, 2002), 79–80.
10. Aaron Berman, *Nazism, the Jews, and American Zionism: 1933–1948* (Detroit, MI: Wayne State University Press, 1990),142–143; Judith Tydor Baumel, *The "Bergson Boys" and the Origins of Contemporary Zionist Militancy* (Syracuse, NY: Syracuse University Press, 2005), 218.
11. Yitshaq Ben-Ami, *Years of Wrath, Days of Glory: Memoirs from the Irgun* (New York: Sheingold, 1983), 284.
12. Ben-Ami, *Years of Wrath, Days of Glory*, 285.
13. Hecht, *A Child of the Century*, 550–551.
14. Hecht, *A Child of the Century*, 551–552.
15. Hecht, *A Child of the Century*, 552.
16. Hecht, *A Child of the Century*, 552.
17. "Des Moines Speech: Delivered in Des Moines, Iowa, on September 11, 1941, this speech was met with outrage in many quarters," *CharlesLindbergh.com*, http://www.charleslindbergh.com/americanfirst/speech.asp
18. Leonard Dinnerstein, *Antisemitism in America* (New York: Oxford University Press, 1995), 136. The book's seventh chapter is entitled "Antisemitism at High Tide: World War II (1939–1945)."
19. Hecht, *A Child of the Century*, 552–553.
20. Mark Cohen, *Not Bad for Delancey Street: The Rise of Billy Rose* (Waltham, MA: Brandeis University Press, 2018), 113-114.
21. Quoted in Ben-Ami, *Years of Wrath, Days of Glory*, 286.
22. "A Letter from Ben Hecht," *PM*, February 22, 1943, 19.
23. Syrjala (as "S. Syrjala") was credited with the design "scheme" and Ayers with its execution. Both were prominent stage designers of the era but from different theatrical worlds. Syrjala was a resident designer of the radical Theatre Union troupe and designed the revue *Pins and Needles* for the Labor Stage. Ayers worked primarily on commercial Broadway productions; during *We Will Never Die*, he was simultaneously in rehearsal for Rodgers and Hammerstein's *Oklahoma!* which opened later that month.
24. My discussion of the *We Will Never Die* musical score relies largely on a recorded radio broadcast of the Los Angeles performance on July 21, 1943. "We Will Never Die: Ben Hecht & Kurt Weill," The Internet Archive, https://archive.org/details/WeWillNeverDieBenHechtKurtWeill.

25. "Significance of References to the Jewish Tradition in the Memorial," "We Will Never Die" Hollywood Bowl official program, 15, Kurt Weill Foundation.
26. For further study of Weill's score for *We Will Never Die*, some written fragments and sketches are housed at the Kurt Weill Foundation in New York and the Irving S. Gilmore Music Library at Yale University.
27. Psalms 22:1 (King James Version). Weill had already set part of this text to the Kol Nidre melody in *The Eternal Road* in a scene dramatizing King David's grief for his dying son. Other than the first line, the *We Will Never Die* version differs completely from the opera's, suggesting Weill revisited this and other psalms in search of language more specific to persecution. For the earlier example, see Werfel, *The Eternal Road*, 113.
28. Adele Berlin et al., *The Jewish Study Bible* (Oxford: Oxford University Press, 2004), 1305.
29. The text of Weill's Kol Nidre arrangement is not in Hecht's script, but is partially audible on the recorded radio broadcast. "We Will Never Die: Ben Hecht & Kurt Weill." Other lines from Psalm 22 paraphrased here include "O my God, I cry in the daytime, but thou hearest not" (Psalms 22:2) and "Deliver my soul from the sword; my darling from the power of the dog" (Psalms 22:20). Another line paraphrases Psalm 25: "According to thy mercy, remember thou me for thy goodness' sake, O Lord." Psalms 25:7 (KJV).
30. Kurt Baum performed the Kol Nidre at the *We Will Never Die* performances in New York, Washington, and Los Angeles. For Baum's background, see Walter Price, "Kurt Baum: Ending on a High Note," *Los Angeles Times*, February 22, 1987.
31. Born in Russia in 1890, Ben-Ami came to New York in 1912 to act in Yiddish Theatre, eventually founding his own company, the Jewish Art Theatre, in 1919. Aside from occasional appearances on Broadway and with Eva Le Gallienne's Civic Repertory Theatre, his career at the time of *We Will Never Die* had been almost exclusively in the Yiddish repertoire.
32. The rabbi tells the audience that this prayer "has risen from the stricken and the dying in all the lands of the earth for many centuries" and "holds the last words of the millions who have died in the massacres by the Germans" (12). The legacy of the Shema as a martyr's prayer goes back to Roman-ruled Judea, when "Jewish martyrs recited it as they went to their deaths." Louis Jacobs, "Shema, Reading of," *Encyclopedia Judaica*, 2nd ed., vol. 18 (Detroit, MI: Thomson Gale, 2007), 455.
33. Weill's setting of the *Shema Yisrael* prayer is another borrowing from his score for *The Eternal Road*, where it is sung at a moment of elation, not martyrdom, when Moses leads his people across the Jordan into the Promised Land at the end of the opera's second act.
34. Intentionally or not, Hecht's idea of reciting names of departed ancestors closely mirrors the Jewish observance of *Yizkor*—part of the Yom Kippur service—a prayer of remembrance and commemoration accompanied by the lighting of yahrzeit candles in memory of the dead.

35. The total number of names in the "Roll Call" varied throughout the pageant's writing, revision, and performance. An early typescript (at the New York Public Library's Billy Rose Theatre Collection) contains 121 names, the published script has 124, and a production script from the Philadelphia performance (at the Morgan Library in New York) shows 118, which matches the Los Angeles radio recording at the end of the run. At each step in the process, a few names appear to have been excised and a few new ones added, but the vast majority remained.
36. Hecht also gives place in the "Roll Call" to founders of modern Zionism (Theodor Herzl, Chaim Weizmann, Max Nordau) and even to Jabotinsky, acknowledging the instrumental role of Bergson and his Revisionist Zionist colleagues in the performance.
37. In his first draft, Hecht even included Christopher Columbus in the "Roll Call," based on legendary rumors of his supposed "Converso" ancestry.
38. Ben-Ami, *Years of Wrath, Days of Glory*, 285.
39. Cecil Roth, *The Jewish Contribution to Civilization* (New York: Harper and Brothers, 1940). Hecht copies Roth, for example, in referring to the nineteenth-century linguist Graziadio Ascoli as "the foremost Italian philologist." Roth, *The Jewish Contribution*, 140, quoted in Hecht, *We Will Never Die*, 19. Other textual similarities include: "Luis Ponce de Leon was perhaps the greatest lyric poet that Spain has produced" (Roth, *The Jewish Contribution*, 111–112) and "Luis Ponce de Leon, the greatest lyric poet of Spain" (Hecht, *We Will Never Die*, 18). Also: "Ludwig Traube, to whom a monument was erected in the court of the Charité ... was the founder of experimental pathology" (Roth, *The Jewish Contribution*, 242) and "Ludwig Traube, founder of the science of pathology whose statue still stands in Paris" (Hecht, *We Will Never Die*, 19).
40. Michael Brenner, *Prophets of the Past: Interpreters of Jewish History*, trans. Steven Rendall (Princeton, NJ: Princeton University Press, 2010), 131–137.
41. In one draft, Hecht even included William Booth, the British-born founder of the Salvation Army, whom Roth's book claims was only possibly from Jewish ancestry. "We Will Never Die" typescript, 14, Billy Rose Theatre Collection, New York Public Library; Roth, *The Jewish Contribution*, 337.
42. "We Will Never Die" typescript, 8, Billy Rose Theatre Collection.
43. "Official Washington Attends 'We Shall [*sic*] Never Die' Pageant," *Washington Post*, April 13, 1943.
44. Hart's use of candles and other sacred imagery might have recalled for some New York theatregoers another religious-themed performance of recent memory—Max Reinhardt's *The Miracle* (1924), for which a Broadway theatre was transformed into a medieval cathedral. Noticing the resemblance, Weill joked, "Moss did a wonderful job of staging. I called him Moss Rein-Hart." Kurt Weill to Ira Gershwin, April 5, 1943, Kurt Weill Foundation.
45. The use of candles in the "Roll Call" also evoked traditional Judaic rituals involving the symbolism of *ner tamid* (the "eternal flame"), such as the yahrzeit candle, lit

on the anniversary of a loved one's death, and the lighting of the menorah during Hanukkah (the "Festival of Lights"). Historically, Hanukkah commemorates an act of political resistance (the revolt of the Maccabees) and Weill underscored the "Roll Call" procession with the traditional Hanukkah melody *Maoz Tsur*, a song whose lyrics explicitly reference persecution and divine vengeance.

46. He began acting on the American stage as Muni Weisenfreund, using the nickname he had adopted since childhood. Once he arrived in Hollywood, Warner Brothers convinced him to make Muni his surname instead.

47. Muni played a Chicano lawyer in *Bordertown* (1935), the eponymous nineteenth-century Mexican statesman in *Juarez* (1939), and a Chinese farmer in the Oscar-winning adaptation of Pearl Buck's *The Good Earth* (1937).

48. At the studio, the two actors became nearly interchangeable, especially when both graduated beyond their early gangster roles to high-prestige historical biographies. Robinson later joked, "The Brothers Warner regarded us as two sides of a coin and did not hesitate to exploit the situation. He played Pasteur and Zola; I could have. I played [Paul] Ehrlich and [Paul Julius] Reuter, he could have." Edward G. Robinson and Leonard Spiegelgass, *All My Yesterdays: An Autobiography* (London: W. H. Allen, 1974), 89.

49. Paul Breines, *Tough Jews: Political Fantasies and the Moral Dilemma of American Jewry* (New York: Basic Books, 1990), 44.

50. Sander Gilman, *The Jew's Body* (New York: Routledge, 1991), 42.

51. Stephen Bloore, "The Jew in American Dramatic Literature (1794–1930)," *Publications of the American Jewish Historical Society* 40, no. 4 (June 1951): 358.

52. One of Strobing's obituaries recalled how his "sporadic stream of telegraph transmissions . . . made him a national hero when the transcripts were read over the radio and reproduced in newspapers three weeks later." "Irving Strobing, Radio Operator on Corregidor, Dies at 77," *New York Times*, July 24, 1997, 21.

53. "Defenders Wept after Shelling, 'Too Much for Guys to Take'—Strobing Ended with Message to Mother," *New York Times*, June 1, 1942, 4.

54. "40,000 at Garden Hail Dramatic Pageant of Jews," *New York World*, March 10, 1943.

55. "We Will Never Die" typescript, 32, Morgan Library. This line does not appear in the published text, but was added by Hecht to this script for the Philadelphia performance in April 1943.

56. Deborah Dash Moore, "When Jews Were GIs: How World War II Changed a Generation and Remade American Jewry," in *American Jewish Identity Politics*, ed. Deborah Dash Moore (Ann Arbor: University of Michigan Press, 2009), 29.

57. Charles Herbert Stember et al., *Jews in the Mind of America* (New York: Basic Books, 1966), 117.

58. Dinnerstein, *Antisemitism in America*, 137, 139.

59. Robert Skloot, "'We Will Never Die': The Success and Failure of a Holocaust Pageant," *Theatre Journal* 37, no. 2 (May 1985): 177.

60. See Breines, *Tough Jews*, 83–87. Abraham Goldfaden's 1885 play *Bar Kochba* (1885) was a staple of the Yiddish Theatre repertory of Hecht's time. Seth L. Wolitz, "Forging a Hero for a Jewish Stage: Goldfadn's *Bar Kokhba*," *Shofar* (Spring 2002): 53–65.
61. Douglas Century, *Barney Ross* (New York: Schocken Books, 2006), xvi.
62. In the weeks and months following *We Will Never Die*, Bergson enlisted Ross himself to appear at various other rallies and fundraisers for his committee. Medoff, *Militant Zionism in America*, 151, 176. See also Century, *Barney Ross*, 151–158.
63. Century, *Barney Ross*, 131, 135. Garfield came close to producing and starring in a Barney Ross biography in 1943 and 1944 until the project was abandoned. Century, *Barney Ross*, 144–146. See also Robert Nott, *He Ran All the Way: The Life of John Garfield* (New York: Limelight, 2003), 196–198.
64. Despite his name change, "Garfield was known to be Jewish, at least by readers of the Jewish American press, where Warner Brothers frequently directed publicity for his films." Bial, *Acting Jewish*, 38.
65. Garfield was initially portrayed in the press as Muni's heir. A 1938 Hedda Hopper column depicts a virtual passing of the torch: "When asked [in 1933] by a newspaper reporter what raw material he saw on Broadway that seemed destined for Hollywood success, Muni unhesitatingly picked John Garfield. . . . A few months ago Muni walked onto a set on the Warner lot and watched John Garfield play a scene. The scene over, Muni walked over to Garfield, complimented him on his performance and thanked him for fulfilling a five-year-old prophecy." "Hedda Hopper's Hollywood," *Los Angeles Times*, September 6, 1938.
66. *Air Force* was the first of five war-era movies in which Garfield played an enlisted man; it was followed by *Destination Tokyo* (1943), *Pride of the Marines* (1945), *Nobody Lives Forever* (1946), and *Gentleman's Agreement* (1947). He also appeared as himself in two Warner Brothers films showcasing the film industry's charitable work on behalf of the military: *Thank Your Lucky Stars* (1943) and *Hollywood Canteen* (1944), the latter a tribute to the servicemen's club he co-founded.
67. In the New York premiere, the Strobing lines in "Jews in the War" were read by Luther Adler. Before Los Angeles, Garfield also appeared in *We Will Never Die* in Chicago, but as one of the pageant's main narrators, replacing Muni and Robinson.
68. While Hecht's written stage directions call for "three Germans" to be visible in the dock, photographs and some reviews indicate that the three seated actors wore uniforms and armbands bearing insignias of all three Axis Powers—Germany, Italy, and Japan. The late change could possibly have been intended to communicate solidarity with the larger U.S. war effort.
69. Hecht, *Child of the Century*, 548–550.
70. Ben Hecht, "Remember Us," *American Mercury*, February 1943, 196–199; "'Remember Us': Condensed from the American Mercury," *The Reader's Digest*, February 1943, 107–110. The article continued to circulate the following year in *The American Mercury Reader*. Lawrence E. Spivak and Charles Angoff, eds. *The American*

    *Mercury Reader: A Selection of Distinguished Articles, Stories, and Poems Published in The American Mercury During the Past Twenty Years* (Philadelphia: Blakiston Company, 1944), 51–54.
71. Hecht's "Remember Us" article has been anthologized as a milestone in early Holocaust reporting in Robert H. Abzug, *America Views the Holocaust, 1933–1945: A Brief Documentary History* (Boston: Bedford, 1999), 146–149.
72. Hecht, *A Child of the Century*, 550.
73. "Memorial to Slain Jews Stirs Throng of 15,000," *Philadelphia Record*, April 23, 1943.
74. Matthew Causey, "Symbolism," in *The Oxford Companion to Theatre and Performance*, ed. Dennis Kennedy (Oxford: Oxford University Press, 2011).
75. "One of the dead raises his head. He speaks in emotionless tones. (The voice is that of an actor off stage.)" Ben Hecht, "We Will Never Die" typescript, 26, Billy Rose Theatre Collection. The final published script does not call for offstage voices.
76. "We Will Never Die: Ben Hecht & Kurt Weill"; "The 'We Will Never Die' Pageant," United States Memorial Holocaust Museum, accessed October 14, 2021, https://encyclopedia.ushmm.org/content/en/article/the-we-will-never-die-pageant.
77. Tanya Pollard, "Tragedy and Revenge," in *A Companion to English Renaissance Tragedy*, ed. Emma Smith and Garrett A. Sullivan Jr. (Cambridge: Cambridge University Press, 2010), 59.
78. Katherine Eisaman Maus, introduction to *Four Revenge Tragedies* (Oxford: Oxford University Press, 1995), ix.
79. Although the published *We Will Never Die* script assigns the call for the Kaddish to the narrators, on the radio recording of the Los Angeles performance, Ben-Ami is heard giving this concluding speech. "We Will Never Die: Ben Hecht & Kurt Weill."
80. Known as the third Madison Square Garden, this incarnation was located between 49th and 50th streets on the west side of Eighth Avenue. The building was demolished in 1968.
81. Hecht, *A Child of the Century*, 576.
82. Edward Barry, "Pageant Stirs 15,000 to Vow: Jew Must Live," *Chicago Daily Tribune*, May 20, 1943. Hymie Epstein's heroics were recounted contemporaneously in the *Chicago Daily News*. See George Weller, "Hymie Epstein Wouldn't Quit, Hero in Guinea," in *Weller's War: A Legendary Foreign Correspondent's Saga of World War II on Five Continents* (New York: Three Rivers Press, 2009), 393.
83. *Casablanca*—based on an unproduced antifascist 1941 play by Murray Burnett and Joan Alison—first premiered in Hollywood in November 1942. Two other films about resistance movements opened in December: *Reunion in France* and *Commandos Strike at Dawn*, starring Paul Muni. March 1943 brought *Assignment in Brittany* and *The Moon Is Down*—the latter based on John Steinbeck's popular novel about the Norwegian resistance. For more on the resistance film genre, see Bernard F. Dick, *Star-Spangled Screen: The American World War II Film* (Lexington: University Press of Kentucky, 1996), 146–187.

84. The scene's other narrator was also associated with the resistance genre: the Greek actress Katina Paxinou, who played a Spanish Republican partisan in the film of Hemingway's *For Whom the Bell Tolls*, which had just opened on July 14, 1943, one week prior to the Hollywood Bowl performance.
85. "To the Conscience of America," *New York Times*, December 5, 1942.
86. Waxman, a German Jewish refugee, came to the United States in 1935. He had experienced Nazi persecution firsthand when he was assaulted in the streets of Berlin by Nazi demonstrators. Tony Thomas, *Film Score: The Art and Craft of Movie Music* (Burbank, CA: Riverwood Press, 1991), 35.
87. Loesser spent most of the 1940s in Hollywood, where he supported the war effort writing shows for servicemen and morale-boosting songs like "Praise the Lord and Pass the Ammunition" (1942). See Thomas Riis, *Frank Loesser* (New Haven, CT: Yale University Press, 2008), 39–49.
88. *We Will Never Die* Hollywood Bowl souvenir program, 27, Kurt Weill Foundation.
89. The American songwriter Sam Coslow received the official screen credit for lyrics to "No Surrender" in *Hangmen Also Die*. But as Sally Bick demonstrates, Coslow was hired only to render Brecht's German lyrics into acceptable Hollywood English. Sally Bick, "A Double Life in Hollywood: Hanns Eisler's Score for the Film *Hangmen Also Die* and the Covert Expressions of a Marxist Composer," *Musical Quarterly* 93, no. 1 (2010): 131–132.
90. Rotsten is listed as "Assistant to Mr. Hart" in the Madison Square Garden program. The Hollywood Bowl program still credits Hart as director but also includes the credit "Staged by Herman Rotsten." *We Will Never Die* Hollywood Bowl souvenir program, 8, Kurt Weill Foundation. An article in the *Los Angeles Daily News* also confirms that "Herman Rotsten directed the local performance for Hart." "Stage Review," *Los Angeles Daily News*, July 22, 1943.
91. The Los Angeles program credits "Actors of Actors' Laboratory for their participation in the Warsaw Scene." *We Will Never Die* Hollywood Bowl souvenir program, 8, Kurt Weill Foundation.
92. Delia Nora Salvi, "The History of the Actors' Laboratory, Inc. 1941–1950" (PhD diss., University of California, Los Angeles, 1970), 241.
93. Salvi, "The History of the Actors' Laboratory," 41–44.
94. Both voice-over lines were spoken by Paul Stewart, an alumnus of Orson Welles's Mercury Theatre.
95. Attilio Favorini, *Voicings: Ten Plays from the Documentary Theatre* (Hopewell, NJ: Ecco Press, 1995), xviii–xix.
96. Hecht, *A Child of the Century*, 576.
97. According to Hecht:

> The invitations went out under the high sponsorship of their Excellencies, the Ambassadors and Ministers of eight of the United Nations overrun by the Germans. Representatives of forty nations occupied the boxes, decorated with their respective

flags. Mrs. Roosevelt headed as distinguished an audience as ever attended an unofficial function in the Nation's Capital. The Chief Justice of the Supreme Court of the United States, Harlan F. Stone, headed a delegation of seven of the nine Justices. Secretary of the Navy, Frank Knox, and Jesse Jones, Secretary of Commerce, represented the Cabinet. Thirty-eight United States Senators joined hundreds of Congressmen and government officials in standing at the bier of the massacred.

Hecht, *We Will Never Die*, 9.

98. "'My Day' by Eleanor Roosevelt: A Comprehensive Electronic Edition of Eleanor Roosevelt's 'My Day' Newspaper Columns," Eleanor Roosevelt Papers Project, George Washington University, accessed July 9, 2012, http://www.gwu.edu/~erpapers/myday.
99. Wyman and Medoff, *A Race against Death*, 49–50.
100. The five venues hosting the pageant on tour each held a capacity crowd of at least 15,000 spectators.
101. Hecht, *A Child of the Century*, 576.
102. Wyman, *The Abandonment of the Jews*, 91. Wyman cites *Radio Daily* as a source, which I have confirmed for the New York and Washington performances. "Coast to Coast," *Radio Daily*, March 11, 1943, 8; "'We Will Never Die' On WNIX Next Monday," *Radio Daily*, April 9, 1943, 2.
103. During the Warsaw Ghetto scene, a narrator says, "Remember these names—Trawinke, Oswiecim, Tremblinka. . . . These were the organized extermination camps." Oswiecim was the original Polish name for Auschwitz before the Germans renamed it. "Tremblinka" was a common variant spelling of Treblinka in contemporary news reports.
104. The newsreel is posted on the website of the United States Memorial Holocaust Museum, on their page devoted to *We Will Never Die*. "The 'We Will Never Die' Pageant," United States Memorial Holocaust Museum, accessed October 14, 2021, https://encyclopedia.ushmm.org/content/en/article/the-we-will-never-die-pageant.
105. Hecht, *A Child of the Century*, 551.
106. Hecht, *A Child of the Century*, 587.
107. Hecht, *A Child of the Century*, 583.
108. Hecht, *A Child of the Century*, 584.
109. MacAdams, *Ben Hecht*, 235.
110. Hecht, *A Child of the Century*, 518.

# 3  THE ASSASSINATION OF "LORD MOISHA"

1. Maurice Samuel, *The World of Sholom Aleichem* (New York: Schocken Books, 1943), 3.
2. Alisa Solomon, *Wonder of Wonders: A Cultural History of Fiddler on the Roof* (New York: Metropolitan Books, 2013), 53.
3. Hecht, *1001 Afternoons in New York*, 51. The original article, titled "How Do You Do," appeared in *PM* on May 12, 1941.

4. Copyright Registration for *The World of Sholom Aleichem*, Box 36, Folder 25. MS-89. Maurice Samuel Papers. American Jewish Archives, Cincinnati, Ohio; "We Will Never Die" typescript, 9, Ben Hecht Papers, Newberry Library, Chicago. The earlier draft is at Billy Rose Theater Collection, New York Public Library.
5. Ben Hecht, "Tales of Capering, Rueful Laughter," *New York Times*, July 7, 1946.
6. Hecht, "Tales of Capering."
7. Hecht, *Guide for the Bedevilled*, 61–62.
8. Despite inconsistencies in Hecht's own accounts, Hoffman determines that his parents and their immediate relatives came either "from Minsk or from outside Kremenchug in the Ukraine." Hoffman, *Ben Hecht*, 12.
9. Hecht, *Guide for the Bedevilled*, 62; Hecht, *Child of the Century*, 87.
10. Hecht, A Child of the Century, 519.
11. Hecht, A Child of the Century, 109.
12. Hecht, *We Will Never Die*, 34.
13. Seth Wolitz, "The Americanization of Tevye or the Boarding of the Jewish *Mayflower*," *American Quarterly* 40, no. 4 (December 1988): 520.
14. According to the *New York Times*, "the stage presentation was a tableau, written by Ben Hecht and staged by the Radio City Music Hall staff under the direction of Leon Leonidoff, with music by Erno Rapee, which told the story of the peoples of the world and their faith and courage in the struggle against aggression." "President Is Heard in War Fund Plea," *New York Times*, October 6, 1943.
15. Margaret Mayorga, ed., *The Best One-Act Plays of 1943* (New York: Dodd, Mead, 1944), 46. Hecht's script for *A Tribute to Gallantry* was published in this popular annual anthology the following year. All subsequent citations from the play are from this published text.
16. Wittingly or not, Hecht's theatrical gesture here also recalls Irwin Shaw's popular 1936 antiwar play *Bury the Dead*, a staple of late 1930s agitprop repertoire, in which dead soldiers from an unnamed conflict (resembling World War I) refuse to be buried until politicians end all war.
17. "War Fund Drive Is Opened in City," *New York Times*, November 16, 1943.
18. Bertha Gersten, quoted in Solomon, *Wonder of Wonders*, 43.
19. Solomon, *Wonder of Wonders*, 74.
20. Hecht, *A Child of the Century*, 521.
21. Hecht, *A Child of the Century*, 517, 536.
22. "Palestine (Terrorist Activities), Volume 404: Debated on Friday 17 November 1944," U.K. Parliament website, accessed February 21, 2023, https://hansard.parliament.uk/commons/1944-11-17/debates/f5523f61-f28e-4eb1-92d0-810abd22e821/Palestine(TerroristActivities).
23. Quoted in Citron, "Pageantry and Theatre," 346.
24. Ben Hecht, *A Jewish Fairy Tale*, Palestine Statehood Committee Papers, MS 690, Series III, Manuscripts and Archives, Yale University Library, 2. All subsequent citations from this work are from this typescript.

NOTES TO PAGES 71–80

25. Wolitz, "The Americanization of Tevye," 519. Wolitz adds: "Sholem Aleykhem's last image is that of Tevye, passive, betrayed, alone, without [his wife] Golde (dead), without family, traveling without any destination, made a Wandering Jew" (530).
26. Advertisement for *A Jewish Fairy Tale*, *New York Post*, December 4, 1944. Secunda is most famous for writing the music to "Bay Mir Bistu Sheyn," which became a hit popular song when it was translated into English in 1938.
27. "Palestine (Terrorist Activities)," U.K. Parliament website, https://hansard.parliament.uk/commons/1944-11-17/debates/f5523f61-f28e-4eb1-92d0-810abd22e821/Palestine(TerroristActivities).
28. As the play goes on, Hecht's "clues" about the true identity of "God" become increasingly obvious. The character even repeats verbatim lines interpolated from the real Churchill's speech of November 17, including the reference to Jewish underground fighters as "gangsters worthy of Nazi Germany" (12–13), and paraphrases Churchill's talk of "those, like myself, who, in the past, have been consistent friends of the Jews and constant architects of their future" as, "I find it necessary to the architecture of the Jewish future that all Jews should feel guilty" (13).
29. Advertisement, *New York Post*, December 4, 1944.
30. Hecht here mockingly echoes phrases from one of Churchill's most famous orations, his June 1940 speech after the British withdrawal from Dunkirk ("we shall fight on the beaches . . . we shall fight in the fields and in the streets").
31. Tevya refers to his new mission as being literally a "Messiah": "It's better to be a Messiah on earth than a Tevya in Heaven. Who can deny this?" (16).
32. *Favorite Tales of Sholom Aleichem* (New York: Avenel, 1983), 654, 659.
33. Breines, *Tough Jews*, 47.
34. Quoted in Breines, *Tough Jews*, 145.
35. During the war years, Szyk became, in Hecht's words, the Bergson committee's "one-man art department," providing several illustrations for the group's advertising campaigns. Hecht, *A Child of the Century*, 566. He first used this drawing (which he entitled "Tears of Rage") for a 1942 newspaper ad promoting Bergson's Committee for a Jewish Army.
36. "Steps to Save Jews Urged at Rally Here," *New York Times*, December 5, 1944.
37. *A Jewish Fairy Tale* was performed at Philadelphia's Academy of Music on February 8, 1945, along with the rest of Bergson's program. Luther Adler again played Tevya, Ruth Chatterton was the narrator, and her husband John (Barry) Thompson played the Churchill role. Staging was credited to another member of the Adler family, Charles Adler. Advertisement, *Philadelphia Inquirer*, February 4, 1945.

## 4  THE DEATH OF TEVYE AND THE BIRTH OF ISRAEL

1. Ben Hecht, *A Flag Is Born* (New York: American League for a Free Palestine, 1946), 46–48. Further citations of this edition are given in the text.
2. Earl Wilson, "It Happened at Night," *New York Post*, September 5, 1946, 36.

3. "Gillette Denies Aid to Terrorists: Says Funds from 'A Flag Is Born' Are Not Used," *New York Times*, December 5, 1946.
4. "Give Us the Money . . . We'll Get Them There!," advertisement, *New York Post*, April 19, 1946.
5. *A Flag Is Born* souvenir program, Kurt Weill Foundation, New York.
6. Robert Garland, "'A Flag Is Born' Premieres at Alvin Theatre," *New York Journal-American*, September 7, 1946.
7. The name change appears to have been a very late revision. "Goldie" persists through all three typescript drafts of the play in Hecht's Newberry Library papers, as well as in Luther Adler's director's script at the Billy Rose Theater Collection.
8. Jeffrey Shandler, *While America Watches: Televising the Holocaust* (New York: Oxford University Press, 1999), 23.
9. Shandler, *While America Watches*, 23. Emphasis added.
10. *A Flag Is Born* typescript, 65, Ben Hecht Papers, Newberry Library, Chicago.
11. "The year 1945 might be considered the symbolic end of large-scale Yiddish theater in America. For decades New York's Yiddish theatrical world centered on the Cafe Royale on Second Avenue and Twelfth Street, next door to the Yiddish Art Theater. . . . But in 1945 it served its last cup of tea." Diner, *Jews of the United States*, 282.
12. *A Flag Is Born* souvenir program, 3, Kurt Weill Foundation, New York.
13. Robert Garland, "'A Flag Is Born' Premieres at Alvin Theatre," *New York Journal-American*, September 7, 1946; Claudia Cassidy, "'Lute Song' Returning to Studebaker on Jan. 22," *Chicago Daily Tribune*, January 5, 1947.
14. Ben-Ami also acted for Hecht as the Rabbi in *We Will Never Die*. After his American tour of *A Flag Is Born*, Ben-Ami produced the play (in Yiddish) in Buenos Aires, where he regularly performed for one of the world's last sizable Yiddish-speaking audiences.
15. Sidney J. Harris, "'A Flag Is Born' Aims at a Nation's Heart," *Chicago Daily News*, December 27, 1946.
16. Nahma Sandrow, "Yiddish Theater and American Theater," in *From Hester Street to Hollywood: The Jewish-American Stage and Screen*, ed. Sarah Blacher Cohen (Bloomington: Indiana University Press, 1983), 22.
17. Sandrow, "Yiddish Theater and American Theater," 22.
18. Amos Oz, *The Silence of Heaven: Agnon's Fear of God* (Princeton, NJ: Princeton University Press, 2000), 104.
19. Claudia Cassidy, "On the Aisle," December 27, 1946.
20. Cyrus Durgan, "The Stage," *Boston Daily Globe*, February 19, 1947.
21. William Hawkins, "Hecht's 'A Flag Is Born' Moving Plea for Jews," *New York World-Telegram*, September 7, 1946.
22. Denning, *The Cultural Front*, 9.
23. Typescripts of *A Flag is Born*, Ben Hecht Papers, box 9, folders 267–271, Newberry Library, Chicago.

24. Tellingly, Weill's leitmotif underscoring the character's key moments is labeled "Partisan Theme"—the word "partisan" appearing nowhere in the play but linking the character to antifascist resistance fighters of the thirties and forties.
25. Citron reads this moment as a Brechtian alienation effect: "The shift from the sentimental, melancholy flashback to the direct, angry accusation was abrupt and violent. . . . Spectators who had wept during Zelda's vision were softened, disarmed and absolutely vulnerable. David's furious speech, coming out of nowhere, exploited that vulnerability." Citron, "Ben Hecht's Pageant-Drama," 87.
26. Marlon Brando and Robert Lindsey, *Songs My Mother Taught Me* (New York: Random House, 1994), 108.
27. Quoted in Peter Manso, *Brando: The Biography* (New York: Hyperion, 1994), 185.
28. Brando and Lindsey, *Songs My Mother Taught Me*, 108.
29. Hecht has Tevya call the angel by its Hebrew name, "Malachamuvis," normally transliterated as *malakh ha-mavet*.
30. At the soldier's entrance, the script mentions a music cue of "martial music threaded with the Hatikva theme" (45). Two years after the play, in the fall of 1947, Weill wrote a setting of the "Hatikvah" anthem at the behest of the soon-to-be Israeli president Chaim Weizmann. The later piece may be "a recycled, if minimally tweaked or expanded, instrumental piece from *A Flag Is Born*." Neil Levin, liner notes, *In Celebration of Israel*, Milken Archive of American Jewish Music, Naxos CD, 2006.
31. "SECOND SOLDIER: We are the Hebrew army of Palestine. We are the soldiers of the Haganah and the *Irgun*. THIRD SOLDIER: We are the army of the Sternists" (46).
32. According to Atay Citron, during the final scene, "Rows of soldiers [were] seen on a slide which is projected on the backdrop." Citron, "Pageantry and Theatre," 394. A *New York Post* reporter, visiting a rehearsal, describes "phantom soldiers I saw projected from a 2,000-watt motor-driven machine to the back wall of the theatre." Harriet Johnson, "Heckled and Hectic Hecht: Elusive Noted Dramatist Difficult to Locate on 'Flag Is Born' Set," *New York Post*, August 29, 1946.
33. Malcolm Cowley, "While They Waited for Lefty," *Saturday Review*, June 6, 1964, 18.
34. Brooks Atkinson, "Drama: Craftsmanship," *The New York Times*, September 15, 1946.
35. Brando and Lindsey, *Songs My Mother Taught Me*, 98.
36. Brando and Lindsey, *Songs My Mother Taught Me*, 107, 100.
37. "[Garfield] is generally considered to be the first 'rebel' actor in film history; the one who opened the door for all the other cinematic anti-heroes to step through. Marlon Brando, Montgomery Clift, Steve McQueen, Paul Newman, Robert DeNiro and many others walked through that door." Robert Nott, *He Ran All the Way: The Life of John Garfield* (New York: Limelight Editions, 2003), xi. In a documentary about Garfield, the actress Lee Grant calls him "the precursor to Brando and [James] Dean." *The John Garfield Story* (Turner Entertainment, 2003), VHS.
38. See Sam Stagg, *When Blanche Met Brando: The Scandalous Story of* A Streetcar Named Desire (New York: St. Martin's Griffin, 2006), 28–29.

39. Claudia Cassidy, "Lute Song Returning to Studebaker on Jan. 22," *Chicago Tribune*, January 5, 1947; Philip R. Davis, "A Lawyer on the Aisle," *Chicago Daily Law Bulletin*, undated clipping, Kurt Weill Foundation.
40. Michael Denning makes a compelling case for reading Lumet's social issue films as later "embodiments of a Popular Front structure of feeling." Denning, *The Cultural Front*, 26.
41. Bial, *Acting Jewish*, 52. For more exploration of links between the Method and Jewish and Yiddish Theatre traditions, see David Krasner, "I Hate Strasberg: Method Bashing in the Academy," in *Method Acting Reconsidered: Theory, Practice, Future*, ed. David Krasner (New York: St. Martin's Press, 2000), 30–34.
42. Strasberg first experimented with Stanislavsky-inspired techniques by teaching amateur actors at New York's Chrystie Street Settlement House, a hub of the Lower East Side Jewish immigrant community.
43. Brando forever maintained that Stella Adler was his primary teacher and disavowed any influence from Strasberg, with whom he barely worked. After the Group Theatre dissolved in 1941, Adler began teaching her own brand of Stanislavsky-inspired socially conscious theatre-making at the New School for Social Research, where Brando first studied with her.
44. Bial, *Acting Jewish*, 53. Sandrow argues that the American Yiddish theatre itself became another conduit for the Stanislavsky "system," especially given the influx of immigrant Jewish artists from Russia and Eastern Europe. Sandrow, *Vagabond Stars*, 205, 268.
45. Kazan was not Jewish, but another Group Theatre alumnus who became a prominent acting teacher in the postwar years was: Sanford Meisner.
46. "The Method actors believe that their own emotions can be appropriate to the character because people of all races, religions, and nations experience similar emotions in similar ways." Bial, *Acting Jewish*, 53.
47. Fred Fehl, William Stott, Jane Stott, *On Broadway* (New York: Da Capo, 1980), 96. Quoted in Manso, *Brando*, 184.
48. Medoff, *Militant Zionism*, 160.
49. After Quentin Reynolds left the original cast, a succession of actors replaced him as the play's narrator, including Ruth Chatterton and Alexander Scourby on Broadway and author Louis Bromfield in Chicago.
50. The Bogart story is related by actor Rudy Makoul, an ensemble member of the cast (billed in the program as "Rudolph McKool") who took over the Speaker role for most of the tour. Rudy Makoul, *Hollywood, Sight Unseeing* (Victoria, BC: Trafford, 2004), 119.
51. The *Philadelphia Record* even compared the play (unfavorably) to the short propaganda films by the Office of War Information, for which Hecht actually worked: "The movie shorts distributed by the O.W.I. were simpler, more direct fare." "Ben Hecht's 'A Flag Is Born' Opens at Erlanger Theatre," *Philadelphia Record*, January 29, 1947.
52. Brooks Atkinson, "The Play," *New York Times*, September 7, 1946.

53. George Jean Nathan, *The Theatre Book of the Year 1946–1947: A Record and Interpretation* (New York: Knopf, 1947), 55.
54. Elinor Hughes, "The Theater," *Boston Herald*, February 19, 1947.
55. Howard Barnes, "The Theaters," *New York Herald Tribune*, September 7, 1946.
56. Sydney J. Harris, "'A Flag Is Born' Aims at a Nation's Heart," *Chicago Daily News*, December 27, 1946.
57. Harriett Johnson, "'A Flag Is Born' Is a Court Where Jews Plead Cause," *New York Post*, September 14, 1946.
58. Elliot Norton, "Thrilling Pageant in Debut," *Boston Post*, February 19, 1947.
59. John Chapman, "'A Flag Is Born' an Impassioned Drama Urging a Free Palestine," *New York Daily News*, September 7, 1946.
60. Garland, "'A Flag Is Born.'"
61. George Freedley, "The Stage Today: 'A Flag Is Born' Has Message for Jews, Non-Jews Alike, Which Must Be Heard," *New York Morning Telegram*, September 9, 1946.
62. Helen Bower, "'A Flag Is Born' Outright Propaganda," *Detroit Free Press*, January 21, 1947.
63. Claudia Cassidy, "On the Aisle," *Chicago Tribune*, December 27, 1946.
64. Nat Kahn, "Hecht-Weill's 'Flag Is Born' Socks Hard as Palestine Propaganda," *Variety*, September 11, 1946.
65. Manuscript of fundraising appeal for *A Flag Is Born*, Ben Hecht Papers. Luther Adler gave the speech during most of the New York run and Sidney Lumet did so on tour.
66. *A Flag Is Born* clippings folder, Billy Rose Theatre Collection, New York Public Library.
67. Unsigned, undated clipping from *PM*, *A Flag Is Born* clippings folder, Billy Rose Theatre Collection.
68. Citron, "Pageantry and Theatre," 364. Also see Brando and Lindsey, *Songs My Mother Taught Me*, 109–111; Manso, *Brando*, 186; and Medoff, *Militant Zionism*, 154.
69. Longtime Broadway producer Jules J. Leventhal lent his professional expertise behind the scenes and was credited as "In Charge of Production."
70. Quoted in Citron, "Ben Hecht's Pageant-Drama," 92.
71. Medoff, *Militant Zionism*, 160.
72. In another tributary gesture, in April 1947 Jewish detainees reportedly staged their own production of *A Flag Is Born* (translated into Hebrew) in a British-run displaced persons camp in Cyprus. Citron, "Ben Hecht's Pageant-Drama," 93.
73. "Play Mrs. FDR Backs Branded Pro-Terrorist," *Chicago Daily Tribune*, December 3, 1946.
74. Citron, "Pageantry and Theatre," 417–419.
75. Wald, *Trinity of Passion*, 22.
76. See Medoff, *Militant Zionism*, 179.
77. "An End to Silence" (appended to *A Flag Is Born* script), Luther Adler Papers, Billy Rose Theatre Collection.
78. "A highlight of the evening was the presence of several hundred members of the newly organized George Washington Legion, sponsored by the league." "Chavez De-

nounces U.S. On Palestine," *New York Times*, May 14, 1948. Unbeknownst to the participants, Israeli independence would be declared just two days after the event.

79. Wolitz, "The Americanization of Tevye," 530.
80. In his study of Uris's novel, Matthew Silver acknowledges that "the production of *A Flag Is Born* presaged techniques utilized by Uris and *Exodus*." M. M. Silver, *Our Exodus: Leon Uris and the Americanization of Israel's Founding Story* (Detroit, MI: Wayne State University Press, 2010), 21.
81. When casting the role of Ari Ben Canaan for his 1960 film of *Exodus*, Otto Preminger (himself a Jewish European émigré) chose yet another actor schooled in method acting, Paul Newman, who trained at the Actors Studio. The Method became a theatrical language through which to perform male "Muscular Judaism" in postwar American popular culture.

## 5 PASSION PLAY FOR A JEWISH "TERRORIST"

1. Letter from Menachem Begin to Ben Hecht, Ben Hecht Papers, box 55, folder 1059, Newberry Library, Chicago.
2. Baumel, *The "Bergson Boys,"* 222.
3. Bruce Hoffman, *Anonymous Soldiers: The Struggle for Israel, 1917–1947* (New York: Knopf, 2015), 373.
4. Begin dated the letter "Tammuz 5707," referring to the tenth month of the Hebrew calendar (equivalent to late June or early July of the Gregorian calendar) and the Jewish year equivalent of 1946–1947 C.E.
5. Begin also posits an even larger audience than a theatrical performance, implying Hecht might use his Hollywood clout to make a film about Gruner: "I believe that such a play would be suitable not only for the stage but also for the screen, through the medium of which one can reach the hearts of millions of people throughout the world." Letter from Menachem Begin to Ben Hecht, Ben Hecht Papers, Newberry Library.
6. Weill to Maxwell and Mab Anderson, June 22, 1947, Kurt Weill Foundation.
7. Quoted in Medoff, *Militant Zionism*, 158. Canadian customs cited a legal provision against importing "treasonable and seditious material." "Custom Censor," *Newsweek*, November 10, 1947, 74.
8. See Medoff, *Militant Zionism*, 160–163.
9. "'A Flag Is Born,'" *The Answer*, September 1946, 20. *The Answer* was the in-house newsletter for Bergson's American League for a Free Palestine.
10. Hecht, *A Child of the Century*, 614–615; Hoffman, *Anonymous Soldiers*, 412.
11. Ben Hecht, "Letter to the Terrorists of Palestine," *New York Herald-Tribune*, May 15, 1947, 17.
12. Hoffman, *Anonymous Soldiers*, 413.
13. James Reston, "Britain Prods U.S. to Stop Funds to Defy Palestine Law," *New York Times*, May 20, 1947. With this story, the controversy stirred by Hecht's editorial literally made front-page news.

14. "Halt in Palestine Agitation Here Requested by Truman," *New York Times*, June 6, 1947. During 1946 and most of 1947, the United States remained neutral regarding Palestine. Truman showed little interest in supporting Zionism until 1948, when he did support and immediately recognize the new state of Israel that May.
15. Leonard Lyons, "Lyons Den," *New York Post*, June 7, 1947. Hecht's reply, as reported by Lyons, was: "Despite the fact that he is President . . . Truman is entitled to his opinion."
16. Hecht, *A Child of the Century*, 594.
17. Matt Lebovic, "How a Small Pogrom in Russia Changed the Course of History," *The Times of Israel*, April 9, 2018, accessed March 9, 2023, https://www.timesofisrael.com/how-a-small-pogrom-in-russia-changed-the-course-of-history.
18. "*The Terrorist* (Ben Hecht)," box 128, folder 5, Erwin Piscator Papers, Special Collections Research Center, Southern Illinois University Carbondale. All citations from the play are from this typescript.
19. Michael Brenner, *Prophets of the Past: Interpreters of Jewish History* (Princeton, NJ: Princeton University Press, 2010), 55.
20. Hecht, *A Guide for the Bedevilled*, 89.
21. Brenner, *Prophets of the Past*, 65.
22. Roth, along with other Jewish historians of the 1920s and 1930s, "waged a passionate battle against the nineteenth-century reduction of the Jewish past to a 'history of suffering.'" Brenner, *Prophets of the Past*, 104.
23. Hecht, *A Guide for the Bedevilled*, 69. Hecht claims to have written the play after a brief epiphany while covering the Zionist Organization of America's 1919 convention as a Chicago reporter. Hecht says it was "performed by a Little Theater group" (possibly the Playwrights Workshop company he was briefly involved with in Chicago), but it was never published and no script is extant.
24. The director of *The Terrorist* was Moe Hack, an experienced Broadway producer and craftsman as a stage manager and lighting designer. (He designed the lighting for *We Will Never Die*.) The music was by Isaac Van Grove, who had been Kurt Weill's music director for *We Will Never Die* and *The Eternal Road* and who had scored Meyer Weisgal's two Zionist pageants in the early 1930s.
25. Advertisement for *The Terrorist*, *New York Post*, September 15, 1947, 17; Advertisement, *New York Post*, September 20, 1947, 15.
26. Chatterton had been involved with previous Bergson events, having acted as a replacement narrator in performances of both *A Jewish Fairy Tale* and *A Flag Is Born*.
27. Advertisement for *The Terrorist*, *New York Post*, September 19, 1947, 40.
28. After *A Flag Is Born*, Hecht took on several new movie assignments as if to compensate for all the income he forwent during his wartime activism. His name appears on three films released in 1947 alone.
29. Quoted in Citron, *Pageantry and Theatre*, 445.
30. Martin Gilbert, *Israel: A History* (New York: Morrow, 1998), 1942.

31. Jeffrey Brown Martin, *Ben Hecht: Hollywood Screenwriter* (Ann Arbor: UMI Research Press, 1985), 159.
32. Hecht, *A Child of the Century*, 606.

## CONCLUSION

1. Bill Krohn, *Hitchcock at Work* (London: Phaidon, 2000), 102.
2. Ben Hecht Papers, box 26, folder 657, Newberry Library, Chicago. This archive includes Hecht's completed script for *Simone*, as he titled his adaptation.
3. Dinnerstein, *Antisemitism in America*, 150–151.
4. Moss Hart wrote the screenplay adaptation for *Gentleman's Agreement* based on Lauren Z. Hobson's novel. For background on John Garfield's performance in the film, see chapters 2 and 4.
5. Anita Gates, "Hollywood's Slow Awakening to Holocaust's Horrors," *New York Times*, April 5, 2005.
6. See Lawrence Graver, *An Obsession with Anne Frank: Meyer Levin and The Diary* (Berkeley: University of California Press, 1995).
7. Meyer Levin, *In Search* (New York: Horizon Press, 1951), 305–306.
8. Edward G. Robinson and Leonard Spigelgass, *All My Yesterdays: An Autobiography* (London: W.H. Allen, 1974), 156. Despite this claim in Robinson's later memoir, he still acted in Hecht's 1952 film *Actors and Sin* (written and directed by Hecht), so the exact timing of the two men's falling out is not clear.
9. Ben Hecht, *A Jewish Fairy Tale* typescript, Palestine Statehood Committee Papers, MS 690, Series III, Manuscripts and Archives, Yale University Library.
10. Ellen Schiff, *Awake and Singing, New Edition: Six Great American Jewish Plays* (New York: Applause Theatre and Cinema Books, 2004); Julius Novick, *Beyond the Golden Door: Jewish American Drama and Jewish American Experience* (New York: Palgrave Macmillan, 2008).
11. "This book is about the great attempt by Jewish American playwrights to dramatize American experience by dramatizing Jewish American experience." Novick, *Beyond the Golden Door*, 7. "The American Jewish stage tells the story of Jews in America and, increasingly, of Jews in the world." Schiff, *Awake and Singing*, 23.
12. Lara Shalson, *Theatre and Protest* (London: Bloomsbury 2017), 29.
13. Elinor Hughes, "The Theater," *Boston Herald*, February 19, 1947.
14. Shalson, *Theatre and Protest*, 29.
15. Tricia Olszewski, "'A Flag Is Born': Dreaming of a Jewish Homeland," *The Washington Post*, April 3, 2004.
16. Tricia Olszewski, "'A Flag Is Born': Dreaming of a Jewish Homeland," *The Washington Post*, April 3, 2004.
17. Elliot Norton, "Thrilling Pageant in Debut," *Boston Post*, February 19, 1947.
18. Brooks Atkinson, "Drama: Craftsmanship: 'The Front Page' and 'A Flag Is Born' Are Compared in Technique," *New York Times*, September 15, 1946, 21.

# Bibliography

Abzug, Robert H. *America Views the Holocaust: 1933–1945: A Brief Documentary History*. Boston: Bedford, 1999.

Avishai, Bernard. *The Tragedy of Zionism: Revolution and Democracy in the Land of Israel*. New York: Farrar, Straus and Giroux, 1985.

Ben-Ami, Yitshaq. *Years of Wrath, Days of Glory: Memoirs from the Irgun*. New York: Sheingold, 1983.

Berlin, Adele, Marc Zvi Brettler, and Michael Fishbane. *The Jewish Study Bible*. Oxford: Oxford University Press, 2004.

Berman, Aaron. *Nazism, the Jews, and American Zionism, 1933–1948*. Detroit, MI: Wayne State University Press, 1990.

Bernstein, Matthew. *Walter Wanger: Hollywood Independent*. Minneapolis: University of Minnesota Press, 2000.

Bial, Henry. *Acting Jewish: Negotiating Ethnicity on the American Stage and Screen*. Ann Arbor: University of Michigan Press, 2005.

Birdwell, Michael. *Celluloid Soldiers: Warner Brothers' Campaign against Nazism*. New York: New York University Press, 1999.

Bloore, Stephen, "The Jew in American Dramatic Literature (1794–1930)." *Publications of the American Jewish Historical Society* 40, no. 4 (1951): 345–360.

Brando, Marlon, and Robert Lindsey. *Songs My Mother Taught Me*. New York: Random House, 1994.

Breines, Paul. *Tough Jews: Political Fantasies and the Moral Dilemma of American Jewry*. New York: Basic Books, 1990.

# BIBLIOGRAPHY

Brenner, Michael. *Prophets of the Past: Interpreters of Jewish History*. Translated by Steven Rendall. Princeton, NJ: Princeton University Press, 2010.

Buhle, Paul. *From the Lower East Side to Hollywood: Jews in American Popular Culture*. London: Verso, 2004.

Buhle, Paul, and David Wagner. *Radical Hollywood: The Untold Story behind America's Favorite Movies*. New York: The New Press, 1982.

Callow, Simon. *Orson Welles*. Vol. 2, *Hello Americans*. New York: Viking, 2006.

Carr, Steven Alan. *Hollywood and Anti-Semitism: A Cultural History up to World War II*. Cambridge: Cambridge University Press, 2001.

Century, Douglas. *Barney Ross*. New York: Schocken Books, 2006.

Ceplair, Larry. *Under the Shadow of War: Fascism, Anti-Fascism, and Marxists, 1918–1939*. New York: Columbia University Press, 1987.

Ceplair, Larry, and Steven Englund. *The Inquisition in Hollywood: Politics in the Film Community, 1930–1960*. Urbana: University of Illinois Press, 2003.

Citron, Atay. "Ben Hecht's Pageant-Drama: *A Flag Is Born*." In *Staging the Holocaust*, edited by Claude Schumacher, 70–93. Cambridge: Cambridge University Press, 1998.

———. "Pageantry and Theatre in the Service of Jewish Nationalism in the United States, 1933–1946." PhD diss., New York University, 1989.

Dean, Joan FitzPatrick. *Pageant*. London: Bloomsbury, 2021.

Denning, Michael. *The Cultural Front: The Laboring of American Culture in the Twentieth Century*. London: Verso, 1998.

Dick, Bernard F. *The Star-Spangled Screen: The American World War II Film*. Rev. ed. Lexington: University Press of Kentucky, 1996.

Diner, Hasia R. *Jews of the United States, 1654 to 2000*. Berkeley: University of California Press, 2004.

———. *A New Promised Land: A History of Jews in America*. New York: Oxford University Press, 2003.

———. *We Remember with Reverence and Love: American Jews and the Myth of Silence after the Holocaust, 1945–1962*. New York: New York University Press, 2009.

Dinnerstein, Leonard. *Antisemitism in America*. New York: Oxford University Press, 1995.

Doherty, Thomas. *Hollywood and Hitler, 1933-1939*. New York: Columbia University Press, 2013.

———. *Hollywood's Censor: Joseph I. Breen and the Production Code Administration*. New York, Columbia University Press, 2009.

*Dr. Ehrlich's Magic Bullet*. Directed by William Dieterle. Warner Archive Collection, 2009. DVD.

Drew, David. *Kurt Weill: A Handbook*. Berkeley: University of California Press, 1987.

Edelman, Marsha Bryan. *Discovering Jewish Music*. Philadelphia: Jewish Publication Society, 2003.

*Encyclopaedia Judaica*. Edited by Fred Skolnik and Michael Berenbaum. 2nd ed. Detroit, MI: Thomson Gale, 2007.

# BIBLIOGRAPHY

Erdman, Harley. *Staging the Jew: The Performance of an American Ethnicity, 1860–1920.* New Brunswick, NJ: Rutgers University Press, 1997.

Fehl, Fred, William Stott, and Jane Stott. *On Broadway.* New York: Da Capo, 1980.

Fetherling, Doug. *The Five Lives of Ben Hecht.* Toronto: Lester and Orpen, 1977.

Fischer-Lichte, Erika. *Theatre, Sacrifice, Ritual: Exploring Forms of Political Theatre.* London: Routledge, 2005.

*Foreign Correspondent.* Directed by Alfred Hitchcock. Warner Home Video, 2004. DVD.

Fussell, Paul. *Wartime: Understanding and Behavior in the Second World War.* New York: Oxford University Press, 1989.

Gabler, Neal. *An Empire of Their Own: How the Jews Invented Hollywood.* New York: Doubleday, 1988.

Gilbert, Martin. *Israel: A History.* New York: Morrow, 1998.

Gilman, Sander. *The Jew's Body.* New York: Routledge, 1991.

Gorbach, Julien. *The Notorious Ben Hecht: Iconoclastic Writer and Militant Zionist.* West Lafayette, IN: Purdue University Press, 2019.

Hecht, Ben. *A Child of the Century.* 1954. Reprinted by New York: Primus, 1985.

———. *A Flag Is Born.* New York: American League for a Free Palestine, 1946.

———. *A Guide for the Bedevilled.* New York: Charles Scribner's Sons, 1944.

———. *Let Freedom Ring.* Directed by Jack Conway. MGM/UA Home Video, 1994. VHS.

———. *1001 Afternoons in New York.* New York: Viking, 1941.

———. *To Quito and Back.* New York: Covici, Friede, 1937.

———. *We Will Never Die: A Memorial Dedicated to the 2,000,000 Jewish Dead of Europe.* New York: Committee for a Jewish Army of Stateless and Palestinian Jews, 1943.

Hecht, Ben, and Charles MacArthur. *Fun to Be Free: Patriotic Pageant.* New York: Dramatists Play Service, 1941.

———. "It's Fun to Be Free." In *Best One-Act Plays of 1941,* edited by Margaret Mayorga, 237–254. New York: Dodd Mead, 1942.

Hoberman, J. *Bridge of Light: Yiddish Film between Two Worlds.* Hanover, NH: Dartmouth College Press, 2010.

Hoberman, J., and Jeffrey Shandler, eds. *Entertaining America: Jews, Movies, and Broadcasting.* Princeton, NJ: Princeton University Press, 2003.

Hoffman, Adina. *Ben Hecht: Fighting Words, Moving Pictures.* New Haven, CT: Yale University Press, 2019.

Hoffman, Bruce. *Anonymous Soldiers: The Struggle for Israel, 1917–1947.* New York: Alfred A. Knopf, 2015.

*Hollywood: An Empire of Their Own.* Directed by Simcha Jacobovici. Arts and Entertainment Home Video, 2005. DVD.

Kaplan, Martin, and Johanna Blakely, eds. *Warners' War: Politics, Pop Culture and Propaganda in Wartime Hollywood.* Los Angeles: Norman Lear Center Press, 2004.

# BIBLIOGRAPHY

Kowalke, Kim, Jurgen Schebera, Christian Kuhnt, and Alexander L Ringer. "*The Eternal Road* and Kurt Weill's German, Jewish, and American Identity." *Theater* 30, no. 3 (2000): 83–95.

Krasner, David, ed. *Method Acting Reconsidered: Theory, Practice, Future.* New York: St. Martin's Press, 2000.

Kuhnt, Christian. "Approaching the Music for *A Flag Is Born.*" *Kurt Weill Newsletter* 20, no. 1 (Spring 2002): 8–10.

———. *Kurt Weill und das Judentum.* Saarbrücken: Pfau, 2001.

Lawrence, Jerome. *Actor: The Life and Times of Paul Muni.* New York: Samuel French, 1974.

*The Life of Emile Zola.* Directed by William Dieterle. Warner Home Video, 2005. DVD.

MacAdams, William. *Ben Hecht: A Biography.* New York: Barricade Books, 1999.

Makoul, Rudy. *Hollywood, Sight Unseeing.* Victoria, BC: Trafford Publishing, 2006.

Manso, Peter. *Brando: The Biography.* New York: Hyperion, 1994.

Martin, Jeffrey Brown. *Ben Hecht: Hollywood Screenwriter.* Ann Arbor: UMI Research Press, 1985.

Martins, Olga J. *Hollywood's Commandments: A Handbook for Motion Picture Writers and Reviewers.* New York: H. W. Wilson, 1937.

McCarthy, Mary. *Sights and Spectacles.* Farrar, Straus and Cudahy, 1956.

McGilligan, Patrick, and Paul Buhle. *Tender Comrades: A Backstory of the Hollywood Blacklist.* New York: St. Martin's Griffin, 1997.

Medoff, Rafael. *Militant Zionism in America: The Rise and Impact of the Jabotinsky Movement in the United States, 1926–1948.* Tuscaloosa: University of Alabama Press, 2002.

Miller, Arthur. *Collected Essays.* New York: Penguin, 2016.

Moore, Deborah Dash. *GI Jews: How World War II Changed a Generation.* Cambridge, MA: Harvard University Press, 2006.

———. "When Jews Were GIs: How World War II Changed a Generation and Remade American Jewry." In *American Jewish Identity Politics*, edited by Deborah Dash Moore, 23–44. Ann Arbor: University of Michigan Press, 2009.

*The Mortal Storm.* Directed by Frank Borzage. Warner Archive Collection, 2010. DVD.

Nahshon, Edna. "From Geopathology to Redemption: *A Flag Is Born* on the Broadway Stage." *Kurt Weill Newsletter* 20, no. 1 (Spring 2002): 5–8.

———. "Jewish American Drama." In *The Cambridge History of Jewish American Literature*, edited by Hana Wirth-Nesher, 242–257. New York: Cambridge University Press, 2016.

Nannes, Caspar. *Politics in the American Drama.* Washington, D.C.: Catholic University Press of America, 1960.

Navasky, Victor S. *A Matter of Opinion.* New York: Picador, 2006.

Norwood, Stephen. "American Jewish Muscle: Forging a New Masculinity in the Streets and in the Ring, 1890–1940." *Modern Judaism* 29, no. 2 (May 2009): 167–193.

Nott, Robert. *He Ran All the Way: The Life of John Garfield.* New York: Limelight, 2003.

# BIBLIOGRAPHY

Novick, Julius. *Beyond the Golden Door: Jewish American Drama and Jewish American Experience*. New York: Palgrave Macmillan, 2008.

Pollard, Tanya. "Tragedy and Revenge." In *A Companion to English Renaissance Tragedy*, edited by Emma Smith and Garrett A. Sullivan Jr., 58–72. Cambridge: Cambridge University Press, 2010.

Presner, Todd. *Muscular Judaism: The Jewish Body and the Politics of Regeneration*. London: Routledge, 2007.

Robinson, Edward G., and Leonard Spiegelgass. *All My Yesterdays: An Autobiography*. London: W. H. Allen, 1974.

Ross, Steven J. "*Confessions of a Nazi Spy*: Warner Bros., Anti-Fascism and the Politicization of Hollywood." In *Warners' War: Politics, Pop Culture and Propaganda in Wartime Hollywood*, edited by Martin Kaplan and Johanna Blakely, 49–59. Los Angeles: Norman Lear Center Press, 2004.

Roth, Cecil. *The Jewish Contribution to Civilization*. New York: Harper and Brothers, 1940.

Salvi, Delia Nora. "The History of the Actors' Laboratory, Inc. 1941–1950." PhD diss., University of California, Los Angeles, 1970.

Samuel, Maurice. *The World of Sholom Aleichem*. New York: Schocken Books, 1943.

Sandrow, Nahma. *Vagabond Stars: A World History of Yiddish Theater*. Syracuse, NY: Syracuse University Press, 1995.

———. "Yiddish Theater and American Theater." In *From Hester Street to Hollywood: The Jewish-American Stage and Screen*, edited by Sarah Blacher Cohen, 18–27. Bloomington: Indiana University Press, 1983.

Schebera, Jürgen. *Kurt Weill: An Illustrated Life*. New Haven, CT: Yale University Press, 1995.

Schiff, Ellen, *Awake and Singing, New Edition: Six Great American Jewish Plays*. New York: Applause Theatre and Cinema Books, 2004.

Shalson, Lara. *Theatre and Protest*. London: Bloomsbury, 2017.

Shandler, Jeffrey. *While America Watches: Televising the Holocaust*. New York: Oxford University Press, 1999.

Silver, M. M. *Our Exodus: Leon Uris and the Americanization of Israel's Founding Story*. Detroit, MI: Wayne State University Press, 2010.

Skloot, Robert. "*We Will Never Die*: The Success and Failure of a Holocaust Pageant." *Theatre Journal* 37, no. 2 (May 1985): 167–180.

Smith, Wendy. *Real Life Drama: The Group Theatre and America, 1931–1940*. New York: Grove Weidenfeld, 1990.

Solomon, Alisa. *Wonder of Wonders: A Cultural History of Fiddler on the Roof*. New York: Metropolitan Books, 2013.

Stember, Charles Herbert. *Jews in the Mind of America*. Edited by George Salomon. New York: Basic Books, 1966.

Symonette, Lys, and Kim H. Kowalke, eds. *Speak Low (When You Speak Love): The Letters of Kurt Weill and Lotte Lenya*. Berkeley: University of California Press, 1996.

Troy, Gil. "From Literary Gadfly to Jewish Activist: The Political Transformation of Ben Hecht." *Journal of Ecumenical Studies* 40, no. 4 (Fall 2003): 431–439.

Wald, Alan. *Trinity of Passion: The Literary Left and the Antifascist Crusade*. Chapel Hill: University of North Carolina Press, 2007.

Waldau, Roy S. *Vintage Years of the Theatre Guild, 1928–1939*. Cleveland: Case Western Reserve University Press, 1972.

Wenger, Beth S. "Constructing Manhood in American Jewish Culture." In *Gender and Jewish History*, edited by Marion A. Kaplan and Deborah Dash Moore, 350–366. Bloomington: Indiana University Press, 2011.

———. *History Lessons: The Creation of American Jewish Heritage*. Princeton, NJ: Princeton University Press, 2010.

Werfel, Franz. *The Eternal Road: A Drama in Four Parts*. Translated by Ludwig Lewisohn. New York: Viking, 1936.

Whitfield, Stephen J. *In Search of American Jewish Culture*. Hanover, NH: Brandeis University Press, 1999.

———. "The Politics of Pageantry, 1936–1946." *American Jewish History* 84, no. 3 (September 1996): 221–251.

Wolitz, Seth. "The Americanization of Tevye or Boarding the Jewish Mayflower." *American Quarterly* 40, no. 4 (December 1988): 514–536.

Wyman, David S. *The Abandonment of the Jews: America and the Holocaust, 1941–1945*. New York: Pantheon, 1984.

Wyman, David S., and Rafael Medoff. *A Race against Death: Peter Bergson, America and the Holocaust*. New York: New Press, 2002.

Zalampas, Michael. *Adolf Hitler and the Third Reich in American Magazines, 1923–1939*. Bowling Green, OH: Bowling Green State University Popular Press, 1989.

# Index

*Note: Page references in italics indicate figures*

*Abandonment of the Jews, The* (Wyman), 3
*Acting Jewish* (Bial), 3
Actors' Laboratory Theatre, 52–53
Actors Studio, 96–97, 245n81
Adler, Celia, 8, 83–84, 92
Adler, Luther: actor in *We Will Never Die*, 49, 235n67; director of *A Flag is Born*, 8, 83, 93, 97; Tevye roles, 77, 119, 240n37; training, 96
Adler, Stella: actor in *We Will Never Die*, 98; director of *A Jewish Fairy Tale*, 77; mentor to Brando, 95, 243n43; training, 96
agitprop: conversion narratives, 93–94, 110–111; Hecht use of, 8, 26, 29, 52–54, 79, 88, 91–93, 239n16; offstage uses, 100; Piscator and, 53
America First Committee, 25
American diaspora, challenges to: in *A Flag is Born*, 91–93, 99–100; targeting entertainment industry, 18–19, 31–32; in *The Terrorist*, 114; through Jewish identity, 20, 30; in *We Will Never Die*, 36–37, 47–48, 53–54

American Jewish Congress, 31
*American Landscape* (Rice), 18
American League for a Free Palestine, 69, 100–101, 106, 114
American Revolution invocations, 25–26, 80, 101–103
*American Way, The* (Kaufman/Hart), 18
antifascism: anti-imperialism overlap, 87–88; Hecht efforts toward, 6, 20–21, 22–23, 26–27, 29; Popular Front efforts toward, 23–24; Production Code and, 15, 21; scarcity of Jewish voices, 18; supporters, 17–18
anti-immigrant sentiment in U.S., 2, 16
anti-imperialism, 87–88
antisemitism: depicted onstage and in film, 6, 9, 15, 17–18, 46, 74, 111–112; Jewish visibility and, 15–16, 18–19, 33; military service and, 44; Production Code and, 21–22, 225n4
appeasement, 25
Arab-Jewish relations, 9–10, 89–90
archetypes of Jewish identity, 6, 64, 75–77, 76, 79–80, 103–104
Arnold, Edward, 50

255

# INDEX

Atkinson, Brooks, 5, 122–123
*Awake and Sing!* (Odets), 16, 227n6
Ayers, Lemuel, 35, 231n23

Bankhead, Tallulah, 25
Bar Kochba, Simon, 45, 235n60
*Bar Kochba* (Goldfaden), 235n60
Barnes, Howard, 98
Baruch, Bernard, 116
"Battle Hymn of the Ghetto" (Waxman/Loesser), 52
Baum, Kurt, 36, 232n30
Begin, Menachem, 9, 105–106, 118, 245nn4–5
Bellamy, Ralph, 50, 77
Ben-Ami, Jacob, 29, 36, 84, 97–98, 232n31, 241n14
Ben-Ami, Yitshaq, 31–32, 39
Ben-Gurion, David, 70, 115, 118
*Ben Hecht* (ship), 100, 107
Benny, Jack, 25
Bergson, Peter: "Action, not pity" motto, 34, 36, 90; American League for a Free Palestine, 69, 100–101, 106, 114; appeals to non-Jews, 101–103; Committee for a Jewish Army, 31–32, 49, 240n35; condemnation of Churchill speech, 70; lobbying campaigns, 3, 30, 55; relationship to Hecht, 7, 30–31, 68–69; response to Gruner hanging, 107
Berlin, Irving, 25, 39
Berman, Aaron, 31
Bial, Henry, 3, 16, 96
biblical material, 4, 38, 85–86
*Birthright* (Maibaum), 17
Bogart, Humphrey, 26
Bohnen, Roman, 52–53
Brando, Marlon, 90, 91–93, 92, 95–96, 97, 242n37
Brecht, Bertolt, 51, 52, 117–118
Breines, Paul, 41–42, 75
Brenner, Michael, 113
Britain: actions against Hecht, 107, 115–116, 245n13; Mandate in Palestine, 69, 80, 115; provoked by Hecht, 64–65, 73–74, 87–90; Zionist loss of faith in, 69
Bromberg, J. Edward, 52–53
*Bury the Dead* (Shaw), 239n16

*Call the Next Case*, 57–59
Cantor, Eddie, 25
*Casablanca* (Curtiz), 51, 236n83
Cassidy, Claudia, 99
Century, Douglas, 45
Chapman, John, 98–99
Chatterton, Ruth, 115, 240n37, 246n26
*Child of the Century, A*, 32
Churchill, Winston, 7–8, 70, 71–74, 240n28, 240n30
cinema: antisemitism depicted in, 9, 46; Holocaust films, 118–119; influence on *We Will Never Die*, 50–52; screenplays with Hecht participation, 19–20, 22–23, 41, 117, 228n17. *See also individual actors and film titles*
Citron, Atay, 100, 242n25
Committee for a Jewish Army, 31–32, 49, 240n35
*Common Man, The*, 58
Communist Party, 17, 23–24
*Confessions of a Nazi Spy* (Litvak), 41
conversion narratives, 93–94, 110–111
*Counselor-At-Law* (Rice), 40
Coward, Noël, 20
Cowley, Malcolm, 95

*Daily Worker*, 22
Denning, Michael, 24, 227n8
Dewey, Thomas, 33
*Diary of Anne Frank, The* (Goodrich/Hackett), 9, 119
diaspora, 46–47, 65–66, 75, 82–83, 112–113. *See also* American diaspora, challenges to; archetypes of Jewish identity
*Dimitroff* (Kazan and Smith), 17
Diner, Hasia, 10, 83
Dinnerstein, Leonard, 33, 118
Douglas, Melvin, 25
*Dr. Ehrlich's Magic Bullet* (Dieterle), 22, 41

Eddy, Nelson, 22
Eisler, Hans, 52
Epstein, Hymie, 50, 236n82
Erdman, Harley, 2, 15–16
*Eternal Road, The* (Werfel/Weill), 4–5, 33, 35, 85, 232n33
*Exodus* (Uris), 77, 103–104, 245nn80–81

# INDEX

Favorini, Attilio, 53
Federal Theatre Project, 5, 42, 52, 53
Ferber, Edna, 32
Feuchtwanger, Lion, 117–118
*Fiddler on the Roof* (Harnick and Stein/Bock), 63, 77, 103, 119
Fiedler, Leslie, 228n20
Fight for Freedom, 25, 230n44
Fischer-Lichte, Erika, 4
*Flag is Born, A*: appeals to non-Jews, 101–103; audiences and tour, 97–98; biblical visions, 85–86; bridge symbol, 8, 103–104; conversion of David to Zionist cause, 93–95, 94; "Council of the Mighty" scene, 86–90, 89; critical reception, 98–99; death of Zelda and Tevya, 93; ending scene, 78; *An End to Silence* adaptation, 103; fundraising and offstage political work, 99–100; impact of Holocaust descriptions, 81–82; Jewish protests against, 101; opening tableau, 81; passing of torch to Muscular Judaism, 64, 90–93, 92; poster art, 102; proceeds used for Palestine, 100, 107; symbols of old world, 83–85; Zionist message, 82–83
*Flight to the West* (Rice), 18
*Flowering Peach, The* (Odets), 227n6
Ford, Henry, 16
*Foreign Correspondent* (Hitchcock), 22–23, 229n37
*Front Page, The*, 19
Fussell, Paul, 28

Garfield, John: film persona, 45–46, 118, 235nn63–66; Jewish identity, 34, 235n64; precursor to Brando, 95–96, 242n37; training, 96
Garland, Robert, 99
*Gentlemen's Agreement* (Kazan), 9, 46, 95–96, 118
"Get Thee Out" (Sholem-Aleichem), 70–71
*Golden Boy* (Odets), 16
Goldfaden, Abraham, 84, 235n60
*Gone With the Wind* (Fleming), 19–20, 228n17
Gorbach, Julien, 4
Graetz, Heinrich, 112–113
Greenberg, Hayim, 46

Group Theatre, 45, 52, 96, 243n45
Gruner, Dov, 105–106
*Guide for the Bedeviled, A*, 4

Halevi, Judah, 108–109
*Hangmen Also Die* (Lang), 51, 52, 237n89
Harris, Jonathan, 94, 115
Harris, Sidney J., 98
Hart, Moss, 33, 39–40, 40, 46, 118, 247n4
"Hatikvah," 35, 43, 78, 94, 103, 242n30
Hayes, Helen, 25
Hecht, Ben, works: *Call the Next Case*, 57–59; *A Child of the Century*, 32; *The Common Man*, 58; *An End to Silence*, 103; *Foreign Correspondent*, 22–23, 229n37; *The Front Page*, 19; *Gone With the Wind*, 19–20, 228n17; *A Guide for the Bedeviled*, 4; *It's Fun to Be Free*, 25–27, 230n47; *A Jew in Love*, 20, 228n20; *Let Freedom Ring*, 22; "My Tribe is Called Israel," 30; *Perfidy*, 118; *To Quito and Back*, 21; *The Red Door*, 114, 246n23; *Scarface*, 41; *The Scoundrel*, 20; *Stagecoach*, 19–20, 228n17; "A Thousand and One Afternoons in New York," 29; *A Tribute to Gallantry*, 66–68; *The Visions of Simone Machard*, 117–118. See also *Flag is Born, A*; *Terrorist, The*; *We Will Never Die*
Hecht, Jenny, 117
Hecht, Rose Caylor, 22, 228n23
Herut Party, 31, 89–90, 118
*History of the Jews* (Graetz), 112–113
Hitchcock, Alfred, 22–23, 117
Hoffman, Adina, 4, 228n20, 228n23
Hollywood: casting of Jews in ethnic roles, 41, 234n47; Popular Front organizations in, 24, 34, 41; Production Code, 2, 15, 21–22, 225n4; reluctance about antifascism, 24. See also cinema
Hollywood Anti-Nazi League, 24, 34, 41
*House I Live In, The* (Maltz), 118
House Un-American Activities Committee, 24, 229–230n41

Ingersoll, Ralph, 24, 29
*International Jew, The* (Ford), 16
International Ladies Garment Workers Union, 17, 25

# INDEX

Irgun Zvai Leumi, 10, 69, 80, 89–90, 101, 105–106, 107–108
isolationism, 24, 28, 32–33, 85–86
*Israel Reborn* (Weisgal), 4
*It's Fun to Be Free*, 25–27, 29, 230n47

Jabotinsky, Vladimir, 30–31
Jacobs, Louis, 232n32
*Jazz Singer, The* (Raphaelson), 16
*Jew in Love, A*, 20, 228n20
*Jewish Contribution to Civilization, The* (Roth), 39, 233n39
*Jewish Fairy Tale, A*: confrontation with God/Churchill, 71–74, 240n28, 240n30; production history, 77; summary, 7–8; Tevya introduction, 70–71; Tevya's doubts, 74–75; Zionist message, 75–77
"Jews in the War" scene in *We Will Never Die*, 41–46
Johnson, Harriett, 98
*Judgment Day* (Rice), 18
*Jumbo*, 33

Kahn, Nat, 99
Kaufman, Beatrice, 32
Kaufman, George S., 18, 32
Kazan, Elia, 17, 95–96
Kennedy, Joseph P., 24
King David Hotel bombing, 80
Kook, Hillel. *See* Bergson, Peter
*Kultur* (Phillip), 17

Labor Stage, 25, 52
Lang, Fritz, 51
Lazarus, Emma, 39
League of American Writers, 24
League of Nations, 69
Leslie, Joan, 50
*Let Freedom Ring*, 22
Levin, Meyer (author), 119
Levin, Meyer (war hero), 44, 118
Levy, Maurice, 50
Lidice massacre, 51, 67
*Life of Emile Zola, The* (Dieterle), 21, 41, 88
Likud Party, 3, 31, 89–90
"Little Theatre" movement, Chicago, 20
Living Newspaper plays, 5, 42–43, 47, 53

Loesser, Frank, 52, 237n87
Luce, Clare Boothe, 18
Lumet, Sidney, 92, 94, 96, 119
Lyons, Leonard, 107

MacArthur, Charles, 19, 25
Magnes, Judah, 101
Mandate in Palestine, British, 69, 80, 115
*Margin for Error* (Luce), 18
McCrea, Joel, 23
Medoff, Rafael, 3, 31
Meredith, Burgess, 25, 50
Method Acting, 96–97, 243n44, 245n81
Miller, Arthur, 2
Moore, Deborah Dash, 44
Motion Picture Artists Committee, 24
Moyne assassination, 69–70, 72
Muni, Paul: Brooks Atkinson on, 122–123; contrast with Brando, 95, 97; ethnic roles, 234n47; in *A Flag is Born*, 8, 83, 88, 89; interchangeability with Robinson, 234n48; Jewish identity, 34, 40–41, 54, 234n46; political affiliations, 24; precursor of Garfield, 235n65; in *We Will Never Die* newsreel, 55–56, 57
Muscular Judaism: in *A Flag is Born*, 64, 86, 90–95, 92, 94; Method Acting and, 245n81; Revisionist Zionism and, 30; in *We Will Never Die*, 34, 41–46

Nahshon, Edna, 2, 16
Nathan, George Jean, 19, 98
National Origins Act, 2
National War Fund, 66
Navasky, Victor, 10
Norton, Elliot, 98, 122
*Notorious* (Hitchcock), 117
Novick, Julius, 18

Oakland, Simon, 115
Odets, Clifford, 16, 17, 93, 227n6
*Old Country, The* (Sholem-Aleichem), 64
Oz, Amos, 86

pageantry, 4, 5, 25–27, 34
*Pawnbroker, The* (Lumet), 119
*Perfidy*, 118
Philipp, Adolf, 17

# INDEX

*Pins and Needles* (Rome/Arendt et al), 17, 52, 227n8
Piscator, Erwin, 53
*PM*, 24, 29–30, 63–64
Popkin, Henry, 2

Rains, Claude, 50
"Raisins and Almonds" (Goldfaden), 84
Raphaelson, Samson, 16
Raziel, David, 75
*Red Door, The*, 114
Reinhardt, Max, 4–5
"Remember Us" (article), 46–47
"Remember Us" (scene), 47–49, 65–66, 235n68
Revisionist Zionism, 3, 9–10, 30–31. *See also* Zionism
Reynolds, Quentin, 81
Rice, Elmer, 17–18, 40
Robinson, Bill "Bojangles," 25
Robinson, Edward G., 24, 34, 40–41, 54, 118–119, 234n48, 247n8
"Roll Call" scene in *We Will Never Die*, 5, 38–41, 40, 64, 233nn35–37, 233n41, 233–234n45
*Romance of a People, The* (Weisgal), 4
Roosevelt, Eleanor, 54–55, 101, 237–238n97
Roosevelt, Franklin Delano, 23, 32, 55, 58–59, 66, 100
Rose, Billy, 33, 116
Ross, Barney, 45, 235nn62–63
Roth, Cecil, 39, 233n39, 246n22
Rotsten, Herman, 52, 237n90

Salomon, Haym, 25–26, 39
Samuel, Maurice, 63
Sandrow, Nahma, 84, 85
satire, political, 8, 87
*Scarface*, 41
Schaeffer, Louis, 52
Schiff, Ellen, 227n7
Schwartz, Maurice, 68, 83
*Scoundrel, The*, 20
screenplays with Hecht participation, 19–20, 22–23, 41, 117, 228n17
Secunda, Sholom, 71, 240n26
Shalon, Lara, 121–122
Shandler, Jeffrey, 82
Shaw, Irwin, 239n16

Sholem-Aleichem, 38, 63–64. *See also* Tevye (character)
*Shulamith* (Goldfaden), 84
Sidney, Sylvia, 49, 55
Sinatra, Frank, 118
Skouras, Spyros, 116
Smith, Art, 17, 52–53
Solomon, Alisa, 63
*Stagecoach*, 19–20, 228n17
*Staging the Jew* (Erdman), 3
stereotypes of Jews, 20, 29, 30, 41–42, 228n20. *See also* Muscular Judaism
Stern Gang, 69–70
*Stranger, The* (Welles), 118–119
Strasberg, Lee, 96
Strobing, Irving, 42–43, 234n52
Supreme Court, 54, 237–238n97
Symbolism: in *A Flag is Born*, 8, 93, 103; in *The Terrorist*, 109; in *We Will Never Die*, 29, 48–49
Syrjala, Sointu, 35, 231n23
Szyk, Arthur, 75, 76, 240n35

*Terrorist, The*: catalogue of atrocities against diaspora, 112–113; commission by Begin, 9, 105–106, 245nn4–5; execution, 113; introduction of Tevya and Halevy, 108–110; Passion Play implications, 113–114; prison drama, 9, 110–112; production team, 246n24; summary, 8–9
Tevye (character): avatar for Eastern European diaspora, 63, 83; in *Fiddler on the Roof*, 103, 119; in *A Jewish Fairy Tale*, 7, 70–75; Schwartz interpretation, 68; in *The Terrorist*, 108; in *We Will Never Die*, 63–64. *See also Flag is Born, A*
Theatre Guild, 21
"Thousand and One Afternoons in New York, A" (column), 29
*Till the Day I Die* (Odets), 17
*To Quito and Back*, 21
*Tough Jews* (Breines), 75
*Tribute to Gallantry, A*, 66–68, 239n14
Truman, Harry, 107, 246n14

United Kingdom. *See* Britain
United Nations, 58, 87, 89, 115
Uris, Leon, 77, 103–104, 245nn80–81

# INDEX

visibility, Jewish: Hecht efforts toward, 2–3, 40; isolationism and, 32; paucity of in popular culture, 1–2, 15–16, 18–19; Production Code barriers to, 21–22, 225n4

*Visions of Simone Machard, The* (Brecht), 117–118

*Waiting for Lefty* (Odets), 93, 227n6
Wald, Alan, 101
Wandering Jew. *See* archetypes of Jewish identity
Wanger, Walter, 23, 229n37
Warner Brothers, 16, 24, 34, 41, 45, 88, 234n46, 234n48
"Warsaw Ghetto" scene in *We Will Never Die*, 50–54, 238n103
*Watch on the Rhine* (Hellman), 18
Waxman, Franz, 51–52, 237n86
Weill, Kurt: *The Eternal Road*, 4–5, 232n33; *A Flag is Born*, 85, 242n30; *It's Fun to Be Free*, 33; political affiliations, 24; quoted, 54, 107; *We Will Never Die*, 33, 35–36, 43, 232n27, 233–234n45
Weisgal, Meyer, 4, 34
Welles, Orson, 118–119
Werfel, Franz, 4–5
*We Will Never Die*: audiences and tour, 49–50; cast, 33–34; "Jews in the War," 41–46; memorial service setting, 35–36, 37, 49; newsreel about, 55–56, 56, 57; opening prologue, 29; performance in DC, 54–55, 121, 237–238n97; poster by Arthur Szyk, 76; production team, 33, 35, 52, 231n23; "Remember Us" (article), 46–47; "Remember Us" (scene), 47–49, 65–66, 235n68; "Roll Call," 5, 38–41, 40, 64, 233nn35–37, 233n41, 233–234n45; solicitation of Broadway community, 32; summary, 7; "The Victory of Their Dying," 36–38; "Warsaw Ghetto," 50–54, 238n103

"When That Man is Dead and Gone" (Berlin), 25
*Where is My Child?* (Leff/Lynn), 84
Whitfield, Stephen J., 4
Winchell, Walter, 20
Wise, Stephen, 28
Wolitz, Seth, 66, 240n25
*World of Sholom Aleichem, The* (Samuel), 63
Wyman, David, 3

Yiddish Theatre: "facing in" art form, 16–17, 227n7; influence on *A Flag is Born*, 8, 79, 83–85; influence on *A Jewish Fairy Tale*, 77; influence on Method Acting, 96, 243n44; Jacob Ben-Ami and, 36, 232n31; Maurice Schwartz and, 68, 83; Muni and Robinson in, 40–41, 97; symbolic end, 241n11

Zanuck, Darryl F., 116
Zionism: in America, 10, 78; Churchill's wavering support of, 70; diaspora and, 75, 82–83, 113; factions of, 9, 31, 101; in *A Flag is Born*, 64, 79, 82–83, 90; "Hatikvah" anthem in Hecht plays, 35, 43, 78, 94, 103; Hecht attitude toward, 68–69, 118; in *A Jewish Fairy Tale*, 75–77; in *The Red Door*, 114; in *We Will Never Die*, 35. *See also* Irgun Zvai Leumi; Muscular Judaism
Zionist Organization of America, 4, 31

# About the Author

GARRETT EISLER received his PhD in theatre from the Graduate Center of the City University of New York (CUNY). He has written several articles for *American Theatre* magazine and his scholarship has been published in *Journal of American Drama and Theatre*, *Studies in Musical Theatre*, *New England Theatre Journal*, and *The Eugene O'Neill Review*. He has taught in theater programs at New York University's Tisch School of the Arts, The New School's Eugene Lang College, Brooklyn College, and Boston University. As a theater professional, he has worked as the literary manager for Syracuse Stage and has written dramatic criticism for the *Village Voice* and *Time Out New York*. From 2005 to 2013, he wrote the theater blog *The Playgoer*, a collection of reviews, reporting, and essays on the theater of the day.